BEFORE THE FIVE FRONTIERS

BEFORE THE FIVE FRONTIERS

Panama
From 1821-1903

by
Alex Perez-Venero

AMS PRESS
NEW YORK

FIRST AMS PRESS EDITION, 1978.

Library of Congress Cataloging in Publication Data

Perez-Venero, Alex.
   Before the five frontiers.

   Bibliography: p.
   Includes index.
   1. Panama—History—To 1903. I. Title.
F1566.45P47   972.87   77-78317
ISBN 0-404-16003-4

To my wife,
Mirna

Contents

Introduction

". . . for if any people have suffered their
history, it is our people."—Juan Materno Vásquez

As we survey the history of Panama from its independence
from Spain in 1821 (when Panama chose to be part of Colombia) until just before its final independence from Colombia in
1903, we are struck by the continual suffering, economic and
spiritual, of Panamanians at the hands of extraneous political
elements. The main highlights of the history of the Isthmus
seem to relate either to desires for self-government (usually in
the direction of commercial aspirations) or to regrets and disappointments at the outcome of such enterprises. Bitterness directed at the restricting shackles imposed from Bogotá sours into
resentment against the interventionist policies of the United
States. The patterns that echo from the nineteenth century into
the twentieth can lead us to a better understanding of the formation of the national outlook of Panama today. In other words,
a study of the nineteenth century is an essential prerequisite
for the understanding of modern Panama. One who starts out
with the premise that Panama as an entity did not exist before
1903 and that Panama owes its identity to the United States will
find that bias and prejudice limit his comprehension of the feelings, ideals, philosophies, desires, wants and aspirations of the
Panamanians today. Moreover, the excitement of the nineteenth
century makes it worthy of a history of its own.

The purpose of the author in writing this history of the Isthmus during the nineteenth century is to demonstrate to the
reader that Panamanian leaders have always felt that their isthmus was a separate entity with its own political, social and eco-

nomic philosophies. Panama, in reality, was not a natural but an artificial part of Colombia. This history will allow the English-speaking student to observe nineteenth century Panama from the point of view of original sources and contemporary Panamanian opinions and interpretations as well as from the traditional English-language books. The author hopes that his study will stimulate not only himself but others to further research.

In dealing with historical surveys written by Panamanian historians, the author has cross-checked as frequently as possible (especially when information appeared to be misleading or incomplete) with the original sources (cited either in footnotes or in the bibliographies of the histories) or with more traditional histories available in Panama, Colombia and the United States. Several errors in dates have been discovered, not only in Panamanian sources but also in North American books which were based on certain less reliable Panamanian histories. The perpetuation of such errors has been avoided here, though verification with original documents has not been possible for all statements made. As incongruencies or contradictions were found, they have been exposed in the footnotes or resolved by using other sources and additional information within the text.

In searching for material, the author has been generously aided by historians in Panama who donated either books or the use of their libraries, as for example, Rubén Darío Carles. The staff of the National Library in Panama, that of the University of Panama, and Mrs. Evelyn Price of the Canal Zone Library were most cooperative and courteous in allowing the author the use of their facilities. Members of the author's family and friends in Panama provided many new books which have been important in assessing the modern interpretations of Panamanian historians and intellectuals. Several old and valuable memoirs and biographies which, because they were limited editions in Spanish are no longer readily available, were donated to the author through the years and form an important source of information for parts of this work. Many old articles and books relating to events on the Isthmus were available in the Louisiana State University Library and the author found these items very useful in cross-checking more recently-published sources.

The bibliography, though selective, represents material accumulated during the last seven or eight years and includes many Panamanian and Colombian sources difficult to obtain in the United States. The knowledge of their existence, as well as their use as sources for the text, will, it is hoped, enlighten, guide and stimulate more exhaustive research concerning specific subjects and events related to Panama.

CHAPTER I

Independence and Aftermath

While the major areas of Latin America were signing declarations of independence from Spain, Panama, within the jurisdiction of the viceroyalty of Nueva Granada,[1] remained loyal to the Spanish Crown and refused to second these movements for independence. It is not strange, then, that Panama served as a strong base for the loyalists in their expeditions against the rebels (patriots) in South America, and that because of upheavals in other areas of Nueva Granada, Panama would serve as capital of that viceroyalty for a time.[2] Due not only to their loyalist support but also to their strategic positions on the Isthmus, Panama (on the Pacific) and Portobelo (on the Atlantic) became royalist strongholds and depositories of war machinery, and consequently they also became targets of rebel aggression during the wars for independence.

The Isthmians, as was the case in other areas of Latin America, were divided among themselves. For economic reasons many former loyalists were flung into the arms of the rebel cause. While Ferdinand VII of Spain had allowed free commercial activity on the Isthmus (*ca.* 1813) the Panamanians had prospered, and such cities as Panama and Portobelo had again become warehouses for merchandise bound from foreign ports to Central and South America. But the greed of the merchants of Cádiz and their successful lobbying for exclusive franchises on the Isthmus were to count among the final blows to the prosperity of Panama and, consequently, to the royalist cause there.[3]

1

Unfortunately for the relatively few Panamanian rebel colo-
nists, Spain had regained much of the military strength which
she had lost under the Napoleonic regime. By 1815 (after retak-
ing Venezuela) Spain reconquered Nueva Granada, quickly aveng-
ing herself on many of the leaders of the liberation movement
there.[4] Furthermore, in 1817, Don Alejandro Hore became governor of Panama, ruling the Isthmus despotically and trying to
retain it for the Crown at all cost. Under his rule, the patriots
had difficulty maintaining their military conquests for any length
of time. One of their unfortunate expeditions was against Portobelo and was led by the Scottish noble, General Gregor Mac-
Gregor, who was successful at first, but ultimately was crushed
by Hore.[5] This victory was to bring grave consequences to the
loyalists in their struggle against the patriots. The death of Hore
in 1820 and the economic losses the Isthmus had been suffering
somewhat reduced the ranks of the royalist following, which
nevertheless remained in the majority.[6]

In 1820, Fernando VII was forced to uphold the Constitution of 1812 (which he had scorned since 1814). The new Constitutional Government adversely affected the movement for
independence on the Isthmus by removing many of the reasons
for loyalists to convert to the patriot cause. The new government
in Spain appointed Brigadier Pedro Ruiz de Porras to succeed
Hore as governor of Panama. Porras and his followers created a
favorable image of constitutional government under Spain
through political clubs, newspaper articles about the Government and free elections of Cabildo members and representatives
of the provinces. With regard to the patriots, however, this taste
of freedom only reinforced their aspirations for complete separation from Spain. Unfortunately for all the Isthmians, Spain became concerned about these comparatively liberal manifestations
under Porras in Panama and decided to replace him with the last
Viceroy of Nueva Granada, Juan de Sámano y Urribarry. Sámano
had found refuge in Jamaica when the patriots recovered Nueva
Granada. He arrived in Panama in December of 1820,[7] and restored the oppressive rule that the Panamanians had had to en-
dure under Hore, thus undermining the loyalty of many an Isth-

mian toward the Crown. Sámano's government was characterized as cruel and bloody, full of persecutions, jailings, terror and
heavy censorship. Fortunately for the Isthmians at that time, his
rule was short-lived, for he died soon after taking power.[8]

By 1821, the Spanish Crown was so intensely worried about
the emancipation struggle in America that it reinforced the defensive position of the Isthmus and sent Field Marshal Juan de la
Cruz Murgeón y Achet, the last governor of Panama named by
the King of Spain, to try to reconquer the areas of Quito and
Nuevo Granada, promising him the vice-royalty if he should re-
capture at least two-thirds of those territories. Impelled by this
promise, Murgeón weakened the Isthmian defenses while forming his own military expedition. Finding that the treasury was
depleted, he exhausted the funds of the *confradías* and of the
church in the form of "loans," and finally left on his ill-fated
expedition to the coast of Esmeralda in October of 1821.[9]

PANAMA DECLARES ITS INDEPENDENCE FROM SPAIN

Before leaving, Murgeón had been forced to find a replace-
ment to occupy the governorship. Unable to find a well-known
Spanish loyalist to leave in charge of the Isthmus, he settled for
the Isthmian-born governor of the Province of Veraguas in Panama, Colonel José de Fábrega.[10] Fábrega was the first native
Isthmian to hold such high office. Although he understood why
many of his fellow countrymen were so embittered by the apparent hopelessness of their positions as second class citizens in
their own land, he was loyal to the Crown and particularly affil-
iated to the Constitutional party of Spain. Thus, he represented
a certain type of security to the royalists, and simultaneously a
hope for the patriots; moreover, he was a guarantee of peace to
both. Therefore he was selected by Murgeón to head the Government.[11]

However, Fábrega took command at a time when the whole
of Hispano-America was breaking away from Spain. Central
America had just declared itself independent; royalists in Vene-

zuela had just declared themselves restricted to the plaza in Puerto
Cabello; and Cartagena had ended the siege by opening its doors
to the army of Montilla.[12] In Panama, where taxations imposed
by the need to pay for Murgeón's expedition had plunged the
Isthmus further into economic misery, soldiers in the interior
abused and jailed many innocent victims of these forced contri-
butions; and patriots in the city of Panama, taking into consideration the probable reluctance of Fábrega to shed the blood of
fellow countrymen, prepared to gain liberation. To undermine
resistance from the garrison, patriots decided to foment desertion in the ranks of the military with bribes from various prominent citizens distributed through probable collusion between
the patriots and a high-ranking military chief in the city.[13]

Such was the state of affairs when on November 10, 1821
an uprising in Villa de los Santos supporting the independence
movement touched off a series of similar events in towns like
Pesé and Natá. These spontaneous uprisings were soon supported
ardently by many Isthmians, and the outburst of the revolution
initiated at Villa de los Santos soon advanced to the very walls
of the fortified city of Panama. The Government there responded
to the *ultimatums* of the interior towns by cutting off all communication with them and even with other towns in the Province
of Panama itself. Within the city arrests were made, and persecutions ensued; a show of force was attempted with the mobiliza-
tion of the remaining troops at strategic spots in the city. Other
precautionary measures were taken. All this must have deeply
concerned Colonel Fábrega. He was charged with the delicate
duty of preserving the Isthmus for the Crown. He had to prepare to defend it from Colombian liberators who could swoop
down upon the Isthmus at any time. These were in a vengeful
mood over the imprisonment and penalties still being suffered
by MacGregor's men who had been captured at Portobelo and
Chagres in 1819 and by other patriots of similar fates. And now
within the Isthmus itself, at Fábrega's very door, Panamanians
were clamoring for emancipation.[14]

Among other recourses, Fábrega turned for advice to the
Asamblea Provincial (Provincial Congress) which advised him to

call together a council composed of civil, ecclesiastical, commercial, military and other high public elements. This Fábrega did, and the meeting was held November 20 in his own home. It was agreed that representatives from all the interior towns would meet on December 20, a measure that Fábrega approved because it would halt all aggression (the outcome of which he could not be certain), and it would delay any punitive measures against the rebels. Then too, Fábrega was actually more worried about attack from the sea by expeditions sent to Panama than he was by the local uprisings. The irony of his faulty judgment in this case was that his opponents at home proved to be more dangerous than the attackers from abroad.

The meeting planned by Fábrega never took place. Panamanians of the interior were too inflamed over the prospect of freedom to wait, and many towns reinforced the determination which first had exploded at Villa de los Santos.[15]

In the meantime, troops continued to desert in the city of Panama in such numbers that there were hardly enough men left to guard the cells and man the barracks. On the night of the 27th of November some 60 soldiers deserted with their arms; the Government, faced with apparently unsurmountable troubles, began taking last minute steps to oppose the rebellion that was seething. Remaining loyalist forces were assigned to strategic places throughout the city, but ignoring their rather passive efforts, the people invaded the principal plaza and the barracks, and asked for a meeting of the Cabildo to decide the future of their Isthmus. The next day, at the invitation of the members of the Cabildo, a meeting took place at the Casa Consistorial.[16] Long discussions ensued concerning the cause of republicanism on the Isthmus and whether to join Colombia. This last measure was agreed upon in part because of the worship of their hero, Simón Bolívar. Finally, the delegates approved the motion to declare the Isthmus free and independent of Spanish domination, and to unite it to Gran Colombia. The Declaration was announced on the 28th of November, 1821, from the balcony of the town hall to the waiting multitude in the plaza, and was received with cheers.[17]

The Declaration that was heard in Panama City was soon imitated in the Province of Veraguas where the insurrections of Los Santos and of Nata had taken place. The Bishop of that area supported the Declaration not only morally but materially, even offering to mortgage church property for the cause.[18]

When Bolívar received the news of the Isthmian declarations in January of 1822 in his headquarters in Popayán, he sent one of his *aides de camp* to present to the people of the Isthmus the congratulations he felt they deserved on liberating their country.[19]

THE UNION WITH COLOMBIA

The decision to incorporate themselves with Gran Colombia was the beginning of a period of great turmoil for the Isthmians, for Bolívar and his government were going to have to face not only the disorder that had reigned during the revolution against Spain, but also the anarchy and turmoil which were to rack the liberated countries for years to come. Nevertheless, the Isthmians were inflamed with patriotic zeal and were willing to support Bolívar's continuing campaigns against the Spanish until the battle of Ayacucho in 1826, which was to prove the final and decisive blow to the Spaniards.[20]

After declaring its independence in 1821, Panama continued to be governed by Colonel Fábrega until formal recognition by Colombia when, because of his personal wishes, he was reinstated as governor of the province of Veraguas, a position he had held before the independence of Panama. The Department of the Isthmus was created by a decree on February 9, 1822 with the same boundaries that the provinces had had when known as the Comandancia General de Panama under Spanish rule. Colonel José María Carreño, a Venezuelan, was appointed as Intendant General of the new department and Governor of the province of Panama.[21] Upon his arrival on the Isthmus in 1822, the constitution ratified the previous year by the Congress of Cúcuta was proclaimed.[22] Soon the authority of the Colombian Government extended itself to all the territorial boundaries of the Isthmus, even to the Islands of San Blas where the Indians recognized Carreño in compliance with the desires of their own Capitán Cuipana, principal *cacique* of the region.[23]

The military problems in areas of Spanish South America permitted only military matters on the Isthmus to be uppermost in Carreño's mind. In order to protect the Isthmus and at the same time not to interfere with or use the troops that marched regularly through the Isthmus on their way south to fight against Spain, Carreñno, upon the advice of Bolívar, organized a locally-manned cavalry regiment and a body of 700 infantrymen. Although this battalion, known as *Istmo,* was principally organized for guarding the Isthmus, Bolívar ordered it to participate in liberating activities in Peru against General José de Canterac in June of 1824. *Istmo* was incorporated into veteran battalions in South America and took part in the famous battle of Junín where the enemy's cavalry was almost destroyed, and in the battle of Ayacucho where General Antonio José de Sucre destroyed the last Spanish force of any consequence and ended Spanish rule in the New World.[24]

During the course of the Peruvian Campaign,[25] the ports of Panama on the Atlantic and on the Pacific were in constant movement with the arrival and departure of Colombian battalions headed for the war in South America. Consequently, the public treasury was faced with difficulties, because it had become totally depleted in furnishing provisions and transportation for troops to Peruvian ports. The victory at Ayacucho actually worsened the economic capacity of the Isthmians because of the continuous influx of defeated Spaniards for whom it was necessary to furnish transportation to Havana; then too, as time progressed, troops of the liberating army began to return to the Isthmus. Some of them were sent to La Chorrera, a short distance from Panama City, to restore their strength.

The methods that Carreño adopted to remedy these problems, including exacting almost doubled taxes, resulted in opposition against him. Carreño (a man of little talent, accustomed to the arbitrary ways of the military camp) used force when necessary to carry out his plans. Due to Carreño's methods, the Colombian cause was beginning to be unpopular on the Isthmus, but his power was diminished at the beginning of 1826 when the command of the Isthmus was divided for administrative purposes between civil and military authorities. Carreño kept the military command as Commandant General (he had been promoted to Brigadier General) and Juan José Argote, a man of principle who did try to stabilize administrative matters, was given civil command with the title of Intendant, a post he held until late in 1826. Argote was well-liked on the Isthmus and had worked for Panama's independence from Spain. He was a man of tact, educated and firm in his political opinions, yet he was the first of a series of leaders to suffer the turbulence of the era and its continual stigma of plays for power.[26]

It was during this period that Bolívar was able to hold his long-planned Latin American Congress on the Isthmus.[27] The idea of an alliance among the recently emancipated peoples of America was conceived by Bolívar at least as early as 1816, but the meeting to discuss such an idea could not be held until after independence had been won. On June 22, 1826, delegates from Colombia, Mexico, Peru and the United Provinces of Central America met in Panama. Chile, Bolivia, Brazil and the provinces of Río de la Plate declined to attend the Congress. England and the Low Countries sent representatives as observers only. One of the delegates from the United States died on the way and the other arrived when the Congress had already adjourned. As Bolívar had foreseen soon after the sessions got under way, the results of the Congress of Panama were not promising.[28]

It was also about this time that Bolívar became alarmed by the anarchy that was threatening the various Latin American countries. As a measure against such anarchy, Bolívar elaborated for Bolivia a constitution in which the term of the president was for life and in which the president could choose his successor. After having been approved by the Bolivian Congress, this constitution was also adopted by Peru. In search of supporters for this constitutional measure, various agents and friends of Bolívar were traveling through the provinces of Colombia. Thus, in Sep-

tember of 1826 Antonio Leocadio Guzmán arrived in Panama
and succeeded in getting the support of Carreño who in turn
put pressure on a Junta de Notables (which he himself had hur-
riedly promoted and which was composed of public employees
and private citizens) to approve an act asking for the "dictatorship" of Bolívar and the adoption of the Bolivian code in Colombia. At first, the Junta brazenly refused to consider the Bolivian constitution, and changed the agenda of the proceedings
to seek instead public approval for an interoceanic railroad and
Bolívar's support for it. Carreño was upset by this arrogant action and stirred up passions with public displays and parades
favoring Bolívar's dictatorship. The result was that at its next
meeting the Junta did proclaim its support of Bolívar.[29] Nevertheless, resistance to the Bolivarian program continued, even
though Carreño was able to secure this formal support. A newspaper appeared in the capital with the title *El Círculo Istmeño*.[30]
It voiced passionate opinions, mostly of an economic order,
against the proposed "dictatorship."[31] Argote, whose efforts at
stabilization were in continual clash with Carreño, resigned under
pretext of illness from the civil government, primarily because
of disagreements regarding the Bolivian Constitution. Liberals
were alarmed that the granting of absolute powers to Bolívar
would mean the destruction of the division of powers. They
soon found a powerful ally in Manuel Muñoz, a Venezuelan
appointed in February of 1827 as head of both the civil and
military government of the Isthmus.[32] Muñoz was sympathetic
to the ideas of *El Círculo Istmeño* and the political club of the
same name, to their criticism of the Bolivian statutes and
their idea of separation from Nueva Granada.[33] However, Muñoz
was forced to resign within a few months, apparently because of
disturbances in Los Santos related to a premature attempt at secession, for which he and the "Círculo Istmeño" were blamed.[34]
With this, the anti-Bolivarian group fell temporarily silent.
Muñoz was replaced by the Prefect of Veraguas, Colonel Fábrega,
until the following December (1827) when Colonel José Domingo Espinar, a native of Panama, arrived as General Commandant with civil powers. In the view of the Isthmians Espinar

abused his powers by his censorship and despotic rule. In March of 1828, the civil part of the government was placed under the command of General José Sardá, a native of Spain, who assumed those duties as Intendant of the Department, and whose rule from 1828 to the end of 1829, though not productive for the Isthmians, was at least more peaceful than it had been under Espinar alone.[35]

Both Espinar and Sardá were in favor of the Bolivian Statutes, the first because he had served loyally under Bolívar, and the second because he was partial to presidency for life and to a monarchy, principles for which he later lost his life. The only hope left for the Liberals in Panama under the rule of Espinar and Sardá was the Convention of Ocaña which was to be held in March of 1828, the same month Sardá came into power.[36] This convention had been arranged by the various political factions to discuss and decide on reforms of the existing government.

As if these problems were not enough, Spain was apparently making one final effort to reconquer her lost colonies. In preparation for any possible attacks from Spanish forces in Cuba, Sardá was forced to recruit an army in the interior of Panama while Espinar was absent. Zulia, Magdalena and Panama were combined into one military department under the command of General Mariano Montilla. Fortunately for Gran Colombia, the efforts of Spain were directed at Mexico.[37] Furthermore, the political horizons of Colombia were becoming more and more clouded. General Páez had revolted in 1826 in Venezuela, partly in reaction to the seemingly over-ambitious designs of Bolívar, and had thus initiated the dissolution of Colombia.[38] During 1827 revolts in Peru and even in Bolivia had led to the abjuration of the Bolivian constitution, which supported the presidency of Bolívar for life. Nevertheless, Bolívar continued his proposal to be declared president for life as stipulated in the Bolivian constitution. At the Convention of Ocaña in April of 1828, antagonisms flared between the Liberals and the Conservatives of Colombia. The Liberals, supporters of General Francisco de Paula Santander, had a majority among the delegates and were making efforts to prevent the reform of the constitution that would give Bolívar what in their opinion was excessive power. Sardá in Panama backed Bolívar's decision to rule for life, and this outraged Liberals there.

In spite of Liberal protests, Bolívar assumed the dictatorship in August. On September 25, 1828 conspirators assaulted the Presidential Palace in Bogotá with the intention of killing the Liberator, whom they accused of attempting to crown himself monarch of Colombia. The conspirators were captured and sentenced: some were executed but this did not deter protest in all parts of Colombia against dictatorial government.[39]

Other events and complications were affecting Bolívar's position as "dictator." A Peruvian army of 8,000 men under the command of General José de la Mar invaded Colombia, bombarded Guayaquil and then took possession of it. Peruvians also blockaded the coast of Panama and took some merchant ships from the port of Panama, whose defensive forces had been increased to 1,000 men. Bolívar wisely gave command of the forces opposing the Peruvians in Guayaquil to the hero of Ayacucho, General Sucre, who defeated the enemy in Ecuador near Loja on February 27, 1829.[40]

Having thus ended the war with Peru, and having put down revolts in the Cauca and Antioquia, Bolívar convened a congress in Bogotá in January of 1830 before which he gave up his supreme rule. The Congress accepted his resignation and named as President and Vice-President of the Republic, Doctor Joaquín Mosquera and General Domingo Caicedo respectively. A few days later Bolívar retired to his quinta, *Fucha.*[41]

TWO ATTEMPTS TO SECEDE FROM NUEVA GRANADA

The new vice-president took over the duties of president in the absence of Mosquera. He renamed as Military Commandant of the Isthmus the man who had already held that post from 1827 to 1829, General José Domingo Espinar. Espinar remained in Panama from 1830 to 1831, during which time much turmoil beset the Isthmus, not only from internal sources but also from troubles in the central government of Colombia.[42]

Fábrega, now a general, had again taken over the Province of Panama as prefect, a post equivalent to the *intendencia* held by Sardá. Espinar arrived again as head of the military, but he became outraged when Mosquera, now in full power as President, transferred him instead to Veraguas. Mosquera named as Military commandant of Panama one of his own Liberals, Colonel José Hilario López, and as civil head, José Vallarino Jiménez.[43] Espinar's reaction, including exiling Vallarino and refusing to accept his authority, only brought about criticisms from the Liberal wing on the Isthmus. Espinar, however, had the backing of the garrison and the masses who still idolized Bolívar, whose loyal supporter he had been. Hoping to give further support to Bolívar, Espinar asked for a formal act favoring independence from the government of Bogotá, but he was snubbed by several prominent men who had the moral support of Fábrega himself. Further enraged, Espinar jailed and finally exiled several important figures of the Isthmus. The inevitable occurred when on the 10th of September, 1830 a riot in Panama between the two factions gave Espinar the opportunity to seize complete governing powers, even those of Fábrega, whom he had confined to Veraguas.[44] In spite of the apparent support of the masses, Espinar had actually lost the respect of many Isthmians because he exiled many leaders, persecuted others, closed the presses, and attempted to rule in such a manner that the glories he had won during the struggle for emancipation from Spain were dimmed in the eyes of the people.

Meanwhile, in the interior of Nueva Granada a counter-revolution broke out in which Sucre was murdered. In Bogotá, leaders of the *coup d'état* against the Constitution of 1830 sought the renewed leadership of Bolívar, who refused the offer. The rebels forced President Joaquín Mosquera to appoint General Rafael Urdaneta as Secretary of War. When Mosquera could not stabilize the situation, the municipal council of Bogotá called on Urdaneta to head the government.[45]

The anarchy that was seemingly rampant throughout Nueva Granada was encouraged in Panama by Espinar's grudges against the government of Mosquera. This produced desires on the Isthmus to become a fourth state (along with Venezuela, Ecuador and Nueva Granada) in a federation, or to secede entirely from Nueva Granada and seek protection from some European power.[46] Finally, on September 26, 1830 the Junta called by Espinar to declare Panama independent from Nueva Granada justified this action by explaining that the Isthmus was neither economically nor morally bound to Nueva Granada.[47] The appearance of this justification this early in the history of Panama after its independence from Spain, marked the beginning of what was to become a trend in the thinking of various factions and groups on the Isthmus. Succeeding attempts to separate the Isthmus from Nueva Granada were to bear the mark of this justification as a witness to a growing sense of belonging apart. Nevertheless, as the use of this justification was in its embryonic stage at this time, the Junta expressed its desire that Bolívar himself would come to the Isthmus and be supreme ruler, and put his Colombia together again. In other words, the separation was to be temporary until such time as the Liberator accepted the duties as head of the Isthmus.

The Province of Panama accepted these conditions, but not so Veraguas, where Fábrega had been opposing Espinar since his confinement there. Bolívar, however, advised Espinar to reincorporate the Panamanian territory in Nueva Granada, for the government of Urdaneta, who had Bolívar's support, had been recognized by most of the provinces of Colombia anyway. The death of Bolívar in December of 1830 occurred only six days after the mutual decree that formally reunited the Isthmus with Nueva Granada.[48] Mosquera and Caicedo resumed power on May 3, 1831, but only after having signed an agreement with Urdaneta, who had lost support with the death of Bolívar a few months earlier.[49]

In the meantime, Espinar had continued to govern in Panama. To assure his strength there he embarked upon a plan that was to be his undoing. He decided to force Fábrega, who continued to oppose his government, into exile. Fábrega, agreed to leave rather than plunge his province into bloodshed.[50] Espinar also embarked upon a military tour of the country to gain more military and economic support to protect his government. But Espinar had not counted on betrayal from the officer he had left in charge while he went to Veraguas. The Venezuelan Colonel Juan Eligio Alzuru had been convinced by Espinar's enemies in the capital city of Panama to turn against him. As Espinar approached the capital, he was arrested and put on board a ship that took him to Guayaquil.[51]

As the choice between Espinar and Alzuru turned out, it was a case of Scylla versus Charybdis, for Alzuru's regime was to hatch another attempt at independence from Nueva Granada and make another play for power. Alzuru first restored all the rights taken away by Espinar, maintained some semblance of order and managed to find many sympathizers on the Isthmus; but he was afraid that he might be made to answer for the death of two officers whom he had executed as spies. Furthermore, the central government, already under Mosquera, insisted on the recognition of the authority of José Vallarino, whom Espinar had not permitted to take civil command. Alzuru distrusted Vallarino, and wanted to keep military power at all cost. Besides, he had been influenced by the many exiled officials on the Isthmus, most of them Venezuelans like himself, who had recently taken part in uprisings in Ecuador. For these reasons, Alzuru agitated and inspired the more obvious supporters of independence on the Isthmus, using the same rationalization for such actions that Espinar had used—that the Isthmus had no natural or economic ties with Nueva Granada. Alzuru's argument seemed even more reasonable to the people of the Isthmus now that Ecuador and Venezuela had broken away also.[52]

Alzuru knew that he could not convert Vallarino to this point of view. Therefore, he relieved him of all power so that the Junta that Alzuru had called together to declare independence could do so unhindered. Thus, on the 9th of July, 1831 another declaration of independence from Nueva Granada was read. One of the Junta's provisions was that Fábrega would take over the civil government and Alzuru would remain in charge of the military. Although Alzuru at first seemed to comply with this and other provisions, when Fábrega came to the capital to take charge, he found that Alzuru was instead going to reserve for himself total power on the Isthmus. Apparently, Alzuru was angered and frightened with the arrival in Chagres of a new military commandant, Colonel Tomás Herrera, whom the Bogotá government had appointed in June. The Declaration of Independence had already been read when Herrera reached Panama, and this made Alzuru even more anxious to seek full independence, for he feared retaliation from the central government. Under the pressures he was experiencing, he overreacted toward the Liberals in the city of Panama by confiscating property and exiling prominent individuals; thus, he brought upon himself the wrath of many citizens there.

In the meantime, Herrera, who had been provided with about 160 men of an experienced battalion, decided to ask for reinforcements from Cartagena. From Chagres he went to Portobelo to set up protective measures and reinforcements in case of attack by Alzuru. He found that the commissioners that Alzuru had sent to Portobelo to negotiate a peace settlement were themselves distraught when they heard the news of Alzuru's rampaging despotism. Herrera actually felt that independence from Colombia was in the best interests of Panama, but he did not think the country would prosper under the foreign and destructive elements in power. Alzuru had created such ill-will by his forced draft and persecution, and by exiling Fábrega, Vallarino and many other prominent citizens with such lack of respect for constitutional government, that José de Obaldía and Francisco Picón, the delegates he had sent to Portobelo, abandoned all support of the tyrant and instead embraced the cause of Herrera.[53]

The campaign that Herrera began against the military forces of Alzuru was to be later reinforced by the simultaneous campaigns of the exiled Fábrega and others who managed to land in Veraguas with the aid of the very ship in which they were bound for their exile. Herrera's army, which consisted of volunteers from Portobelo and Palenque in addition to his original force of 160, now counted nearly 700 men. They sailed up the Chagres as far as Gorgona, then marched near Panama City at Farfán,

hoping to engage the enemy there. Only three days later, Fábrega reached Chorrera with about 1500 men whose ranks had
been additionally reinforced with the men whom the despot
kept at Natá under the command of Colonel José Antonio Miró.
Alzuru, on the other hand, had advanced to La Boca, across the
Río Grande, and with the aid of a flotilla of bongos and canoes,
had entered the lands adjacent to Farfán. Alzuru planned to
march behind Herrera to force him against the river. Then he intended to retrace his steps to march to La Chorrera and dispose
of Fábrega's force. But his plan failed because the superior forces
of Herrera overwhelmed him. Alzuru had to retreat, not all the
way back to La Chorrera, but as far as Arraiján, between La
Chorrera and Farfán, a few miles from Panama City. There, he
sentenced the mayor (Alcade) of the place to a violent death
after finding that he had prepared provisions for his enemies. It
was near Arraiján that Alzuru was completely crushed, for Fábrega heard of Herrera's victory at Farfán, and marched upon Alzuru as he had just turned back to Río Grande. After a short
fight in which Alzuru was caught between Fábrega and Herrera,
he was captured and led to the capital. Herrera and his forces
had entered that city the same day of their victory near Farfán,
on the 25th of August, 1831, but had left again to pursue Alzuru.
When Alzuru was brought to the city, he was tried before a military court, and was executed together with some of his main
chiefs before the entire army congregated in the main Plaza on
the 29th of August. Thus ended the second futile attempt to secede from the Central Government in Nueva Granada.[54]

    Although the masses were addicted to secession at this time,
the rash policies of the leaders of these attempts to secede had
only alienated other leaders of the Isthmus from that cause,
leaders who could then only hope for economic stability and
political order from some other source—namely, Nueva Granada.
Such had been the case of Obaldía and Picón in Portobelo, for
example. Fortunately for the Isthmus, a hopeful, though short-
lived reprieve of comparative progress and peace was about to
begin. Under the guidance of Herrera the wounds that the ex-
cesses of past administrations had inflicted upon the little Isthmus began somewhat to heal.

NOTES

1. What is known today as Colombia was also known as the State of Nueva Granada after Independence from Spain. Nueva Granada was part of Bolívar's Republic of Colombia (referred to by many historians as Gran Colombia), together with Ecuador and Venezuela, until the disintegration of that union. In 1858 Nueva Granada was named the Granadine Confederacy; in 1861 it was known as the United States of Colombia, and in 1886, it was named the Republic of Colombia. See: E. Taylor Parks, *Colombia and the United States, 1765-1934* (Durham, N.C., 1935), 481.

2. Ernesto Castillero R. and Juan A. Susto, *Rincón histórico,* Vol. I (Panama, 1947), 97.

    In 1812, Brigadier Benito Pérez, appointed by the regency as Viceroy of Nueva Granada, was forced to establish his base of authority in Panama due to the state of confusion and revolt in Santafé de Bogotá, the viceregal capital. The Tribunal of the *Real Audencia* thus functioned in Panama until about the middle of 1813 when Pérez's successor, Don Francisco Montalvo, established the government in Santa Marta. See: Juan B. Sosa and Enrique J. Arce, *Compendio de historia de Panama,* 2nd ed. (Panama, 1971), 184, hereafter cited as Sosa and Arce, *Compendio.*

    Under the rule of Spain, the General Comandancia de Panama was composed of three provinces—Portobelo, Veraguas, Darién; and two districts—Natá and Alanje. The provinces were ruled by a Governor and a Commandant (Military) and the districts by an *Alcalde Mayor* (Mayor). Panama, the capital, was ruled by a high official in charge of the military (*Comandancia General*) and also of the supreme civil government (*Gobierno Superior Político*).

    The military garrisons stationed in Panama consisted of an artillery company and an infantry battalion. There were also militias in many places throughout the rest of the Isthmus. For example, in Natá there was a battalion of whites and a battalion of *pardos;* in Veraguas there was a white infantry battalion, and in other places were single companies of infantry and artillery. See: Rubén D. Carles, *A 150 años de la independencia de Panama de España, 1821-1971* (Panama, n.d.), v, hereafter cited as Carles, *A 150 años.*

3. Castillero and Susto, *Rincón histórico,* Vol. I, 93-97; Sosa and Arce, *Compendio,* 184-187.

4. It was at this time that Bolívar fled to Jamaica where he wrote his famous *Letter from Jamaica.*

5. Sir Gregor MacGregor managed to escape the counterattack by the

Spanish (commanded by Governor Hore) by throwing a mattress out of the window of his bedroom and jumping into the sea to swim to his ship, *Hero.* See: An Officer Who Miraculously Escaped, *Narrative of the Expedition under General MacGregor against Porto Bello* (London, 1820), 51-52; Jane Lucas DeGrummond, *Caracas Diary* (Baton Rouge, 1954), 307-308, 313; *Niles Weekly Register,* XVI (1819), 55, 128, 158, 318, 335, 384. W.D. Weatherhead, *An Account of the Late Expedition Against the Isthmus of Darien, Under the Command of Sir Gregor MacGregor* (London, 1821), 22-68.

For a short biography of MacGregor see: *The Dictionary of National Biography,* ed. Leslie Stephen, Vol. XII (London, 1949), 539.

Stanley Faye states that ". . . pending the arrival of other vessels he [MacGregor] had proposed to unresponsive officers a privateering campaign, and also another capture of the Isthmus and the digging of a Panama Canal." "Commodore Aury," *The Louisiana Historical Quarterly,* XXIV (July, 1941), 55.

Another expedition, this one against the Island of Taboga, was led by Juan Illingworth in 1819. For a description of this naval maneuver see: Camilo Destruge, *Biografía del General Don Juan Illingworth* (Guayaquil, 1914), 7-36.

6.   Manuel María Alba C., *Cronología de los gobernantes de Panamá, 1510-1967* (Panama, 1967), 133, hereafter cited Alba, *Cronología;* Castillero and Susto, *Rincón histórico,* Vol. I, 98; Ernesto J. Nicolau, *El grito de la Villa (10-Noviembre-1821)* (Panama, 1961), 15, 55; Sosa and Arce, *Compendio,* 185, 189-192, 194.

7.   Castillero and Susto, *Rincón histórico,* Vol. I, 98; Bonifacio Pereira Jiménez, *Historia de Panama,* 3rd ed. (Panama, 1969), 215; Sosa and Arce, *Compendio,* 194-196. Sámano came with the idea of separating Panama from the domain of Nueva Granada and renaming Panama *Tierra Firme* (Captancy General of Tierra Firme). See: Alba, *Cronología* 134-135; Noris L. Correa D., *Apuntes de Historia patria* (Panama, n.d.), 114.

8.   Alba, *Cronología,* 134-135; Correa, *Apuntes de historia patria,* 114; Nicolau, *El grito de la Villa,* 3; Sosa and Arce, *Compendio,* 196.

9.   When Murgeón received the news of Panama's declaration of independence, he decided to change the commands of two of his ships, but the commanders had already begun talks with the patriots to turn the ships over to them with the stipulation that the salaries of the crews would be paid retroactively. By this time, Murgeón was gravely ill in Quito. His illness was apparently the result of a serious fall he had had in the mountains of Esmeralda. The difficult situation in which he

found himself, and the final news that his ships had been turned over to the patriots, proved too much for him. He died April 3, 1822. See: Nicolau, *El grito de la Villa*, 98-100.

The spelling of Murgeón's name fluctuates even within the same book (*El grito de la Villa*) between Mourgeón and Murgeón. This last spelling would represent the Spanish version of the French *ou* sound, and it would be the tendency among Spanish-speaking writers to spell it thus.

10. Alba, *Cronología*, 135-136; Carles, *A 150 años*, vii; Correa, *Apuntas de historia patria*, 115-116; Sosa and Arce, *Compendio*, 197-198.
11. Nicolau, *El grito de la Villa*, 9, 15.
12. Alba, *Cronología*, 135; Correa, *Apuntes de historia patria*, 115; Nicolau, *El grito de la Villa*, 9; Pereira, *Historia de Panamá*, 216; Sosa and Arce, *Compendio*, 198-199.
13. Alba, *Cronología*, 136-137; Nicolau, *El grito de la Villa*, 25, 60; Sosa and Arce, *Compendio*, 198-199.
14. Nicolau, *El grito de la Villa*, 27-28, 55; Sosa and Arce, *Compendio*, 199.
15. Nicolau, *El grito de la Villa*, 56-66.
16. *Ibid.*, 67; Sosa and Arce, *Compendio*, 199-201.

Some of the important officials who attended the meetings at the Casa Consistorial were: the Governor, the Captain General, the Bishop, the Vicar General, provincial representatives, military chiefs and several other members of the administration. See: Sosa and Arce, *Compendio*, 200.

17. Nicolau, *El grito de la Villa*, 67-68; Sosa and Arce, *Compendio*, 200.
18. Correa, *Apuntes de historia patria*, 118.
19. Ernesto Castillero R., *Historia de Panama*, 7th ed. (Panama, 1962), 78.
20. With the words, "I admit that the existing Republic cannot be governed except by the sword," Simón Bolívar prophesied the future history of Colombia—a history of the constant struggle and bloody strife between liberalism and conservatism for control of the government. When either of these two schools of thought was in power, its governmental measures were annulled and reversed by the succeeding administration. Aggravating this constant political strife were the bitter religious and regional disputes. In no other American country did the Church have such a hold on the people. Liberals constantly harrassed the Roman Catholic Church and the Jesuits while Conservatives defended both. These struggles, both political and religious, were and still are predominant issues in Colombian history. See: *Selected Writings of Bolívar, 1823-1830*, ed. Harold A. Bierck, Jr., trans. Lewis Bertran, (New York, 1951), I, 740; Tom B. Jones, *An Introduction to Hispanic American History* (New York, 1938), 360-361; "The Struggle in Col-

ombia," *The Saturday Review,* XCII (September 14, 1901), 326; F.A. Kirkpatrick, *Latin America: A Brief History* (New York, 1939), 253, hereafter cited as Kirkpatrick, *Latin America.*

21. Alba, *Cronología,* 141; Sosa and Arce, *Compendio,* 202.

22. In 1821, an assembly had been held in Cúcuta for the purpose of writing a constitution. The leader of the revolutionaries, Simón Bolívar, had previously argued for a centralized government; without one, he claimed, the enemies of Colombia would have a strong advantage. At the time of the Cúcuta assembly, Bolívar's popularity was at its peak. Under his leadership, the Spaniards had been driven a second time from New Granada and a third time from Venezuela after the failure of federation in both countries. A centralized government was therefore favored by the assembly, and on August 30, 1821 the second of Colombia's constitutions was adopted. By its terms Bolívar was elected President and Francisco de Paula Santander, Vice-President. See: *Selected Writings of Bolívar,* I, 22; William Marion Gibson, *The Constitution of Colombia,* (Durham, 1948), xi-xii, 37; Jesús María Henao and Gerardo Arrubla, *History of Colombia,* trans. and ed. J. Fred Rippy (Chapel Hill, 1938), 519.

23. Pereira, *Historia de Panamá,* 228; Sosa and Arce, *Compendio,* 202.

24. Alba, *Cronología,* 141, 143; Sosa and Arce, *Compendio,* 203-204.

25. The years from 1822 to 1827 found Bolívar in Ecuador and Peru, continuing the fight to drive Spain from South America. During the five-year absence of Bolívar, his vice-president, Francisco de Paula Santander, acted as president of the republic. At first, Colombia was able to make progress toward its development as a nation, especially in the field of education. In 1822, President Santander ordered the establishment of normal schools, and schools for the female population. Even some Indians were to have educational privileges. These advances, plus Santander's attention to the development of agriculture, trade and mining, were soon ended by internal problems—conflicting ambitions among various leaders, the desire to give the masses more education, the clergy's opposition to liberalism, the long absence of Bolívar, financial chaos, and in 1826, rebellion in Venezuela led by José Antonio Páez. See: Henao and Arrubla, *History of Colombia,* 369; Parks, *Colombia and the United States,* 110-111, 117-118.

26. Alba, *Cronología,* 141, 143; Sosa and Arce, *Compendio,* 204-205.

27. Bolívar himself did not attend. See: Moisés Chong M., *Historia de Panamá* (Panama, 1968), 134; Mariano Arosemena, *Apuntamientos históricos (1801-1840),* (Panama, 1949), 168-169, hereafter cited as *Apuntamientos.*

28. Pereira, *Historia de Panamá,* 228-230; Sosa and Arce, *Compendio,* 205-206.

The only transcendental result of this meeting was the inspiration to consider the countries of the Americas as a brotherhood, the basis on which pan-americanism stands even today. See: Alba, *Cronología,* 144.

In the opinion of Mariano Arosemena, who lived at that time on the Isthmus, the enemies of Panama were intimidated by the apparent mutual interest and desire for protection which the American nations seemed to hold in regard to one another, thereby giving the meeting still another positive result. Arosemena, *Apuntamientos,* 170.

29. Arosemena, *Apuntamientos,* 170-171; Sosa and Arce, *Compendio,* 206.

30. The editors of this paper were members of the club of the same name. They were José Agustín Arango, José de Obaldía and Mariano Arosemena. Arosemena, *Apuntamientos,* 178.

31. The main objection to the high concentration of power in the hands of Bolívar and to the Bolivian statutes, related to the continued economic ruin brought about by the powerful Colombian mercantile groups so ably represented in the Bogotanian central government. The Isthmians wanted free trade and were eager to construct an interoceanic highway, but they were thwarted and ignored by the aforementioned group. See: Chong, *Historia,* 133.

32. Alba, *Cronología,* 144; Castillero, *Historia de Panama,* 80; Sosa and Arce, *Compendio,* 206-207.

33. Because Muñoz was related to Bolívar, the supreme government mistakenly considered him loyal to Bolívar's cause. But Muñoz was instead an avid republican who did not agree with such a concentration of power as Bolívar proposed. See: Arosemena, *Apuntamientos,* 178-179.

The desire for a decentralized government was a manifestation of the Liberal philosophy. The Liberals of the nineteenth century based their beliefs on the idea of having freedom from any unnecessary restrictions or policies imposed by government. Liberals all over Colombia were not necessarily in accord as to local regulations, but they all shared the hope that the government and the Church would not interfere and impose the religion, morality and views of a governing few on the entire population.

34. Alba, *Cronología,* 145; Arosemena, *Apuntamientos,* 177; Chong, *Historia de Panamá,* 133; Sosa and Arce, *Compendio,* 206-207.

35. Alba, *Cronología,* 146-148; Arosemena, *Apuntamientos,* 179, 184; Sosa and Arce, *Compendio,* 206-207.

36. Arosemena, *Apuntamientos,* 179, 184, 192. Sardá was sentenced to death in Bogotá for plotting against Santander. He escaped, continued his opposition, was discovered and shot. See: Carles, *A 150 años,* 8-9.

37. Arosemena, *Apuntamientos,* 182-183, 185, 199; Sosa and Arce, *Compendio,* 207.

38. The Páez revolt forced Bolívar to return to Colombia in 1827. He immediately was given full emergency powers to deal with the Páez uprising. Bolívar managed to pacify the Venezuelan hero for the time being; however, opposition to Bolívar developed in Colombia. This opposition was led by Santander, Francisco Soto and others. See: Henao and Arrubla, *History of Colombia*, 375-426; Parks, *Colombia and the United States*, 120-123.

39. Arosemena, *Apuntamientos*, 181, 185-187, 189; Bonifacio Pereira Jiménez, *Biografía del Río Chagres* (Panama, 1964), 237; Pereira, *Historia de Panama*, 237; Sosa and Arce, *Compendio*, 207-208.

    Actually, there was simultaneous support of various forms of government: parties in favor of monarchy, presidency for life within a centralized system of government, dictatorship, republican democracy, federation, and separation of Colombia into three sovereign republics, Venezuela, Ecuador and Nueva Granada. See: Arosemena, *Apuntamientos*, 195.

40. Arosemena, *Apuntamientos*, 190-191, 197-199.

41. Arosemena, *Apuntamientos*, 206-207; Sosa and Arce, *Compendio*, 208-209.

42. Arosemena, *Apuntamientos*, 192; Chong, *Historia de Panamá*, 131; Pereira, *Historia de Panamá*, 243. The date quoted by Sosa and Arce of Espinar's arrival on the Isthmus is 1831 and it does not mesh correctly with other dates they use for other occurrences. It is either printing errors or carelessness on the part of the authors that their dates are sometimes not consistent or accurate.

43. Alba, *Cronología*, 150; Sosa and Arce, *Compendio*, 209. Apparently, one of the reasons that the central government had become suspicious of Espinar was his arrogant refusal to take the oath of loyalty when he took charge of his duties the second time. Also, President Mosquera was not in accord with some of Espinar's ideas [and of course, Espinar was an avid admirer of Bolívar]. See: Arosemena, *Apuntamientos*, 200-201.

44. Alba, *Cronología*, 148; Arosemena, *Apuntamientos*, 201-206; Chong, *Historia de Panamá*, 131-132.

    Espinar had received advice from Caicedo on one occasion, while Caicedo still backed Espinar, to get rid of Fábrega's interference, for he was aware of the innate discord between those two Isthmians. See: Alba, *Cronología*, 149.

45. Arosemena, *Apuntamientos*, 208-209; Sosa and Arce, *Compendio*, 210; Gibson, *The Constitutions of Colombia*, 109-110.

46. So intent were several factions of rich and powerful men of the Isthmus in seceding from Colombia that Espinar found it necessary to prevent them from successfully acquiring the protection they were soliciting from Great Britain. See: Chong, *Historia de Panama*, 133.

However, according to Mariano Arosemena, such an intention was simply a pretext that gave Espinar another excuse to take over the entire Isthmian government and cover up his own desires to secede as a fourth state within Gran Colombia. See: Arosemena, *Apuntamientos*, 132-133.

The United States representatives in Bogotá reminded Washington of the danger of British aggression both at Panama and the Mosquito Coast. These representatives were relieved that the rebellion of 1830 on the Isthmus was crushed, since there was a rumor that Panama had offered to surrender its sovereignty to Great Britain in return for protection against Bogotá. See: Parks, *Colombia and the United States*, 183.

47. Historical sources do not clarify the formation of this *junta;* however, previous examples show that this type of *junta* was formed to perform specific and temporary duties, and was usually composed of leading members of the community.

48. Arosemena, *Apuntamientos*, 204, 206, 209; Carles, *A 150 años*, 11; Pereira, *Historia de Panamá*, 244; Sosa and Arce, *Compendio*, 211-212. Bolívar died on December 17, 1830 on the eleventh anniversary of the creation of Gran Colombia. His death marked the beginning of the first open struggles between liberalism and conservatism. See: Henao and Arrubla, *History of Colombia*, 375-426; Parks, *Colombia and the United States*, 120-123.

49. Arosemena, *Apuntamientos*, 228; Sosa and Arce, *Compendio*, 211-212; Gibson, *The Constitution of Colombia*, 110.

50. Arosemena, *Apuntamientos*, 205; Sosa and Arce, *Compendio*, 212. A letter claimed to have been written by Fábrega to Pablo López of Santiago was intercepted and published in the form of loose sheets. The letter stated Fábrega's fears of Espinar's ambition and also his pledge for support of any acts against Espinar's rule. See: Arosemena, *Apuntamientos*, 206.

51. Arosemena, *Apuntamientos*, 214; Pereira, *Historia de Panamá*, 244; Sosa and Arce, *Compendio*, 212.

52. Arosemena, *Apuntamientos*, 214-215; Pereira, *Historia de Panamá*, 244; Sosa and Arce, *Compendio*, 212-213. Venezuela declared herself independent from Colombia in 1829; Quito did the same in 1830.

53. Arosemena, *Apuntamientos*, 218, 215-220, 222-223; Pereira, *Historia de Panamá*, 249; Sosa and Arce, *Compendio*, 213-215.

54. Arosemena, *Apuntamientos*, 224-226; Sosa and Arce, *Compendio*, 216, 217, 218.

CHAPTER II

The Free State and the Federal State

The optimism that prevailed immediately after Tomás Herrera's victory on the Isthmus in 1831 was to become a fluctuating rather than a stable attitude. Herrera would lead one more very serious and active attempt at permanent separation from Nueva Granada, and Justo Arosemena would continue to work for self-government in Panama in the struggle that would follow regarding the recognition of Panama as a state within a federal system.[1]

THE POLITICAL ORGANIZATION OF NUEVA GRANADA AND ITS EFFECTS ON THE ISTHMUS

The dissolution of Gran Colombia was now a fact. At the end of 1831 a convention met at Bogotá to form the central provinces into the political entity officially known as Nueva Granada.[2] In 1832 the convention elected Francisco de Paula Santander president.[3] The departments were eliminated, the territory was divided into provinces, the provinces into cantons, and the cantons into parishes. The Isthmus continued with its two main divisions —Panama and Veraguas—with Juan José Argote as governor of Panama and General José de Fábrega as governor of Veraguas. Tomás Herrera kept the military command of both areas.[4] The governors and Herrera took great interest in trying to smother all ideas regarding revolution, and tried to instill legal order as firmly as possible in order to advance in a new and prosperous direction.[5] Their preoccupation with unrest was due partly to demonstrations which had taken place early in 1832. These were led by a separatist faction which believed that the welfare of the Isthmus required secession from Nueva Granada, for only then could Isthmians determine how best to stimulate trade in their land without constant regard for the interests of Bogotá. Even though individuals of high esteem agreed with the separatists, many others at this time (including Tomás Herrera) considered such action subversive and non-conducive to long-lasting peaceful economic results for the Isthmians, whom they felt would only have to struggle militarily to remain permanently free from Colombia.

There were two groups of secessionists. One group, led by Mariano Arosemena, wanted Panama to unite with Ecuador; and the other, led by José de Obaldía, wanted a Hanseatic Republic under the protection of Great Britain and the United States. Obaldía tried to enlist the aid of the consuls of these two nations, but he was unsuccessful. The President of Ecuador, General Juan José Flores, encouraged the partisans of the idea regarding union with Ecuador. A premature attempt at secession, early in 1832, spearheaded by adherents of this particular preference, ended in the execution of two officers of the Ninth Battalion: Lieutenant Melchor Durán and a Second Lieutenant by the name of Casana. In this way the voices of discontent were silenced temporarily.[6]

The Isthmus was convalescent, and internal peace and constitutional order seemed for the moment to prevail in spite of the economic problems of the country. When Argote began his term, education was almost non-existent, agriculture was in a sad condition, commerce was at a standstill, and Panama's exploitation of its geographic position was merely an unfulfilled desire. Argote was relentless in his efforts to strengthen the Panamanian economy by various peaceful means. He made serious efforts to organize the tax system and saw to it that the monies collected were properly administered.[7] Argote was able to provide new schools and upgrade old ones. He established the first tallow candle and straw hat factories, but any other plans that he might have had for the economic progress of the province were halted because of an illness that forced him to take a leave of absence in September of 1833.[8]

The Isthmians continued their struggle to improve commerce. Business groups firmly believed that if the Isthmus were a totally free port it would acquire much more commercial activity.[9] Their petitions for free trade were considered by the Central Government, but on June 13, 1833 it merely lowered the tax to 2%, not taking into consideration that the expense of examining cargo and verifying values of merchandise was a fixed cost necessary as long as *any* tax continued to be exacted. Furthermore, ships with cargo destined for other ports continued to bypass Panama because Article 2 of the Law of June, 1833 required them to pay a tonnage fee whenever they docked in ports of Panama even when they did not disembark cargo or passengers. Isthmians continued to demand that an interoceanic route of some kind be developed and that Panama be a free port, with no restrictions whatsoever.[10]

In 1834 the Bogotá government at last partly heeded the wishes of Panamanian elements in favor of making Panama a free port. It decreed that on most products destined to cross the Isthmus or to be embarked later for other ports, the only charges to be collected were to be tonnage and warehouse charges if warehouses were used. Products intended for use by the population of the Isthmus were to be taxed, however, and certain products such as precious metals still were to be under duty.[11] As for interoceanic communication, a new surge of vigor and interest became apparent in government circles of Nueva Granada. In 1835 Portobelo and Panama City were declared absolutely free—no tonnage fees, anchorage fees, not even storage fees. All products could be introduced freely—even liquor. But there was one large obstacle to this declaration: the law was not supposed to go into effect until some sort of transisthmian route was opened.[12]

In the period from 1834 to 1836 the governor of Panama was Manuel J. Hurtado, author of the Act of Independence of 1821 and former Colombian Minister in London.[13] Although modest progress continued under Hurtado, a new wave of criticism was evolving. Local representatives of the provincial government were beginning to feel that rapid progress was checked by the rigorous centralism imposed from Bogotá. The opinion of Mariano Arosemena, at this time a representative in the *Cámara Provincial,* seemed to express this attitude towards a centralized government very clearly:

> The rigorous centralization of those days did not allow the territories to undertake any steps of positive progress, and even on those occasions when success seemed to be within reach, they found themselves not infrequently frustrated by the national government. A central government did not satisfy the demands of the provinces in their diversified interests in the whole of the extensive Neogranadine territory.[14]

Although general peace and relative progress seemed to hover over the provinces of Nueva Granada, they soon vanished as political and economic crises strengthened criticism against domination from Bogotá.[15]

THE RUSSELL AFFAIR

At the end of Hurtado's administration the Isthmus was involved in a sensational incident that almost caused a war between Nueva Granada and Great Britain. It arose over a personal matter between Justo Paredes and Britain's viceconsul, Joseph Russell. In the fight which followed, Paredes was wounded by a sword cut on the left nipple and Russell received blows on his face. Juan A. Diez, judge of the second district court (*juez 2° cantonal*) and cousin of Paredes, arrived at the scene, and even though the two men were already separated, Diez gave Russell such a strong blow with his cane that the Briton had to spend many months in bed.[16] The judge who considered the case condemned Russell to six years in the stockade, assigned him the cost of the trial, and did not penalize Diez for the assault against Russell. Great Britain, aware of the strange sentence, demanded the immediate release of Russell, indemnity to Russell for damages and injuries, dismissal of the judicial authorities who had not complied with their duties, and the re-opening of the consular office which had been closed.

By the time that Pedro de Obarrio took office in February, 1836 as the new governor of Panama, the Russell Affair had worsened. Great Britain had sent a squadron to the Atlantic to blockade the coast of Nueva Granada and a warship to the port of Panama to enforce British demands. Governor Obarrio was forced to take defense measures, for the National Government had resolved not to give way to British pressures. Fortunately, General José Hilario López instigated peaceful measures to end the dispute. Though many Panamanians expressed disdain toward the solution, in December of 1836 the Nueva Granada Government paid an indemnity of 1000 pounds sterling and annulled the sentence given to Russell.[17] The entire affair was apparently viewed by Colombians as an excuse on the part of Great Britain to gain control of the Isthmus of Panama.[18] This could possibly explain Colombia's decision to satisfy Britain's demands and thus avoid further involvement with British forces. However, it appears that if Britain was actually looking for an excuse to take over Panama at this time, the indemnity it required of Colombia would have been greater, to make it almost impossible for Colombia to readily accede to its payment. Since this was not the case, perhaps Colombia's fears were actually unfounded.

POLITICAL TURMOIL AND ECONOMIC DEPRESSION

Notwithstanding the negative publicity surrounding the Russell incident, the administration of Pedro de Obarrio was a dedicated one. Obarrio was able to promote education with the available resources. On July 16, 1836 the first school for girls was opened in the district of Santa Ana, and that year schools in Chepo and on the island of San Miguel were also established. These schools were to be maintained with money from the fifth part of the revenues from liquor.[19]

While popular education made some advance, there were serious setbacks in other areas, due in part to the political situation within the Central Government. In New Granada's presidential elections of 1836, José Ignacio Marquez, a moderate Liberal, won. His victory came as the result of a split in the Liberal Party over two other candidates: General José María Obando and Vicente Azuero, a radical Liberal.[20] Márquez took over the reins of government in 1837. The relative progress which the Liberals had been able to achieve on the Isthmus was stifled by Márquez, according to Liberal views,[21] even though in other parts of the country he followed liberal policies in government, such as encouraging public education, reducing the size of the standing army and stimulating industry.[22] He was aware that the representatives from the Isthmus had whole-heartedly opposed him publicly in the Bogotá Congress and in the news media. His antipathy for the Panamanians, and his political allegiance to other political sectors which had supported him (though according to some reports he was notably impartial) created an air of indifference toward Panama and, thereby, a series of economic regressions. Even the usual legal processes needed to transact serious business were neglected and indeed ceased to exist on the Isthmus for over a year because there was no judicial machinery with final authority from the Central Government.

Since the Isthmus still lacked good means of communication, the new ills compounded the misery and ruin evident everywhere in the provinces of Panama and Veraguas.[23] At this time the designate Minister of Nueva Granada to Ecuador, the well-known man of letters, Doctor Rufino Cuervo, arrived in Panama on his way to his post and was so shaken by the economic decadence of the capital city—numerous buildings in ruins, multitudes of vagrants roaming the streets in search of jobs, prices fallen to unbelievable levels—that in a famous letter to a friend in Bogotá he wrote this sentence: "Anyone who wishes to know Panama had better come quickly because it is ending."[24]

This sad situation was made even worse by the civil war that was developing in Nueva Granada and that threatened to engulf the Isthmus. The political victory of Márquez and his administrative policies had engendered much ill feeling among the Liberals who had lost the election. Intertwined with these antipathies was the strong desire to form a federal government. In 1840 many provinces declared themselves states within a federal system and armed themselves. The resulting fratricidal war was bloody indeed.[25]

THE FREE STATE OF THE ISTHMUS

When the civil war exploded in Nueva Granada, Carlos de Icaza was governor of Panama and Carlos Fábrega was governor of Veraguas. Tomás Herrera was still military leader. The echoes of the war hastened the union of Isthmians against active involvement and strengthened within them a desire to secede completely from Nueva Granada and thus avoid the horrors of war and the economic disasters it always brought to the Isthmus.[26] Some leaders, however, were hesitant about the permanent success of secession at this time. One of these men, Justo Arosemena, (who was later to be greatly instrumental in gaining legal statehood for Panama) realized that final separation without the military strength to uphold such an entity as Herrera proposed was a passionate but unrealistic dream, and he preferred not to participate whole-heartedly in the venture which was destined to end with grave consequences for the leaders of the Isthmus. Instead, he advocated separation only for the duration of the war, and only as a means of maintaining neutrality in it. Justo Arosemena was not a petty man, however, and in spite of his reservations, he did assist in maintaining peace and order in the bureaucratic work of the new nation, the Free State of the Isthmus, becoming an indispensable aid to Tomás Herrera. In the years that followed, his idea of attaining statehood through the legislative processes, was the idea that would predominate on the Isthmus.

Even though later Tomás Herrera was to support such an idea, in 1840 he preferred to attempt irrevocable independence.[27] Herrera's experience on the Isthmus had led him to consider what previously had come to his attention when he had defeated Alzuru—that while Panama's best interests did not lie in its close ties to Nueva Granada, they did not lie in the hands of a selfish and greedy leadership either. This is why he had not always supported independence. But at this moment, the turmoil of war which threatened the Isthmus was too strong, and Herrera perhaps felt that he was now called to be the leader Panama needed. His own words testify to some of the thoughts that were assailing him and to the reasons for his support of independence at this time:

> Certainly, reason and experience attest, as you citizens know, that this country, of singular characteristics in the world, has uselessly waited or would hope to prosper as long as it is subjected to an irregular role as appendix to Nueva Granada, whose high officials have never and will never recognize its needs nor satisfy them. The Isthmus owes to the world's commercial movements those services for which the Supreme Being has destined it, by bringing the oceans close together and by taming the high mountain ranges of the Andes there.[28]

Herrera accepted the request to head the new government as president of the republic. Because the garrison in Panama adhered to the act of separation upheld by the "deliberating" popular assembly of November 18, 1840 that had formed the Free State of the Isthmus, he found no immediate obstacles to his new position. But Governor Carlos Fábrega of Veraguas refused to second the movement until Herrera marched to Santiago with troops.

A convention was held in June of 1841 to proclaim the State and ratify the assembly's act of November 18, to formulate the constitution of the state, and to elect a Chief and Vice-Chief— positions unanimously conceded to Herrera and Icaza. However, Bogotá did not recognize this secession, basing its stand on the claim that Panama had become united with Colombia in 1821 as a part of a federative nation and not as an independent entity. The position of the Central Government acquired strength as it defeated the insurgents in the central parts of Nueva Granada, and re-established itself in these areas. Panama was well aware of its weak military defenses against a solidified army from Nueva Granada.[29]

Besides the obvious lack of arms to combat Nueva Granada, the Panamanians became apprehensive about the possibility of a military take-over by the British in Bocas del Toro and the consequent international repercussions involved. The English wanted control over lands which might be exploited for purposes of building a canal. They had landed in various parts of Central America, and under the pretext of supporting the unification and the claims of the Mosquito Indians, they had also landed in Bocas del Toro on the Isthmus. The question of this abuse of weak nations by a stronger one was aired diplomatically. Papers were compiled and sent to the consul and to the Governor of Jamaica by Mariano Arosemena, Minister of the Treasury; but before any military action developed between Panama and Great Britain, the Isthmians had once again rejoined Nueva Granada.[30]

The Free State lasted about thirteen months, during which time the Government of Nueva Granada crushed military uprisings in the interior of the country and prepared a military expedition to invade the Isthmus. However, General Tomás C. de Mosquera, the hero who had stopped the uprisings, wanted to exhaust all possibilities for a peaceful settlement with the Panamanians before attempting force. Realizing the military weakness of their position, the Isthmians signed a treaty on December 31, 1841 which reincorporated the Isthmus into Nueva Granada.[31]

In spite of assurances to the contrary, Herrera and Icaza were exiled.[32] The Nueva Granadines had misunderstood the intent and motives of Herrera and his followers in this secession, and looked upon it as some sort of *"lesa patria."* Thus, to them, it was appropriate to further subjugate, humilitate and control the Isthmus with greater force than before. The dishonesty with which Herrera was treated only heated Panamanian passions against the Central Government of Nueva Granada. The new governors from Bogotá were not able to restore complete tranquility in the period immediately following reincorporation of the Isthmus. Lack of security, intrigues against those who had been connected with the Free State of the Isthmus, added to the tactics of many Isthmians who hoped to ingratiate themselves with the renewed centralized government, created an air of unrest and ominous ill-will. Even young men like Justo Arosemena had to exile themselves, at least for a year or two, after losing even such non-political positions as that of schoolmaster.[33]

ADMINISTRATION AFTER THE REINCORPORATION OF THE ISTHMUS IN NUEVA GRANADA

Towards the middle of 1842, the Panamanian Miguel Chiari came from Bogotá to assume the governorship of Panama. He was a man of moderate character and high intellect and was considered the individual most able to govern the Isthmus and calm the unrest caused by the end of the Free State. He had held many important public posts within the Central Government. During his short term in office, Chiari opened a school in Portobelo, made the capital more sanitary by constructing an aqueduct, and campaigned vigorously against pettifoggers who entangled and prolonged lawsuits with the idea of exploiting the litigants. Though he was certainly the man for the times, his health and pressing personal problems forced him to resign. Fortunately for the Isthmians, another enlightened man came to replace him as governor in 1843—Colonel Anselmo Pineda from the Province of Antioquia. Pineda founded a philanthropic society whose objective was to promote the betterment of the popular masses, that is, to improve their intellectual, moral and religious education, to eradicate vices, to improve the economic condition of the province, to instill the habit of saving and the love of work. In short, these men represented the Romantic good will which the Enlightenment had made possible. It was Pineda who recalled from Peru the well-educated and enlightened Justo Arosemena to establish his new school system. With the help of men like Arosemena, Pineda established schools on Sundays for the instruction of workers, and various hat-making schools in Penonome, Los Santos and Panama. He brought teachers from

Tolima. In like manner, he opened shoemaking schools in Parita and in Panama; he had the roads and walls of the capital repaired; he built jails, and established a police body to deal with criminals and vagabonds.[34]

It was during this period that world commercial activities had a real influence on the Isthmus of Panama. Since its emancipation from Spain, Europeans had considered Hispanic America a promising market for their goods. However, speculators overrated the buying power of that market, and over-production caused a great number of economic and commercial losses in Europe in 1845. By then, the American continents had savored certain luxuries which they were reluctant to give up, and thus, they continued to create a demand that had not been there before, and which to some degree increased commercial exchange between the Old and the New Worlds.[35] This period, though short, was one of hope and enthusiasm on the Isthmus. The interest that Pineda took in the improvement of institutions, and the new interests in navigation and transoceanic possibilities that were apparent, led to order and peace. The Isthmians forgot momentarily their grievances against the Central Government and instead prevailed upon each other to support the economy and positive activities in Panama.[36]

To supply commercial and mail service between England and the West Indies, the Royal Mail Steam Packet Company was founded in 1839. By 1846 the itinerary came to include the Isthmus. Connections were made with the steamers of the Pacific Navigation Company (chartered in England in 1840 as the result of the efforts of William Wheelwright, an American businessman), using a canoe-and-mule line across the Isthmus. Thus the city of Panama on the Pacific and the town of Chagres on the Atlantic began to show signs of modest economic life, perhaps even something of a commercial renaissance.[37]

President Mosquera named Tomás Herrera governor of Panama in 1845, and he continued in that position until 1849, through part of the administration of Mosquera's successor, General Hilario López.[38] On the local plane, Herrera paralleled López's liberal national reforms.[39]

It was during Herrera's administration that the rush to the gold fields in California began. Consequently, serious negotiations were undertaken for a railroad that would accommodate the potential number of passengers through the Isthmus to and from the West Coast. Herrera increased the port facilities and available methods of transportation, improved school and hospital facilities, and in general was notable and admirable in his efforts to combat the problems that assailed the Isthmus with the influx of such vast numbers of people as the Gold Rush brought to Panama. Among these problems were the serious epidemics of cholera that broke out on the Isthmus.

When Herrera was named Secretary of War by President Lopez in 1849, he left the Isthmus for Bogotá. He was replaced by José de Obaldía, during whose administration detailed plans for the construction of the railroad (already under way) continued to be discussed, and slaves were emancipated (1852).[40]

THE PROVINCES OF CHIRIQUI AND AZUERO ARE CREATED

Important administrative changes occurred about this time in the interior of the Isthmus. The canton of Alanje was separated from the Province of Veraguas in 1849 to form a new political entity—the Province of Chiriquí. In 1850, the new province of Azuero, made up of the cantons of Parita, Los Santos and the district of Santa Maria of the Province of Panama, was legally recognized. The first governors of the new provinces were named by the National Executive Power, but after 1853 the governors of every province were elected by popular vote.[41] Each new province was allotted seven *diputados* to the national congress. Of the four provinces that now made up the Isthmus, the most convulsive was Azuero; its disorder resulted from the plays for power and influence of two powerful families in the province, families separated more by personal antagonisms than politics. Because of the scandalous political behaviour in the Azuero

province, the Granadine Congress eliminated it in 1855 by add-
ing a major part of it to the territory of Veraguas.[42]

ADMINISTRATIONS DURING THE BUILDING
OF THE RAILROAD

Since the history of the railroad will be dealt with in the
next chapter, and the experiences of the Forty-Niners in the following one, it suffices to say here that the civic and political ne-
cessities of the Isthmus were locally bound to those two circumstances. Attempts were made by governors Bernardo Arce Mata
(sometimes spelled Arze de Mata) and Doctor Salvador Camacho
Roldán (both appointed in 1853) to improve the safety of towns
and thoroughfares by providing better policing and public lighting in the streets of Panama City and elsewhere. In order to alleviate the long and costly processes of the law, judges were requested to expedite their cases so that innocent people would
not have to suffer unjust and long imprisonment before their
trials. Not only the traveler, but also cargo, was to be protected,
and assassins and robbers whose imprisonment needed to be as
secure as possible were sent to jail in Cartagena. The Isthmus
was suffering from the depravations of numerous bands of criminals who robbed and murdered to such a degree that there were
daily scenes of blood on the Cruces Trail, especially during the
early years of the Gold Rush.[43] Previously, in 1851, Ran Runnels, an energetic Texan with a knowledge of "border town"
Spanish, had been brought to the Isthmus. He was supported by
the Railroad Company, some maritime enterprises and several
prominent Panamanian citizens in his organization of a police
guard—a sort of vigilante group which became known as the
"Isthmian Guard." Its objective was to rid the Isthmus of bandits. This police guard caught, jailed and even hanged some of
the bandits. On March 1, 1855 when the Government of Nueva
Granada was again able to protect life and property on the Isthmus, this vigilante group was abolished.[44]

Although foreigners were to be forced to obey the laws, they were also given consideration. Many humble but necessary conveniences were created for their use, such as the construction of public toilets. The National Guard had been reorganized to serve as an auxiliary force to the police of the province, and school buildings were repaired. The canton that included the city of Panama had to bear the heaviest share of the cost of provincial administration because of expenses incurred publicly in behalf of the great number of travelers through the city at this time.[45]

Since after 1853 governors on the Isthmus were to be elected rather than appointed, Arce Mata, the governor who had been in office in Panama, ran for election in 1854. Though Arce Mata had been an effective governor, he was the candidate of the Conservatives and lost to the Liberal candidate, José María Urrutia Añino, partly because he did not use his position as governor to enhance his campaign.[46] Unfortunately for the Panamanians, they made an unwise choice in this election.

ADMINISTRATION OF URRUTIA AÑINO

Urrutia Añino began his governorship on January 1, 1855. Shortly thereafter, in the same month, the railroad was basically completed, an event which gave much hope to the Panamanians. However, the problems of maintaining law and order on the Isthmus had become very serious. Troops which would ordinarily have been used to suppress crime, were instead deployed in the central provinces of Nueva Granada to suppress the 1854-1855 Melo Revolt.[47] When the garrison in Panama left in 1855 to put down this revolt, the Isthmus suffered even more depredations at the hands of criminals, and the vigilantes under the leadership of Ran Runnels were necessarily quite active. Urrutia Añino was later blamed for this situation because he had spent several weeks with his family in Natá and had made it impossible, according to his critics, for the wheels of justice and public safety to turn effectively. For this reason he was removed from his position by the then vice-president of the Republic, Doctor Manuel María Mallarino.[48]

THE FEDERAL STATE OF PANAMA

The agitated state of affairs during the Gold Rush as well as the philosophical ideas of the times seemed to favor the yearnings of many Isthmians for an autonomous life for the territory. The failure of separation attempts in 1830 and 1840 had not stamped out these desires. The philosophical history of federalism, an offshoot of European philosophies of the time, was exemplified on the Isthmus in the thoughts of Justo Arosemena, the promulgator of the theories which justified the federal state in Panama,[49] and which he expressed in writing in his famous pamphlet *El Estado Federal de Panamá.* His point of departure was within the framework of a scientific or positivistic approach which considered the interests of society and its freedom the basis of all government. To achieve this, Arosemena argued, sovereignty was undeniably necessary, for the closer freedom was applied to the atom of society (the individual) the truer the freedom achieved.[50] Compared to other federalist philosophies in which the national unity superseded federal rights, and in which secession was intolerable, Arosemena's ideas might have seemed radical;[51] and indeed he was a vocal member of the *gólgota* faction—extreme Liberals—who now considered decadent the Liberal party led by such men as Obando.[52] Arosemena had developed his influence and esteem through his dedicated work as a member of the House in Bogotá. When he was elected Speaker of the House in 1852, he felt that his persuasive powers were at their height and that the time was ripe to introduce his project. Thus in 1853 he introduced a proposal for the creation of the Federal State of Panama. Although impressive, this proposal created much debate. Those who opposed him, including some members of his own family, felt there were several reasons for turning down such an idea. The reforms in the Constitution of 1853 were felt to substantially increase the local voice of the Panamanians in their government, thus limiting negative influences from Bogotá upon their way of life and their economy. Others felt that setting up an independent bureaucracy would not only be expensive, but it would make elections difficult to control and keep honest, and there would not be enough qualified and enlightened Panamanians to fill the necessary bureaucratic positions.[53] The popular masses, for psychological-social causes, were not in favor of statehood.[54] However, Arosemena had some powerful supporters, including General Tomás Herrera who, in spite of previous personal antipathies, was not a petty man and struggled for ideas rather than for personalities. Then too, as time passed new personnel in the Isthmian legislature turned in favor of Arosemena's stand, for in spite of its liberal measures, the Constitution of 1853 was not totally satisfactory to them.[55]

Unfortunately for Arosemena, a *coup d'état* in 1854 delayed further consideration of his plan in Congress, and caused him to lose the valuable support of Tomás Herrera who died during the uprising. This *coup d'état* shook the entire nation on the 17th of April, 1854 while José María Obando was still president. It was led by General José María Melo. Obando, as well as other more traditional Liberals had manifested disapproval of the 1853 reformed constitution[56] and had refused to fire Melo who was involved in a criminal trial. Melo declared himself a dictator when he could not convince Obando to take on such a dire responsibility himself. Tomás Herrera, who was in Bogotá at this time, escaped and hid until the Vice-president, José de Obaldía, had had a chance to find asylum in the legation of the United States. Then Herrera went north, talked the people into supporting the legitimate government and later received the support of many of Melo's own officers.[57] Nevertheless, Herrera was killed trying to squelch Melo's forces.[58] It is possible however, that Herrera's perennial heroism may well have continued to influence the impulse favoring statehood for Panama long after his death.

After the defeat of Melo and the capture of Bogotá, and because of the inability of the different wings of the Liberal Party to get together lastingly, a Conservative, Doctor Manuel María Mallarino, was elected president in 1855. Mallarino, however, not having full control and realizing that the Radicals had helped restore the government, formed a coalition government. Because several provinces under Conservative control wanted statehood during this time, the Conservative Party became federalist. It has been claimed that the former centralists became federalists because the Conservatives were dissatisfied with the separation of Church and State in the Constitution of 1853 and wanted local autonomy in order to afford a safe place for the "victims" of liberalism. However, Conservative adoption of federalism was more a matter of expediency than of principle. By supporting federalism, the Conservatives hoped to get control of the government.[59] All these attitudes, fanned by the brilliant arguments in Congress of Justo Arosemena before Melo's uprising, were the beginnings of the new federalism soon to be diffused throughout Nueva Granada.[60]

For the moment, the political struggles and the absurdities of the military to which he was entirely alien, had dejected the spirit of Justo Arosemena, who was a senator by now, and he declined to return (only for the time being) to his representational duties when the Melo rebellion was over. Thus, he himself abandoned temporarily his great project. However, in 1855, when the military revolt of Melo ended, the political climate in Bogotá was temporarily refreshed. All factions renewed with great vigor their attempts to legislate positive benefits for the Republic. Mallarino, who had assumed the presidency even during the revolution, did so with a conciliatory spirit. Even leaders of the uprising seemed to prefer peace—at least for the time being—to the shedding of blood in trying to contain ideas that were overpowering. By the time Justo Arosemena did return to his work in Congress, the proposals regarding the Federal State of Panama had been confused and mauled and modified, so that he then published his clear and philosophically convincing pamphlet—*El Estado Federal de Panamá,* which could be considered the summation speech in the defense plans of a brilliant attorney. So impressive was it indeed, that its allegations convinced

Congress, which, on February 27, 1855 created the Federal State of Panama.[61]

The Isthmus assumed its new sovereignty with legislative powers in all fields except those relating to foreign relations, the army, navy and war, national postal matters, national debt and the naturalization of foreigners. The new laws specified that laws regulating import duties on the Isthmus were not to be proclaimed without the approval of the state legislature.[62] Elections were held with great civic pride, and on July 15 the Constitutional Convention of the State was called to order in the capital. Even though the majority of the members were Conservatives, they elected Justo Arosemena, champion of the federal system, as Superior Chief of the State. The Convention further divided the state into seven departments: Coclé, Colón, Chiriquí, Fábrega, Herrera, Los Santos and Panamá. The capital of these departments respectively were: Natá, Colón, David, Santiago, Pesé, Los Santos and Panamá.[63] Thus, the Federal State was inaugurated under auspicious skies and the Panamanian people were ready, it seemed, to begin anew.

NOTES

1. Justo was the son of Mariano Arosemena whose memoirs, *Apuntamientos históricos,* are so useful in studying the Isthmian events of this period up to 1840. Both father and son had similar ideas, though Justo was able to make fruitful and carry to higher levels the seeds sown by his father. See: Rodrigo Miró, *Mariano Arosemena* (Panama, 1960), 22.
2. The convention assembled in 1831 to write a constitution for the Republic of Nueva Granada (the present countries of Colombia and Panama). Thirteen provinces, including Panama, were represented. However, political chaos in the south, especially in the Cauca Valley, prevented the provinces of Cauca, Choco, Pasto and Popayan from sending delegates, an omission which would lead to further unrest and political strife in Colombia. See: Gibson, *The Constitutions of Colombia,* 109-110; Henao and Arrubla, *History of Colombia,* 427-439; Kirkpatrick, *Latin America,* 255.
3. The constitutional convention elected Santander as president of the new country and brought him home from exile. Santander, who in modern times is considered the founder of the Liberal Party, was

actually conservative in philosophy. One must understand the basic differences between the liberal and conservative ideologies to appreciate fully Santander's public support of the Liberals, while basically being conservative. The Liberals advocated federalism, limitation of the Church's powers and extension of suffrage. Conservatives, oligarchs, on the other hand, wanted a centralized form of government, which the clergy could help them maintain. Santander sympathized with the Liberals only because he had disapproved of Bolívar's plan to unify New Granada, Venezuela and Ecuador. See: Jones, *An Introduction to Hispanic American History*, 361.
4. Sosa and Arce, *Compendio*, 219-220.
5. Arosemena, *Apuntamientos*, 231, 232.
6. Castillero R., *Historia de Panamá*, 86.
7. Arosemena, *Apuntamientos*, 232-233.
8. *Ibid.*, 244; Sosa and Arce, *Compendio*, 219-220.
9. Even before independence from Spain, Panamanians had promoted free commerce through the Isthmus in one way or another. See Chapter I, which deals in part with the Isthmian petitions to the Crown in the Courts of Cádiz regarding commercial franchises.

One of the greatest defenders and promulgators of commercial improvement on the Isthmus was Mariano Arosemena; himself a businessman, he was aware of the many problems facing economic ventures on the Isthmus. As he abandoned his personal enterprises to become more and more active in public affairs, he transcended his personal interests in favor of commercial success for all of Panama. See: Mariano Arosemena. *Historia y nacionalidad (testimonios éditos e inéditos)*, ed. Argelia Pello de Ugarte (Panama, 1971), xix-xxii.

A more cynical view may suggest that Mariano Arosemena was primarily concerned with his personal commercial success, though this is not to say that more complex motivations were not also present in his actions.
10. Arosemena, *Apuntamientos*, 237-238, 239.
11. *Ibid.*, 244-245, 251-252, 265; Chong, *Historia de Panamá*, 149.
12. Arosemena, *Apuntamientos*, 244, 251-252.
13. Sosa and Arce, *Compendio*, 220-221.
14. Arosemena, *Apuntamientos*, 246.
15. Under the centralized form of government created by the Constitution of 1832, Santander had begun his rule—a rule of peace, stability in fiscal matters, and relative prosperity. Again, as in the years 1822 to 1827, Santander became a champion of education: he opened new public professional and scientific schools in Colombia. He reduced the influence of the Church in educational matters, but he would not pursue a strong policy against the Church, even though he did encourage religious toleration and even Protestant missionaries. Among his other

reforms were the improvement of business and the ending of the conflict with Spain.

Santander managed to lead Colombia through four years of peace
and prosperity, but he failed to achieve peace with the followers of
Bolívar. Indeed, his antagonism toward them led him to exclude them
from public office and even to persecute them. This antagonism between Santander and his enemies was further augmented by his decision to assume in the name of the new country half of the debt created
by Gran Colombia. This situation, in part, led to the defeat of Santander's candidate, José María Obando, in the election of 1837. See: Gibson, *The Constitutions of Colombia,* 111; Henao and Arrubla, *History
of Colombia,* 435-439; Jones, *An Introduction to Hispanic American
History,* 361-362; Kirkpatrick, *Latin America,* 255.

16. Sosa and Arce, *Compendio,* 220-221. The accounts differ, for Mariano
Arosemena *infers* that Russell continued to resist, thus provoking
Diez's attack. See: Arosemena, *Apuntamientos,* 263.

According to another version there was a fight between the two
men, Paredes and Russell, in the streets on the night of November 20th.
Paredes was severely wounded; the cries of his wife attracted people
and Russell was knocked down without ceremony, after having been
disarmed; then he was hurried to prison. See: *Niles Weekly Register,*
LI (February 11, 1837), 369.

The New Orleans *True American* states that in consequence of the
incarceration of the British consul by authorities of Nueva Granada, a
British squadron was blocking some of the ports. See: *Niles Weekly
Register,* LI (February 18, 1837), 385.

17. Arosemena, *Apuntamientos,* 262-264: Castillero R., *Historia de Panamá,* 87; Sosa and Arce, *Compendio,* 221. Some years before, Cartagena was involved in a similar affair when an alcalde and a French colonel (Adolfo Barrot) were at odds with each other. France demanded
apologies by storming the plaza with troops from Martinique. The
overbearing attitude of France elicited the following opinion from
Mariano Arosemena, who implied that this type of reaction on the part
of European governments was all too common: "It has been a practice
of the European governments as regards the South American republics,
to ignore, in times of conflict, the legal and constitutional provisions
for redress. A government based on law as was that of Nueva Granada,
had to prefer, in the incident with France, the blockading and even
bombarding of one of its ports by French marines to presenting itself
before the civilized world degraded and demeaned for evading a few
shots from a cannon." *Apuntamientos,* 242.

18. See: Williarm R. Manning, *Diplomatic Correspondence of the United
States: Inter-American Affairs, 1831-1860,* (Washington, 1935), V,
551-552, 557-558.

19. Castillero R., *Historia de Panamá*, 87.
20. Obando was considered undesirable by many Liberals because of his alleged role in the *"crimen de Berruecos"* (the murder of José de Sucre), and his lack of political talents.

    Azuero represented a small group of radicals, some of whose desired reforms were too far ahead of the times and some too utopian. Although Azuero was one of the leading and most vigorous intellectual and political figures of Colombia, his advanced ideas in matters of religion and politics had brought upon him the enmity even of other Liberals.

    Márquez was of impeccable morality and public renown, with authentic political talents.

    The elections brought no majority to any candidate and the election in the Congress gave Márquez his victory. See: José Dolores Moscote and Enrique J. Arce, *La vida ejemplar de Justo Arosemena* (Panama, 1956), 36-38, hereafter cited as Moscote and Arce, *Justo Arosemena*.
21. Arosemena, *Apuntamientos*, 267.
22. Márquez's administration was almost overthrown when the Congress of 1838 passed a measure that suppressed a few deserted convents in Pasto and set aside their income and half of their property for the support of education in Pasto. Although the measure had been suggested by the bishop of Popayán and supported by representatives of the province, the people of the area involved thought it was an attempt to overthrow their religion. A rebellion led by a priest followed, and the government had to use force in bringing the revolutionists under control. But peace was short-lived: war soon broke out again. This time it was led by the candidate of Santander's party, General José María Obando who claimed to be fighting for a federal system. The government, however, finally defeated Obando in Pasto. Again, the victory was only temporary, for uprisings continued almost all over the country. See: Henao and Arrubla, *History of Colombia*, 440-449; Jones, *An Introduction to Hispanic American History*, 362; Kirkpatrick, *Latin America*, 255-256.

    President Márquez was supposed to have wanted to sell part of the Colombian territory (probably the Isthmus) to the British. See Rob Roy MacGregor, "The Treaty of 1846 (Seventeen Years of American-Colombian Relations) 1830-1846," (Ph.D. dissertation, Clark University, 1929), 140.
23. Alba. *Cronología*, 162; Arosemena, *Apuntamientos*, 267; Castillero R., *Historia de Panamá*, 87; Chong, *Historia de Panamá*, 150; Moscote and Arce, *Justo Arosemena*, 45.
24. Castillero R., *Historia de Panamá*, 87; Sosa and Arce, *Compendio*, 221-223: Translated from the Spanish, which read: "El que quiera conocer a Panamá que venga, porque se acaba."

25. *Ibid.;* Arosemena, *Apuntamientos,* 282-284. See also note 22.
26. Alba, *Cronología,* 159, 161; Pereira, *Historia de Panamá,* 254; Sosa and Arce, *Compendio,* 223-226.
27. Alba, *Cronología,* 159, 161; Chong, *Historia de Panamá,* 154; Moscote and Arce, *Justo Arosemena,* 54; Pereira, *Historia de Panamá,* 254; Ugarte, *Historia y Nacionalidad,* xxvi.
28. Quoted by Chong, *Historia de Panamá,* 151. This is part of a speech Herrera gave to the Congress of the new nation, as President of the Estado Libre del Istmo.

   The writings of Herrera in 1841 are very enlightening with respect to his justifications regarding independence and his acceptance of the presidency at this time. See: Concha Peña, *Tomás Herrera* (Panama, 1954), 69-75, for copy of a speech written by Herrera and published in September of 1841 in *La Gaceta del Istmo,* the official publication of his government.
29. Alba, *Cronología,* 161; Chong, *Historia de Panamá,* 151-152. Pereira, *Historia de Panamá,* 254-255; Sosa and Arce, *Compendio,* 223-226.

   Costa Rica recognized the Isthmian State. Don Pedro de Obarrio was named *plenipotenciario* to Costa Rica. The United States did not recognize Panama even though Panama sent a diplomatic representative to Washington. See: Pereira, *Historia de Panamá,* 254.
30. Alba, *Cronología,* 162-165; Moscote and Arce, *Justo Arosemena,* 53; Arosemena, *Historia y nacionalidad,* xxv.

   The author strongly believes that fear of Britain's designs on the part of the Panamanians had a definite influence on their decision to rejoin Nueva Granada.
31. Pereira, *Historia de Panamá,* 254-255; Sosa and Arce, *Compendio,* 223-226.

   At first Mosquera commissioned Julio Arboleda to speak with the leaders of the Isthmus; when he did not get positive results, he sent two men to negotiate reentry into New Granada; these men were Colonel Anselmo Pineda and Doctor Ricardo de la Parra, commissioned by Doctor Rufino Cuervo and recommended by General Juan José Flores, President of Ecuador.
32. Herrera was stripped of his military rank until 1844 when under Mosquera's regime he was reinstated and promoted to general. See: Chong, *Historia de Panama,* 153; Pereira, *Historia de Panamá,* 255.
33. Chong, *Historia de Panamá,* 155; Moscote and Arce, *Justo Arosemena,* 58-59.
34. Carles, *A 150 años,* 19-20; Moscote and Arce, *Justo Arosemena,* 107-111; Sosa and Arce, *Compendio,* 224-225.

   When Pineda became governor there were only five schools functioning in the province. He increased the number to twelve by opening schools in Macaracas, Penonomé, Parita, Natá and Antón for boys and in La Chorrera and La Villa de los Santos, for girls.

35. Berthold Seemann, *Historia del Istmo de Panama*, trans. Santiago D. McKay (Panama, 1959), 89-90.

36. Moscote and Arce, *Justo Arosemena*, 114.

37. John Haskell Kemble, *The Panama Route, 1848-1869* (Berkeley and Los Angeles, 1943), 3; Seemann, *Historia del Istmo de Panamá*, 90; Sosa and Arce, *Compendio*, 225-226.

38. Sosa and Arce, *Compendio*, 226. Pineda was replaced temporarily in 1845 by José de Obaldía who in turn was replaced for seven months by Joaquín María Barriga.

39. The years 1849 to 1857 saw the Liberals in control of the government. Inspired by the European revolutions of 1848, the Liberals succeeded in electing General José Hilario López to the presidency. López's reforms and anti-clericalism began with his exiling of the Jesuits. He continued his anti-clerical measures by making the bishops and clergy responsible to the ordinary tribunals, not only in criminal and civil cases, but also for failure in their religious duties. Further, he made civil servants out of the clergy, which henceforth would be paid and supervised by the government. Any member of the clergy who protested would be exiled. Such strong measures led to several Conservative revolts which in turn led to stronger anti-clerical measures. Finally, Church and State were separated in the Constitution of 1853. See: Gibson, *The Constitutions of Colombia*, 191-194; Henao and Arrubla, *History of Colombia*, 455-458; Kirkpatrick, *Latin America*, 257.

During López's administration, the contract with the railroad was signed, and work began for the railroad of Panama; together with the Gold Rush to California, it precipitated shady land speculation in which some high officials—even ex-president Mosquera—were involved. See: Moscote and Arce, *Justo Arosemena*, 177-179.

40. Castillero R., *Historia de Panamá*, 91-92; Carles, *A 150 años*, 20; Moscote and Arce, *Justo Arosemena*, 31; Peña, *Tomás Herrera*, 96-97; Sosa and Arce, *Compendio*, 227.

41. Ernesto Castillero R., *Chiriquí* (Panama, 1968), 39; Sosa and Arce, *Compendio*, 232. Santiago Agnew, first popularly elected governor of the Chiriquí was great great grandfather of the author. With the Isthmus as a Federal State, which became a reality in 1855, Chiriquí had four *diputados*, among them Juan Nepomuceno Venero, great grandfather of the author.

42. Sosa and Arce, *Compendio*, 232.

43. *Ibid.*, 233, 235; Alba, *Cronología*, 177.

44. For dates used, see: Joseph L. Schott, *Rails Across Panama* (Indianapolis, 1967), 93; Sosa and Arce, *Compendio*, 235. A careful analysis of the dates used or implied by Sosa and Arce reveals conflicting statements and dates. With the railroad finished in January of 1855, why would crime afterwards increase on the Cruces Trail and why would the Railroad Company expend such energy in protecting it? Obviously,

Ran Runnel's group was formed much earlier. Thus, we accept the dates used by Schott. It may be noted, also, that according to Schott, Runnels was still on the Isthmus in 1856.

45. Carles, *A 150 años*, 21; Sosa and Arce, *Compendio*, 234.

46. Sosa and Arce, *Compendio*, 234.

47. More will be said about this revolt and its effects on the formation of the Federal State of Panama.

48. Carles, *A 150 años*, 21; Peña, *Tomás Herrera*, 123; Sosa and Arce, *Compendio*, 235. Probably the Melo Revolt, related to President José María Obando's disregard of the Constitution of 1853, had a bearing on the upsurge of crime on the Isthmus, because surely troops from Colombia could not be spared to keep law and order on the Isthmus.

49. That we may better grasp the notability of Justo Arosemena's part in the history of Panama, it may be well to note that the best national writers and historians of Panama, of all inclinations and tendencies, have written many pages concerning his work: Ricardo J. Alfaro, Octavio Méndez Pereira, Eusebio A. Morales, Guillermo Andreve, Jose de la Cruz Herrera, J. D. Moscote, J. I. Fábrega, Enrique J. Arce, Diógenes de la Rosa, Catalino Arrocha Graell; and of the younger generation of mature writers: Carolos Manuel Gasteazoro, Rodrigo Miró, Ismael García S., Ricaurte Soler and Alfredo Castillero Calvo. See: Justa Arosemena, *El Estado Federal de Panamá*, ed. Jorge Fábrega P. (Panama, 1965), ix-x.

51. We could perhaps make a contrast to Abraham Lincoln's insistence upon unity later in the United States.

52. Soler, *Pensamiento panameño*, 85; Moscote and Arce, *Justo Arosemena*, 185-187.

53. Moscote and Arce, *Justo Arosemena*, 198-199; Ricaurte Soler, ed., prologue to Arosemena, *Teoría de la nacionalidad* (Panama, 1968), 13.

54. Arosemena, *El estado federal de Panama*, viii.

55. Moscote and Arce, *Justo Arosemena*, 218-219.

56. Gibson, *The Constitutions of Colombia*, 191-194; Henao and Arrubla, *History of Colombia*, 455-458; Kirkpatrick, *Latin America*, 257.

57. Moscote and Arce, *Justo Arosemena*, 218-219; Peña, *Tomás Herrera*, 123-147.

58. Peña, *Tomás Herrera*, 146-147.
      The legitimate forces prevailed, however, and Melo was exiled. Obando was deposed as president but acquitted of treason by the Supreme Court. (Henao and Arrubla, *History of Colombia*, 471-472.) See: Moscote and Arce, *Justo Arosemena*, 228-230, for a partial account of Obando's trial.

59. Gibson, *The Constitutions of Colombia*, 217-221; Henao and Arrubla, *History of Colombia*, 467-472.

60. Moscote and Arce, *Justo Arosemena*, 241.

61. *Ibid.*, 219-221, 224, 227-228, 231; Sosa and Arce, *Compendio,* 236. There appear various discrepancies in several historical works as to the exact date the pamphlet was actually published.

The Estado Federal was abolished in 1885 by Rafael Núñez, then president of Nueva Granada. See: Correa, *Apuntes de historia patria,* 140.

62. Arosemena, *El estado federal de Panamá,* vii; Miró, *Mariano Arosemena,* 21-22; Sosa and Arce, *Compendio,* 237-238.

63. Sosa and Arce, *Compendio,* 237-238.

CHAPTER III

The Panama Railroad

Panama, because of its isthmian geographic position midway between the northern and southern hemispheres, creates a logical culminating point for the world's commerce. Men of various civilized countries of the world have seen this gift of nature and have dreamed about some form of inter-oceanic communication in Panama.[1] One of the first countries to realize the advantage of Panama's geographical position was Spain. Ever since the Spaniards first came to explore Panama, this tiny country has not lacked a mode of communication across its narrow isthmus.[2] The men from Spain, following King Ferdinand's order to establish forts across the isthmus, came upon a small fishing village in November of 1515, which the natives called Panama. While at the village, the Spaniards, under the command of Antonio Tello de Guzmán, were told by the natives that the shortest and best route across the Isthmus was a trail that ran northward from the village of Panama to Porto Bello.[3] Guzmán told Pedro Arias de Avila (or Pedrarias Dávila), a noble from Segovia appointed in 1514 by the King of Spain as governor of Castilla del Oro,[4] of the discovery of the village of Panama and of the trail from the village to Porto Bello. Pedrarias, after waiting some months to see if no better route from sea to sea could be found, ordered Gaspar de Espinosa, who has the dubious honor of being the first European to cross the Isthmus of Panama on an ass, to build a road across the isthmus. But instead of building a paved roadway from Porto Bello to Panama, Guzmán built the road, which averaged three feet in width, from Nombre de Dios to Panama. In 1502 Columbus had founded a small settlement at Nombre de Dios which he had had to leave because of trouble with the Indians. Thus, the settlement founded by Columbus became the Atlantic terminal of the first cobbled roadway across the Isthmus of Panama. The revived Nombre de Dios, for almost a century to follow, had the honor of being the oldest active European-founded city on the mainland of the Americas. This distinction officially lasted until 1597 when by order of King Philip II of Spain it was abandoned. The honor was then transferred to Panama. The paved roadway from Nombre de Dios and the road from Porto Bello joined together near the Río Boqueron which is more than halfway from the Pacific to the Atlantic.[5] Over this system, for more than three hundred years, treasures and merchandise passed on their way to Spain. But soon the time for a cheaper, faster system that could handle larger amounts of traffic on the Isthmus of Panama became inevitable.[6]

One of the first attempts to negotiate the building of a better system, this time a canal, was undertaken by Colonel William Duane, a relative of Benjamin Franklin and a personal friend of the first minister from Colombia at Washington. With the blessings and capital of some United States citizens, Colonel Duane visited Bogotá, the capital of Nueva Granada, from 1822 through 1823. He presented proposals in Bogotá for a canal across Panama. However, these proposals were not accepted.[7] Another attempt to build a faster roadway took place between the years 1827-1829 when a British engineer by the name of John A. Lloyd and Captain Maurice Falmarc, a Swede, surveyed the Isthmus of Panama for the possibilities of a railroad with the encouragement of President Bolívar of Colombia. The two men submitted a report that showed the practicability of a railroad from Chagres, located on the Atlantic, to Panama. However, Bolívar's dream of a railroad across Panama never materialized beyond Lloyd's and Falmarc's report.[8]

The plan of the Panamanians at this time was to create completely free ports as soon as an interoceanic route was completed.[9] Thus, they were eager to encourage capitalists to build. In 1835

a decree gave Charles, Baron de Thierry, the privilege of digging
a canal through the waters of the Río Grande, the Chagres and
the Bahía de Limón. The Baron was to have the canal under
complete personal control for 50 years, at which time he would
turn it over to Nueva Granada.[10] But delays in construction made
the Panamanians aware of certain disadvantages in granting single
concessions of this sort. Therefore, a decree in 1836 announced
that the privilege of opening an interoceanic route of any kind
would be granted—should Thierry not meet his deadline—to any
persons who offered the best advantages to Nueva Granada and
whose plans appeared most feasible.[11]

Previously, in 1835, Senator Henry Clay had introduced a
resolution in the United States Senate, requesting the President
to negotiate treaties, both with Central America and Nueva Granada, for the protection of citizens of the United States who
might attempt to establish a mode of communication between
the Atlantic and Pacific Oceans. In May, 1835, Charles A. Biddle, brother of the famous financier Nicholas Biddle,[12] was appointed by President Andrew Jackson as a special agent to "visit
the different routes on the continent of America best adapted
to interoceanic communication and to report theron with reference to their value to the commercial interests of the United
States."[13] Biddle arrived in Panama in the latter part of 1835
and remained there several months. Accompanied by Don José
de Obaldía, who was a member of the Congress of Nueva Granada and also to be associated with Biddle in the project to build
across the Isthmus, Biddle left for Bogotá where he arrived on
March 13, 1836. While at Bogotá, Biddle negotiated for rights
to build a transisthmian route.[14] Doctor Francisco Sota, President Santander's Secretary of the Treasury, spoke in the Senate
in favor of the concession, pointing out the contribution to the
economic welfare of the Isthmus that this canal would make. He
pleaded for a brotherly relationship between the "mainlanders"
and the Isthmians in order to consolidate the Isthmus more
closely to Nueva Granada. He predicted that without policies of
sympathy and understanding the Isthmians would continue attempts to separate themselves from the Granadine nation, and

would succeed sooner or later.[15] Finally a decree from the Government of Nueva Granada granted to Biddle and his associates a formal concession in accord with the Congressional act of June 6, 1836, to build an interoceanic route under the company name of Biddle, Azuero and Associates. Biddle had actually not been authorized by President Andrew Jackson to acquire such a power, so Biddle then proceeded to the United States in 1836. However, he died on December 21, 1836 before he was able to prepare his report for President Jackson.[16] "In this manner he escaped a severe reprimand from the irate Jackson who had no intention of overlooking Biddle's flagrant misuse of his mission. The concession went to the grave with the man who had obtained it."[17] Ira Bennett claims that Biddle's idea of a railroad could have worked but that it came at an inopportune moment —the Panic of 1837.[18]

In 1838, the right of building a railroad, highway, or canal or a combination of all three across Panama was granted by Nueva Granada to a French company known as Augustin Salomon et Compagnie (Salomon had been an associate of Thierry). However, before the company could begin work, Panama and Veraguas had declared themselves an independent state (*El Estado Libre del Istmo,* 1840), and, as referred to in Chapter II, the situation on the isthmus and in Nueva Granada was precarious and not at all conducive to solid business achievements. By the time Panama rejoined Nueva Granada (December, 1841) the Salomon concession was very unpopular in Panama and in Bogotá, apparently due in part to anti-semitic feelings as well as to the recurring frustration of the Isthmians upon observing that those who were granted concessions, even very generous ones, were not achieving any real success.

Notwithstanding such disappointments, the desire in Panama and Bogotá for a transit system, owned and controlled by the government of Nueva Granada and financed by foreign loans, motivated the government to instruct minister Manuel Mosquera, who was in Europe, to attempt to get loans and to receive a joint neutrality guarantee of the Isthmus from the governments of France, Great Britain, and the United States. However, his attempts did not receive great attention, and in 1842 the Bogotá Congress declared all transit concessions terminated. The following year it specifically mentioned the Salomon Company.

The Salomon interests refused to accept this termination. Their representative in France appealed to the French Foreign Minister, François Guizot, to support their claim (even while Mosquera was seeking the neutrality guarantee). Guizot, although willing to have a canal constructed either by private means or by the government of France, Great Britain and Nueva Granada, refused to support Salomon and Company without new and complete surveys of the route. Therefore, in September of 1843, he sent Napoleon Garella, an engineer, to study and report on the feasibility of a canal across Panama. Garella recommended a canal that would go from the Bay of Boca del Monte, which is located twelve miles west of Panama, to Limón Bay, which is the Atlantic terminal of the present-day canal. But the lack of necessary capital caused the idea of a canal and other related projects to be abandoned.[19]

Panamanians were disgusted with the inability of promoters to secure financial backing, and many of them felt that lack of encouragement from the centralized government in Bogotá was partly to blame. Such was the sad economic condition of Panama. (It was at this time that Rufino Cuervo wrote his graphic message about the condition of Panama to his friend.) The disillusion of the Isthmians resulted in the support of the federalist cause and in the attempt for independence of 1840.[20]

In 1845 Captain W. B. Liot, a representative of the British navy, suggested either the construction of a railroad from Porto Bello to Panama or the building of a macadam highway across Panama. This plan was never carried beyond the suggestion of Liot.[21]

THE BIDLACK TREATY

On December 12, 1846 during the Mexican War, Benjamin A. Bidlack, United States *chargé d'affaires* at Bogotá, and Manuel

María Mallarino, Secretary of State for the government of New Granada, signed the Treaty of Peace, Amity, Navigation, and Commerce. Article 35 of this treaty stated that

> the Government of New Granada guarantees to the Government of the United States that the right of way or transit across the Isthmus of Panama upon any modes of communication that now exist, or that may be hereafter constructed, shall be open and free to the Government and citizens of the United States . . . [which] also guarantees . . . the rights of sovereignty and property which New Granada has and possesses over the said territory. . . .[22]

without any specific instructions, and on the initiative of Nueva Granada, "which had become suspicious of the intentions of Great Britain and France, particularly the former, in the Isthmian region,"[23] Bidlack signed the treaty guaranteeing the neutrality of the Isthmus of Panama, a treaty under which the United States would intervene militarily fifty-seven times, many of these at the request of the central and even the local government.[24] It goes almost without saying that modern Panamanian historians view this treaty as another "pragmatic" tactic of the colossus of the North to insure for itself future concessions and influence at the expense of the Isthmians whose attempts for independence would henceforth be constricted. This attitude is reinforced by the later events in which Great Britain and the United States entered into the Clayton-Bulwer Treaty (1850) to guarantee accessibility of the Isthmus for themselves, as though Panama and even Colombia were but their own colonies over which they must watch and decide issues—issues which would have direct bearing on the Isthmians themselves.[25]

President Polk reluctantly accepted the Bidlack Treaty because of "the departure from established policy which the guarantee of neutrality and sovereignty would involve."[26] When Polk submitted this treaty to the Senate in February of 1847, he argued that

> such a departure was justified by the urgent importance of communication with the Pacific and virtual indispensability of

such a guarantee to the construction and operation of a railroad or canal in the Isthmian region. The object of the treaty,
he said, was commercial, not political. It was not exclusive, for
it secured to all nations the free and equal passage of the isthmus. Any other nation might make a similar guarantee if it
should choose to do so.[27]

However, the Senate, afraid of debate, postponed considering the
treaty until the next working session of Congress. Then, probably
influenced by British activities around Nicaragua and the failure
of the United States to get transit rights across Tehuantepec at
the end of the War with Mexico, the Senate ratified Bidlack's
treaty by a large majority on June 8, 1848.[28]

Secretary of State James Buchanan, following Polk's statement that Bidlack's treaty was not exclusive, asked the British
minister in Washington, John F.T. Crampton, to find out what
Lord Palmerston thought about the neutrality guarantee of Panama. Palmerston never answered. John M. Clayton, Buchanan's
successor, formally requested Great Britain to make a treaty,
similar to Bidlack's, with New Granada. The British did not do
this; however, in a clause of the Clayton-Bulwer Treaty, which
was signed on April 19, 1850, the British agreed to protect,
jointly with the United States, any mode of communication
across Panama, Tehuantepec and Nicaragua.[29]

Meanwhile, the Bidlack Treaty did not discourage the French,
who again attempted the construction of a railroad across Panama. In 1847, the government of Nueva Granada awarded the
first formal contract for the building of a railroad across the
Isthmus of Panama to Mateo Klein, an agent and lawyer for the
Compagnie de Panama, actually the same basic organization of
Salomon and Company. This contract was granted to the French
company for a period of ninety-nine years, with the sole rights
for the building and maintenance of a railroad across Panama,
provided that it be completed within six years. But because the
Compagnie de Panama failed to raise the necessary capital (due
to the revolutionary outbreaks in Europe), the provisions of the
contract expired in June, 1848.[30] The failure by the French
company to construct a railroad in Panama ended, for the time
being, French efforts in Panama. The blow to the Isthmians must

indeed have been cruel, for in mid-1847 the worst decline of a
depression which had encircled all of Nueva Granada assailed
the Panamanians.[31] They began to search desperately for those
who would lift their Isthmus to the calling of its destiny as
bridge between the two oceans. At this opportune moment, en-
trepreneurs and pioneers in the United States were anxious to
have a railroad built across Panama.

THE NEED FOR THE RAILROAD AND
ASPINWALL'S PROJECT

In 1846, the question concerning the proper boundary of
Oregon was settled. The Mexican War had ended by 1848 and
Mexico ceded, by treaty, upper California to the United States.
All this new territory awaited settlement by people from the
eastern part of the United States. There were three routes by
which these easterners could get to the newly-opened lands. The
first route was by land, across 3,000 miles of deserts, prairies,
rivers, mountains, and Indians. The second route was by way of
water, around South America and then up the Pacific coast. It
took at least ninety days to cover the distance of some 12,000
miles.[32] The third route was Vanderbilt's transit system across
Nicaragua. This tiresome route was not a favorite one of pioneers
from the East.[33] Whatever route the emigrants to California
chose, they encountered hardships never before experienced by
them. It was only natural, because of the difficulties of reaching
the Pacific coast, that the desirable class of settlers, farmers and
their families, were not enthusiastic about going West. Also, the
desired emigrants were hesitant about pioneering in an area
where the administration of law and government faced difficulties caused by the tremendous distance and slowness of communications between the seat of the National Government and the
Pacific coast.[34]

The United States saw fit to find a faster, less costly, safer
and easier route for its own citizens in order to enable them to
settle the Pacific territories. Congress, on the recommendations

of the Secretary of the Treasury and the Postmaster General, by
an act of March 3, 1847, authorized the Secretary of the Navy
to make contracts for postal services between New York, Savannah, New Orleans and Chagres, the principal port on the Atlantic
side of Panama, and between the Isthmus and Oregon. The latter
route was granted to William H. Aspinwall, a New York capitalist
(great-uncle of Franklin D. Roosevelt) and his associates. They
immediately formed the Pacific Mail Steamship Company.[35] The
New York, Savannah, New Orleans and Chagres contract was
awarded by the Secretary of the Navy to George Law, another
New York capitalist. This contract looked very promising, since
it connected the principal Atlantic ports of the United States.
But Aspinwall's contract caused other capitalists in New York
to wonder why a man of his capabilities would want the Pacific
route. At the time of the awarding of the contracts, gold had
not yet been discovered in California. Nevertheless, at the time
he had assumed the mail contract, Aspinwall had in mind a railroad across Panama.[36]

   Prior to that time, the only method of going across Panama
was from Chagres up the Chagres River by native boats to Gorgona or Cruces, which were located roughly midway across the
Isthmus. From here one either walked or rode mules or horses
along a road to Panama City. This mode of communication was
extremely difficult and usually took from four to five days in
the rainy season. In view of the hardship and time involved in
crossing the Isthmus of Panama, Aspinwall hoped for a railroad
that would grant him and his associates huge profits and that
would shorten the traveling distance from four or five days to a
matter of hours. The associates of Aspinwall involved in this
scheme were Henry Chauncey, a New York capitalist and John L.
Stephens. Stephens, a graduate of Columbia College of Law,
had gone to Central America in 1839 as *chargé d'affaires* at the
request of President Martin Van Buren to study the different
routes that had been proposed for a canal connecting the Atlantic and Pacific Oceans.[37] His search led him to Panama where
he became so enchanted with the Chagres River that he built a
cottage on its banks some few miles above Bohio and recom-

mended to President Van Buren that the Chagres River area was
the best route of all he had seen. Stephens came back to Panama
in the early part of 1848. This time he came for the sole purpose
of making studies for the railroad of which Aspinwall dreamed.
Along with an engineer named James L. Baldwin, Stephens expected to sight a line for the railroad across the Isthmus of Panama which would not cross any ridges over 600 feet. How excited
he must have been when, together with Baldwin, he found a pass
not over 337 feet above the sea level.[38]

Stephens reported the good news to Aspinwall and Chauncey.
These three men presented to the United States Congress on
December 11, 1848, a memorandum which pointed out to the
American nation the significance of a railroad in Panama in
terms of naval and military purposes as well as the encouragement such a railroad would provide for Latin American and
Pacific coast trade.[39] They made it clear that they could not attempt such a tremendous project without some form of government grant. But this aid, the three men told the Senate, was not
to be in the form of an outright grant. Instead, Aspinwall and
his associates wanted the Secretary of Navy, who at the time
was John Y. Mason,[40] to grant them the authority to draw up a
twenty-year contract to be put into effect as soon as work on
the railroad was finished. The proposed contract would allow
the transportation of all munitions, troops, army and naval supplies, United States mails, and United States public agents across
the Isthmus of Panama on the planned railroad. The price for all
this transportation would not exceed $750,000, which was the
sum paid by the United States to the Collins Line for carrying
its mail from New York to Liverpool.[41] Aspinwall's memorandum was referred to the Senate Committee on Military Affairs;
and on the 14th of December, 1848, the chairman of the committee, Thomas H. Benton of Missouri, introduced a bill in the
Senate that contained all the points that Aspinwall wanted but
limited the price to $500,000,[42] (which was two-thirds of the
amount paid by the United States to the New York-Liverpool
line). Benton's bill also stated that no amount of money would
be paid by the United States until the whole transit of Panama

could be made under the power of steam. Stated also in the bill
was the condition that the construction of the railroad in Panama was to begin one year after the contract between the Secretary of Navy and Aspinwall's associates, and was to be finished
within three years from June 1, 1849.

Benton's bill met tremendous opposition from George Law,
the holder of the mail service between the Atlantic ports of
New York, Savannah, New Orleans and Chagres, because he
wanted the contract. In view of all the opposition to the bill proposed by Benton, Thomas B. King, member of the House of
Representatives and also a member of the Committee on Naval
Affairs, presented to the House on January 16, 1849, Aspinwall's memorandum with the exception that the amount of the
contract be $250,000, instead of the half a million dollars pro-
posed by Benton.[43] Senator Stephen A. Douglas of Illinois on
January 29, 1849 in the Senate proposed a substitute for the
bill introduced by Benton. Douglas' bill stated that the amount
of the contract should not go over $250,000 a year. The bill also
included rates for freight and passengers over the proposed railroad. The rates, which were scaled downward as the years progressed, were to be $8 per ton for freight and $8 per passenger
for the first five years of railroad operations. At the end of ten
years the rates designated for freight and passengers in Douglas'
bill would stop being mandatory. The bill was approved by the
Senate.[44]

The agreement, however, did not stop the debate on opposition to the bill. Most of the objection came from the senators
representing western and southern states. The senators from the
West, with the exception of Douglas, objected because they
feared that the proposed contract would hinder the development
of a trans-continental railroad across their states. The Southern
senators also protested because they wanted the Tehuantepec
route to be chosen for any such mode of communication from
sea to sea. The Tehuantepec route would place the southern port
of New Orleans in a more favorable position. The only area that
did not object to the Douglas bill consisted of the New England
and Atlantic-seaboard states. The senators of this area, including

Daniel Webster, supported the bill loyally. Even though Webster was actually in favor of the Tehuantepec route, he considered it unavailable in view of Mexico's attitude. Actually, the most heated debate opposing the bill for the railroad through Panama came from the group of senators who preferred the Tehuantepec route.[45] Nevertheless, Jefferson Davis, who opposed the bill, had this to say:

> If that people [on the Pacific Coast] are to be bound permanently to the Union, if it is to be made their interest in all time to remain a portion of the United States, then I say it is necessary that a ready and accessible means of communication must be continuous; towns, villages, and hamlets, must extend along the communication, from the seat of the General Government until we stand upon the shores of the Pacific. This must be our ulterior object, and all other measures in reference to the subject must be considered as temporary expedients only.[46]

Many Senators were opposed to the bill because they thought it was helping a monopoly. Finally the Douglas bill was shelved and on February 6, 1849 the Senate turned to different business. The fact that the Senate did not definitely act on any of the proposals having to do with a railroad in Panama caused Aspinwall to write a friend the following:

> I have to thank you for your interesting private letter from Panama which reached me in Washington where I have lost much time this winter in trying to induce favorable action on the part of the Government towards a railroad across Panama; but President-making and slavery were too engrossing to admit of attention being bestowed on this or any other matter of interest to California—and we shall therefore limit ourselves to improving the transit in a more economical way—so that by next year at this time, it may be accomplished in 10 or 12 hours from sea to sea. . . .[47]

FINANCING THE COMPANY

Aspinwall had, however, made informal negotiations with Nueva Granada for a railroad in Panama, prior to December 11,

1848 when he and his associates introduced the Memorandum
calling for a railroad across the Isthmus before Congress. When
the Compagnie de Panama, Mateo Klein's outfit, forfeited the
contract for a railroad across Panama in June, 1848,[48] the president of Nueva Granada authorized the Colombian minister in
Washington to transfer the right for a railroad on the Isthmus to
any organization which could guarantee the long-planned completion. Immediately after the informal negotiations, and while
the debate on Aspinwall's Memorandum was going on in Congress, Aspinwall and his associates were proceeding with the
organization of a railroad company. They announced on December 13, 1848, that subscriptions for capital stock for the Panama
railroad would be taken at the Bank of the State of New York
within a few days, and that the Trustees were to be Cornelius W.
Lawrence, Samuel Jandon, Matthew Morgan, C. A. Davis, William Kent, and General Winfield Scott.[49] On December 28,
1848 in Washington, Aspinwall and associates began formal negotiations for the Panama railroad with the minister from Nueva
Granada.[50] On April 7, 1849 the act which incorporated the Panama Railroad Company passed the legislature of the State of
New York.[51] This act stated that the capital stock for the railroad was not to be less than one million dollars nor more than
five million dollars. The value of the shares would be one hundred dollars each, with the beginning of construction to take
place as soon as a half a million dollars of shares were sold.
The New York Legislature in its Act incorporating the railroad
gave the power of constructing the Panama Railroad to W. H. Aspinwall, John L. Stephens, Henry Chauncey, Governor Kemble,
Thomas W. Ludlow, Joseph B. Varnum, Prosper M. Wetmore,
Horatio Allen, Cornelius W. Lawrence, David Thompson, Samuel S. Howland, Edwin Bartlett, and associates. The legislature
also gave these men the right to operate ships to and from Panama. On June 28, 1849 capital stock for the railroad was issued
in the amount of one million dollars. The shares were sold so
rapidly, due chiefly to New York capitalists, that by three
o'clock of the same day all of the planned capital stock was
subscribed. On July 2, 1849 stockholders elected Thomas Ludlow

president of the Panama Railroad Company and John L. Stephens vice-president. Stephens succeeded Ludlow as president soon afterwards. Colonel A. J. Center was then made vice-president of the company.[52] They and their associates proceeded to complete the organization of the company.

MORE SURVEYING AND A NEW CONTRACT

Meanwhile, during the early part of 1849, Colonel George W. Hughes of the United States Army Topographical Corps was appointed chief engineer in charge of surveying the Isthmus. Hughes and thirty-eight military and civil engineers left New York on January 22, 1849, to begin their search for a lower pass over the mountains. They found one which was only 275 feet above sea level. This was about 200 feet lower than the one found by Garella in 1838 and even lower than the one that Stephens had previously found. This 275 foot pass over the mountains proved later to be the lowest existing pass in the Continental Divide. When news of the discovery of the new gap was heard in New York, in June, 1849 the future of the railroad seemed promising. The original plan for the route of the railroad was first to begin work near Gorgona, in the highlands, some thirty miles from the Atlantic, so that the company could operate steamers carrying passengers from Chagres on the Atlantic to Gorgona. Money from passenger fares would pay for the construction of the railroad from Chagres to Gorgona. The original plan had to be discarded because the river proved much too shallow, even for steamboats drawing 18 inches.[53]

On June 12, 1849 (about the time that news of the low pass reached New York) Stephens, partly because of his knowledge of the Spanish language and temperament, completed the negotiating of a highly favorable agreement, and the Nueva Granada Legislature by decree accepted the contract for the railroad proposed by Aspinwall and his associates. The contract was signed on April 15, 1850 by John L. Stephens (representing the Panama Railroad Company) and Victoriano de Diego Paredes (Secretary of Foreign Affairs of Nueva Granada).[54] This same Colombian later created an awkward situation between Panamanians and North Americans when he publicly proposed, at the official inauguration of the city of Colón (already accepted under that name by the legislature in Panama) on February 27, 1852 that the city be named Aspinwall. Panamanians and other Colombians resented this name so much that the postal department was forbidden to deliver any mail with that name on it. In this way the Panamanians forced the world to recognize the name of the city as Colón, the name in Spanish of Colombus, the discoverer of America.[55]

The contract between Nueva Granada and the Panama Railroad Company was ratified by the Nueva Granada Congress on May 29, 1850. Its principal provisions were:

1. The Panama Railroad Company was granted the exclusive right of building and operating a railroad across the Isthmus for a period of forty-nine years. However, the New Granada government was to have the privilege of purchasing the railroad (a) at the end of twenty years for five million dollars, (b) at the end of thirty years for four million dollars, and (c) at the end of forty years for two million dollars; and it was to notify the company at least one year before the termination of whichever option it chose.[56]

2. The railroad was to be completed from ocean to ocean within a period of six years from the date of ratification of the contract.[57]

3. The railroad was granted exclusive rights for forty-nine years to use the ports situated at both terminals. These were to be free ports, and the Company was to set tolls which it might think proper.[58]

4. The Company could use any means it deemed necessary for the construction and operation of the railroad on which trains could cross the Isthmus in twelve hours or less.[59]

5. The Railroad Company was granted land for a right of way, for its terminal cities, hotels, wharves, warehouses, drydocks and other facilities, the Island of Manzanillo on the At-

lantic, and permanent title to 250,000 acres to be selected from any public lands on the Isthmus.[60]

6. Any legal problem arising between the railroad and New Granada would be settled in the courts of New Granada. (This was eighteen years before Carlos Calvo published the "Argentine Jurist" doctrine (1868) that alien investors have no recourse beyond the courts of the nation to which their capital has migrated.)[61]

7. The Railroad Company would carry Nueva Granada's mail free of charge across the Isthmus. Also, it would pay Nueva Granada five per cent of all money received from other mail contracts.[62]

8. The Company would pay to Nueva Granada three per cent of its net profits.[63]

9. The railroad would carry all troops of Nueva Granada free of charge across Panama.[64]

10. The railroad would be exempt from all taxes by Nueva Granada for a period of twenty years.[65]

The Panama Railroad Company announced on July 14, 1849, that it was ready to accept bids from contractors for construction of the Gorgona-Chagres section of the railroad. George M. Totten (called Colonel even though he had no military rank) and John C. Trautwine were the successful bidders, perhaps because they had had experience in tropical engineering. They had built El Dique, a canal from Cartagena to the Magdalena River. Totten and Trautwine arrived in Panama in January, 1850; and, with great enthusiasm, set up their headquarters and began work on the railroad.[66]

THE ACTUAL BUILDING OF THE RAILROAD—POSITIVE AND NEGATIVE CONSEQUENCES

However, they soon found the jungles and marshes of Panama damping their enthusiasm. The spruce and pine lumber they imported for buildings and railway ties decayed in the hot, wet climate of the tropics as rapidly as it was placed on the ground.

At the same time thousands of prospectors coming through the Isthmus on their way to California caused such a tremendous drain of the labor supply that it was almost impossible to hire workers. As if this were not enough trouble, Totten and Trautwine found that the Chagres River at low water was not navigable at all, and even at high water the flat-bottomed steamers operating in the river carrying supplies from Chagres to Gorgona proved to have too deep a draft. Faced with all these problems, Totten, in February, 1850 wrote New York stating that he was unable to carry out the contract for the building of the railroad. He recommended, however, that instead of Chagres as the Atlantic terminal for the railroad, the Company should select a terminal at Navy Bay on the Atlantic where supplies could be unloaded directly from the ships. On March 12, 1850 the Company decided to follow all of Totten's suggestions, and to retain him and Trautwine as engineers in charge of construction.

In May of 1850 Trautwine, Baldwin, a small group of assistants and a dozen Indians landed on a narrow coral reef which ran around Manzanillo Island, the place chosen as the Atlantic terminal for the railroad. Manzanillo was 650 acres of sunken swamp, with crocodiles playing in smelly mud and mosquitoes looking for blood. Totten had missed this trip because he was in Cartagena recruiting workers for the clearing of the island. Workers on Manzanillo were constantly falling sick with malaria and other tropical fevers. Because of these casualties the company kept agents busy recruiting workers throughout the Caribbean Islands and imported some from China.[67]

Thus, the men who helped to build the Panama Railroad were of many nationalities and races. Jamaicans proved the best workers, but close behind them were Cubans, Cartageneans, Irish from New Orleans, French and Haitians. The thousand or so Chinese laborers were soon overcome with a suicidal mania because their drugs had been taken away from them. Many Chinese hung themselves, others threw themselves on their machetes or weighted down their clothes and then jumped into the Chagres.[68]

People in the Canal Zone and in Panama, even today, repeat the legend "that every tie of the original Panama Railroad cost a life."[69] However, an employee of the railroad in 1860 walked the entire length of track during his vacation and counted 94,326 ties, and there were not that many martyrs. The actual number of deaths was about 12,000.[70]

To put an end to rumors in New York and elsewhere not only of the high death rate but also of bad management, the company built better houses and facilities for its workers, and by March of 1852 it had built seven miles of tracks—all on piles. This was necessary because of the extensive swamps the road traversed. Unexpected relief from the bad situation that the railroad was in came from travelers on their way to California. They began to use the few miles of track, the company hastened to build more, and the public in New York readily bought more stock.[71]

Notwithstanding the prosperity which seemed inevitable for the Isthmians, they suffered another economic crisis in 1851, right on the heels of the one felt in 1847. This crisis was due to the greed and corruption of persons high in the Central Government who had deprived Panamanians of their import duties; they claimed, however, that this was meant to stamp out any ideas Isthmians might have about gaining independence. The Bidlack Treaty had its own way of hamstringing Panamanians, who, because of the treaty, could not successfully revolt against the unjust measures of the Central Government. Only after long legal struggles in the Congress of Nueva Granada were the Isthmians to be granted statehood and thus more control of their local economic situation.[72]

When two parties of workers, one working from the Atlantic to the Pacific and the other, *vice versa,* met on the rainy midnight of January 27, 1855, the first transcontinental railroad in America was temporarily completed. The actual completion took another two years and two million dollars more. When completely finished, the railroad had cost more than $9,000,000, or close to $170,000 per mile.[73]

For many years to come the Panama route, and therefore the railroad, had almost a complete monopoly on the transportation of mail, gold, emigrants and travelers who did not wish to attempt the other routes to California. However, the largest amount of freight for the railroad did not come from the California trade as expected, but came instead from South and Central America. On the original capitalization of one million dollars, the railroad's average dividend from 1853 to 1881 was 16%.[74] Truly it was a dream come true, not only for Aspinwall and his associates, but for the generations that were to use and be grateful for the Panama Railroad.

Nevertheless, many Panamanians were bitter because of the price they had to pay in the long run, for the end of construction meant, practically, the end of prosperity for many workers, even though the railroad was fully exploited thereafter by Panamanian commercial groups, by the United States and by other foreigners. Panamanians who had been lured away from the long-range progress that had begun in a small way in the interior of the Isthmus during the years before the construction found themselves deceived, corrupted and with neither immediate nor future prospects of improving their lot.[75] Rogelio Sinán, a distinguished contemporary author and poet of Panama, referred to the drain of manpower from the basic and longer-lasting improvements of rural economy when he wrote:

> All that living sap which is the farming community turned itself innocently toward the crossings of the metal road. Men, women, children, attracted by the insane lure of the mermaid, abandonned what they considered their static rural sadness to change it for a miserable urban joviality. In the cities formed on the transit zone these phantoms of maize begin to mold themselves to a life of urgency and sweat, huddled in dirty rooms full of stench, where at last they let themselves be devoured by the insatiable cosmopolitan city.[76]

The terrible depression of 1847, however, encouraged many Panamanians to look favorably upon the construction of the railroad and its availability afterward for the expansion of commerce and consequent uplifting of the economy. This and the treachery of the Central Government toward her step-daughter, Panama, in taking from her the import duties in 1851, fanned the flaming desires of many Isthmians to be recognized as a state within Nueva Granada in order to manage more effectively their own economic growth. Finally, in 1855 when their statehood was recognized and the railroad was completed, Panamanians did sense the beginning and the promise of a new era; an era that, as it turned out, would tragically disappoint their dreams and hopes.

NOTES

1. Fessenden N. Otis, *Illustrated History of the Panama Railroad* (New York, 1861), 15.
2. Ira E. Bennett, *History of the Panama Canal* (Washington, 1915), 86.
3. John E. Minter, *The Chagres* (New York, 1948), 87.
4. *Ibid.* Castilla del Oro was the name given by Columbus to Panama. See: Bennett, *History of the Panama Canal,* 480.
5. Minter, *The Chagres,* 38-40; 87-90.
6. Bennett, *History of the Panama Canal,* 86.
7. See: Colonel William Duane, *A Visit to Colombia in the Years 1822 and 1823* (Philadelphia, 1826), iv.
8. Bennett, *History of the Panama Canal,* 86. Mr. Lloyd had served for some time before on General Bolívar's personal staff. He received from Bolívar the special commission to survey the Isthmus of Panama "in order to ascertain the most eligible line of communication across it, whether by road or canal." (*House of Representatives,* Report No. 145, 30th Cong. 2 sess., p. 455. There appears in this report a section entitled "Notes Respecting the Isthmus of Panama: by M. A. Lloyd.").

   According to Arosemena, *Apuntamientos históricos,* 161-162, this survey occurred in 1825. However, several other sources, one of which quotes the writings of Lloyd himself, say the dates are from 1827 to 1829, which actually seems more reasonable in view of the fact that Bolívar was so busy with the independence movement and fighting in 1825. See: Parks, *Colombia and the United States,* 182; Gerstle Mack, *La Tierra Dividida,* (Panama, 1971), 135-137.

   Regarding the correctness of sources in reference to this period in general, and to dates used, John Haskell Kemble, *The Panama Route,* and the source Kemble uses, Ernesto Castillero R., *Historia de Panamá,* are not always correct. The author has found that this last source is not entirely reliable for details. It appears as though Castillero writes from memory, without cross references or original documents perhaps.
9. Already in 1835, a North American, Dr. J. H. Gibbon, had stated that a Free Port in Panama would activate world commerce and especially

that of the United States, whose citizens were already owners of 60% of all the commerce on the Pacific, or so it was believed. See: Angel Rubio, *La ciudad de Panamá* (Panama, 1950), 51; Juan Antonio Susto, ed., *2 relaciones de viajes al Istmo de Panama en 1835:* "J. H. Gibbon" trans. by Ricardo J. Alfaro (Panama, 1961), 15-16, hereafter cited as Susto, *2 relaciones.*

10. Arosemena, *Apuntamientos,* 252-253; Chong, *Historia de Panamá,* 150. Thierry was English-born, but of French parents. According to J.H. Gibbon, his title was doubtful (or so he implies in his diary) and he was a little "touched"; his contract with Nueva Granada would have never been acceptable to any truly great capitalist, wrote Gibbon. See: Susto, *2 relaciones,* 21-22.

11. Arosemena, *Apuntamientos,* 257.

12. Bennett, *History of the Panama Canal,* 86; J. Fred Rippy, *The Capitalists and Colombia* (New York, 1931), 38.

13. James Fred Rippy, *The Capitalists and Colombia* (New York, 1931), 38; *Senate Document* No. 429, 59 Cong., 1 Sess. (Ser. 4919), 4.

14. *Ibid.*

15. Castillero R., *Historia de Panamá,* 85-86.

16. Arosemena, *Apuntamientos,* 257; Rippy, *The Capitalists,* 38.

17. Rippy, *The Capitalists,* 39. For a detailed account of the proceedings relating to Charles Biddle's mission see: U.S. House of Representatives. 30th Cong., 2 sess., Report No. 145, *Canal or Railroad Between the Atlantic and Pacific Oceans.*

For an account of the instructions by the United States Government to Charles Biddle, see pp. 241-244.

Concerning the ill-feeling created by Biddle because of his violation of the instructions, see pp. 269-324.

See letter of Charles Biddle to John Forsyth, stating his views: pp. 271-277. Here Biddle mentions that confidence in Thierry's plan was destroyed, that the feeling was that his scheme was impracticable.

In a note from Robert McAfee, *chargé d'affaires* of the United States, to Lino de Pombo, Minister of Foreign Affairs of Nueva Granada, McAfee states that Biddle put up $1 million as a guarantee for completion of a road to be opened across Panama. See p. 268.

Biddle's own note, in defense, received November 15, 1836, states that the stock of the company which was granted the concession would be divided as follows: "Two-thirds of the stock is the property of Charles Biddle and such citizens of the United States as he may associate with him; the remaining one-third is the property of the Nueva Granadians. The office of the company is to be in Philadelphia, and all installments are to be paid there; and the number of directors is to be in the same proportion as the quantity of stock." See p. 273.

Such entering into a contract by a diplomatic representative of the United States was prohibited. John Forsyth expresses it in a note from him to Robert McAfee dated Sept. 23, 1836. See pp. 269-270.

Charles Biddle had the support of the Society of Friends of the Country, which was made up of prominent citizens of the Isthmus. (Arosemena, *Apuntamientos,* 278). In a letter to Biddle on Dec. 4, 1835, the signatures appearing are of Blas Arosemena, Mariano Arosemena, and José de Obaldía, and in a later letter, the name Tomás Herrera appears. (See pp. 278-280, 310). They state that Thierry's scheme for a canal was not practical and that they believed a railroad would fulfill the dream of the Isthmus. The fact that many such prominent persons of the Isthmus were actually members of the company, standing to gain financially in the event of successful completion of the railroad, may well lead to the supposition that their patriotic motives were at least partially questionable.

18. Bennett, *History of the Panama Canal,* 86.
19. Arosemena, *Apuntamientos,* 282; Bennett, *History of the Panama Canal,* 86-87; Gerstle Mack, *The Land Divided* (New York, 1944), 127-130; Minter, *The Chagres,* 89; Parks, *Colombia and the United States,* 196-200; *U.S. House of Representatives,* 30th Cong., 2 sess., Report No. 145; regarding Salomon and Company, see p. 454; concerning practicability of a ship canal, see pp. 70, 73, 509, 590. Garella received aid and help from Colonel Anselmo Pineda, Governor of Panama; see p. 509.
20. Alba, *Cronología,* 159; Arosemena, *Apuntamientos,* 282-289; Chong, *Historia de Panamá,* 151.
21. Bennett, *History of the Panama Canal,* 86. Captain W.B. Liot was the colonial superintendent of the Royal Mail Steam Packet Company which had a cargo, mail and passenger service between England and the Caribbean. See: Mack, *The Land Divided,* 131.

    See: W.B. Liot, *Panama, Nicaragua and Tehuantepec; or Considerations upon the Question of Communication Between the Atlantic and Pacific Oceans* (London, 1849).
22. Diogenes A. Arosemena, *Documentary Diplomatic History of the Panama Canal* (Panama, 1961), 35; Bennett, *History of the Panama Canal,* 87; Robert R. Russel, *Improvement of Communication with the Pacific Coast as an Issue in American Politics, 1783-1864* (Cedar Rapids, 1948), 54.

    Benjamin A. Bidlack was apparently moved by a letter from Secretary of State James Buchanan which requested him to use his influence with Nueva Granada to prevent it from granting privileges to any other nation which might prove injurious to the United States. See document No. 1818 in: William R. Manning, *Diplomatic Correspondence of the*

United States: Inter-American Affairs, 1831-1860, Vol. 5 (Washington, 1935), 357-365. See also: Eugene I. McCormac, *James K. Polk: A Political Biography* (Berkeley, 1922), 709; J. Fred Rippy, *The Caribbean Danger Zone* (New York, 1940), 60-61.
23. Russel, *Improvement of Communication*, 54.
24. Alba, *Cronología*, 170; Arosemena, *Documentary Diplomatic History*, 31; John E. Fagg, *Latin America* (New York, 1963), 535; Russel, *Improvement of Communication*, 54.
25. Alba, *Cronología*, 171; Chong, *Historia de Panamá*, 160-161.
26. Russel, *Improvement of Communication*, 54-55. There is no doubt that the acquisition of California was to Polk the most important objective of the expected war with Mexico. See: William Brandon, *The Men and the Mountain: Fremont's Fourth Expedition* (New York, 1955), 22. George Bancroft, Polk's first Secretary of the Navy said that Polk's ambition was to acquire California. See: Norman A. Graebner, *Empire on the Pacific: A Study in American Continental Expansion* (New York, 1955), 84.
27. This could be shown to be not wholly true from Buchanan's letter to Bidlack. See: Manning, *Diplomatic Correspondence*, Vol. 5, 357. For an overall effect of the Bidlack treaty on relations between the Isthmus and Colombia and Bidlack's own initiative see the following books: Jules Dubois, *Danger Over Panama* (Indianapolis, 1964), 21-39; Sheldon B. Liss, *The Canal: Aspects of United States-Panamanian Relations* (South Bend, 1967), 11-21.
   For an excellent study of relations between the United States and Panama see: Lawrence O. Ealy, *The Republic of Panama in World Affairs, 1903-1950* (Philadelphia, 1951) and William D. McCain, *The United States and the Republic of Panama* (New York, 1965).
28. Dubois, *Danger Over Panama*, 22; Russel, *Improvement of Communication*, 54-55.
29. Russel, *Improvement of Communication*, 55. The Clayton-Bulwer Treaty of April 19, 1850, was to bind the United States not to acquire any territory in the region of possible ocean-to-ocean transit or to erect any fortifications there or to obtain control exclusively over any area. A partial repudiation of the above obligations took place between 1856-1857 and 1869-1870. After 1880 the attitude of the United States towards the Clayton-Bulwer treaty was one of open defiance.
   In 1856-1857, after the so-called "Watermelon War," Secretary of State William Marcy stated that the United States had to land marines because Colombia had failed to protect the transit of passengers. As we shall see in Chapter V, he demanded indemnity. Furthermore, he attempted to acquire the island of Taboga and other islands in the Bay

of Panama. What he really wanted was the transfer to the United States of all Colombia's rights as defined in the charter of the railroad and to create two quasi-independent governments, one at Colòn and the other at Panama. See: Parks, *Colombia and the United States*, 194-262; Rippy, *The Caribbean Danger Zone*, 60-65. But the best example of violations can be seen during the Thousand Day's War in Panama, which will be dealt with in the last chapter of this work.

It is obvious that the United States, faced with three different treaties (Bidlack, the Railroad Contract, and Clayton-Bulwer) would choose the treaty and interpret it in a manner most convenient to it at a given time.

30. Joseph B. Bishop, *The Panama Gateway* (New York, 1913), 45; Frederic J. Haskin, *The Panama Canal* (Garden City, 1913), 102; Kemble, *The Panama Route, 1848-1869* (Berkeley and Los Angeles, 1943), 178.

31. Alba, *Cronología*, 169.

32. Bennett, *History of the Panama Canal*, 87; "Panama Railroad in Second Century of Service," *Illinois Central Magazine*, XXXXV (November, 1956), 10.

   See: *Two Years Before the Mast*, a novel by Richard Henry Dana, Jr., published in 1840 and which revolutionized the treatment of seafaring men. Dana was only nineteen when, in 1834, he left Boston aboard a trading brig for the long, difficult voyage around Cape Horn, but his book remains today a thrilling tale of life under the sail.

33. Earl Harding, *The Untold Story of Panama* (New York, 1959), 1. One reason for the undesirability of the Nicaraguan route during the years 1855-1857 was due to the filibustering activity of William Walker in Nicaragua. See: Rippy, *The Capitalists*, 39.

34. Bennett, *History of the Panama Canal*, 87; Otis, *Illustrated History*, 16.

35. *Illinois Central Magazine*, 11; Russel, *Improvement of Communication*, 55-56.

36. Bennett, *History of the Panama Canal*, 87; Kemble, *The Panama Route*, 178-179. James Marshall discovered gold in upper California on January 24, 1848.

37. Stephens' exploration of the Mayan ruins of Chiapas in Yucatan reflected his love for archaeology, which prompted him to write two volumes on the subject which are still important works. See: John L. Stephens, *Incidents of Travel in Central America, Chiapas, and Yucatan*, ed. Richard L. Predmore (New Brunswick, 1949).

38. Bennett, *History of the Panama Canal*, 87-88; Kemble, *The Panama Route*, 179; Minter, *The Chagres*, 255-257.

39. Their memorial, entitled "Memorial of W.H.S Aspinwall, John L. Stephen, and Henry Chauncey, in reference to the Construction of a Railroad across the Isthmus of Panama," was presented before the 30th Congress, 2nd session. *Congressional Globe*, 30 Congress, 2 Sess., 20-

21; Kemble, *The Panama Route*, 179-283; Elena Ronan, "All Aboard," *Americas*, III (January, 1951), 25; Russel, *Improvement of Communication*, 56.

The need to overcome the vast distances between the East and the West and to hold the West together in the Union was a pressing factor to the Americans during the 1840s-1850s. The answer, according to the expansionists, was a transcontinental railroad. The railroad would bring economic and military power to the United States over the Pacific Ocean and throughout the world. See: Graebner, *Empire on the Pacific*, 90-100.

40. John D. Hicks and George E. Mowry, *A Short History of American Democracy* (Boston, 1956), xv.

41. *Congressional Globe*, 30 Cong., 2 Sess., 20-21; Kemble, *The Panama Route*, 179-181.

42. *Ibid.* Thomas Benton, father-in-law of John Charles Frémont, was one of the most powerful men in Washington. He was also one of the leaders of the expansionist group in Congress—devoted to the cause of turning the eyes of America to the unopened and undeveloped west. See: Brandon, *The Men and the Mountain*, 14-15.

43. Kemble, *The Panama Route*, 180; Russel, *Improvement of Communication*, 58.

44. *Congressional Globe*, 30 Cong., 2 Sess., 382; Kemble, *The Panama Route*, 180; Mack, *The Land Divided*, 149.

45. *Congressional Globe*, 30 Cong., 2 Sess., 398-402, 411-415, 457-463; Kemble, *The Panama Route*, 180-181; Ronan, "All Aboard," 25; Russel, *Improvement of Communication*, 59.

46. Russel, *Improvement of Communication*, 58-59.

47. Kemble, *The Panama Route*, 180-181; Ronan, "All Aboard," 25.

48. Bishop, *The Panama Gateway*, 45.

49. Kemble, *The Panama Route*, 180-183.

50. *Ibid.*, 181; Rippy, *The Capitalists*, 39.

51. Bennett, *History of the Panama Canal*, 88; Mack, *The Land Divided*, 149; Minter, *The Chagres*, 256.

52. Kemble, *The Panama Route*, 183; Mack, *The Land Divided*, 149-150; *The Panama Canal, Twenty-Fifth Anniversary* (Balboa Heights, 1939), 40; Ronan, "All Aboard," 25.

53. Bennett, *History of the Panama Canal*, 88; Mack, *The Land Divided*, 151; Rippy, *The Capitalists*, 40.

54. Chong, *Historia de Panamá*, 161; Kemble, *The Panama Route*, 181; Minter, *The Chagres*, 256.

55. Castillero R., *Historia de Panamá*, 97-98. The argument is reminiscent of a contemporary one regarding the Bridge of the Americas, across the Panama Canal. The Americans have named it the "Thatcher Ferry Bridge" and the Panamanians insist it should, by its very nature, be called the "Bridge of the Americas" (in Spanish *El Puente de las Americas*).

56. *Ibid.;* Otis, *Illustrated History,* 397-398. Article II is in the appendix of this book where there is a translation of the original contract.
57. Otis, *Illustrated History,* 398-399. (Article V of the contract.)
58. *Ibid.,* (Article IX of the contract).
59. *Ibid.,* (Article XIV of the contract).
60. *Ibid.* Involved in the land speculation which unfortunately erupted on the Isthmus were people as admired and important as the ex-president of Nueva Granada, Tomás Cipriano Mosquera. He was heavily censured on the Isthmus by his compatriots for his part in such dishonest activities. See: Moscote and Arce, *Justo Arosemena,* 155, 177-178; Seemann, *Historia del Istmo de Panamá,* 89.
61. Kemble, *The Panama Route,* 182; Harold F. Peterson, *Argentina and the United States, 1810-1960* (New York, 1964), 258.
62. Kemble, *The Panama Route,* 182; Otis, *Illustrated History,* 405.
63. Minter, *The Chagres,* 257.
64. Kemble, *The Panama Route,* 182.
65. Joseph L. Schott, *Rails Across Panama* (Indianapolis, 1967), 12.
66. Bennett, *History of the Panama Canal,* 88; Kemble, *The Panama Route,* 184; Mack, *The Land Divided,* 151; Minter, *The Chagres,* 259; Oran, "Tropical Journeyings," *Harper's New Monthly Magazine,* XVIII (January, 1859), 148.
67. *Ibid.*
68. Bennett, *History of the Panama Canal,* 90; Rubén D. Carles, *Crossing the Isthmus of Panama* (Panama, 1946), 28-30; Minter, *The Chagres,* 271-272.
69. Chong, *Historia de Panama,* 165; Minter, *The Chagres,* 273.
70. *Ibid.;* Schott, *Rails Across Panama,* 173.
71. Russel, *Improvement of Communication,* 60.
72. Alba, *Cronología,* 169, 175, 181-183. This source does not elaborate the situation concerning import duties. Apparently, import duties were still being collected, but the Panamanians were not receiving their fair share. Of course, the idea they had been fighting for, at least in some circles, of a free port was not being carried out; thus they were not getting the advantages of a duty-free port, for the point of not charging duties was to stir up more commercial traffic in the area. It must have been a frustrating situation for Panamanian businessmen indeed.
73. Bennett, *History of the Panama Canal,* 88-100; Haskin, *The Panama Canal,* 96; Minter, *The Chagres,* 272; Ronan, "All Aboard," 46; Russel, *Improvement of Communication,* 61.
74. Rippy, *The Capitalists,* 43; Russel, *Improvement of Communication,* 61; *Senate Document,* No. 429, 59 Cong., 1 Sess., (Ser. 4919), 237.
75. Chong, *Historia de Panamá,* 165-166.

76. Rogelio Sinán, "Rutas de la novela panameña," *Letras de Panama* (December 1, 1947), 7. The negative aspects of Panama's fate in her dealings with North Americans fires the imagination of many other contemporary Panamanian writers. One of the most vehement complaints is that of Rodolfo (Fito) Aguilera, Jr., whose protagonist in *Historia de una vida vulgar* (Panama, n.d.) unleashes momentarily his anti-American feelings: "I remember, whenever I see a gringo, the Panama Canal, which cruelly ruptured, without conscious reparation, the virginity of our Isthmus. I can almost see the ardent and gigantic phallus of the Saxon, and hanging from it, the bleeding and torn hymen of my poor land." p. 64.

CHAPTER IV

The Forty-Niners Through Panama

On January 24, 1848 James Marshall discovered gold on the American River in Upper California. This discovery came at an opportune moment, for the Mexican War was over and men who were unwilling to settle down were looking for new excitement. Furthermore, the 1840s, a period of hard times, had left the East in a financial crisis. Mortgages had spread to almost every phase of commercial and private life. It is no wonder, then, that the communities of the East, in order to alleviate the financial straits in which they found themselves, were ready to send their young men West in search of gold.[1] Doctors, lawyers, professors, mechanics, thieves, gamblers, murderers, clerks and clergymen sold, abandoned or mortgaged what was not already mortgaged (their farms, practices, homes or anything they had established) in order to go West in search of gold.[2]

Of the various routes to California, the Panama route, with ships leaving either from New York or New Orleans, was the shortest, quickest and most travelled. It was also the most expensive, because it required the outlay of cash for the purchase of tickets on steamers and for the expenses of the transit across Panama. It attracted the reckless, the impatient, and gold-seekers not accustomed to hardships, so that gamblers, speculators, murderers, cheap politicians and prostitutes were in the majority along this route.[3] Ship after ship brought thousands of Forty-Niners to Panama from 1848 until 1869, when at last the first transcontinental railroad in the United States was completed.

This tremendous number of travelers "turned sleepy Panama into a roaring city of saloons, brothels, dance halls, and gambling dens."[4] Along with undesirables, each shipload of gold-seekers brought material prosperity to Panama. The little Isthmus, covered with dense, wet and hot jungles and fever-breeding mosquitoes, had not known such commotion and wealth since the early days of the Spaniards.[5]

Before Aspinwall and his associates began building their Panama railroad, Aspinwall's Pacific Mail Steamship Company, on October 6, 1848 sent its steamer-sailing ship *California* to the Pacific Coast of the United States by way of Cape Horn. The *California,* built in the shipyards of William H. Webb (the leading New York shipbuilder of the time) was some two hundred feet in length, with a beam of about thirty-four feet and a tonnage of over one thousand. Two boilers supplied steam, and power was augmented by sails. At this time, the West Coast was so sparsely settled that the ship, big as it was, carried very few passengers in comparison to its total capacity.[6]

When the *California* left New York, the rush for the gold fields of California had not yet begun. The ship sailed with a handful of passengers en route to Brazil, Chile and Peru. None of the few passengers were on their way to California. The ship reached Río de Janeiro twenty-two days out from its port of embarkation, setting a new record for the run, and it reached Callao, Peru, on December 27, 1848. Stories of the tremendous amount of gold in California had reached Callao before the ship docked. The desire for a share of this wealth encouraged many Peruvians to board the almost-empty *California* for San Francisco. The ship set sail for Panama on January 10, 1849, where she arrived a week later to find a port wild with gold-seekers. They had been brought there by a small steamer, the *Falcon,* and six other vessels.[7]

While the *California* was sailing around Cape Horn, the United States Mail Steam Line chartered the *Falcon* to carry passengers to Panama, where it was to make connection with the *California.* The *Falcon* left New York on December 1, 1848 with only twenty-nine passengers for California. Most of these

were government employees and missionaries. The *Falcon*'s
next port-of-call was New Orleans. By the time it left New Orleans on December 18, 1848, it carried 193 passengers. The news
of the discovery of gold in California had spread over the United
States, and everyone was trying to get to the gold fields. Of the
193 passengers that left the port of New Orleans aboard the *Falcon,* some 150 were southern backwoodsmen, carrying pans
pots, axes and whatever kind of equipment they thought necessary for digging gold. The *Falcon* had berths for only one hundred additional passengers. However, the remaining gold seekers
refused to leave the ship. The captain of the *Falcon* threatened
to use force, but backed down when the backwoodsmen spat
tobacco juice on the deck and brandished their revolvers. Finally,
the captain had to place bunks in the hold and in the dining room.

The *Falcon* arrived at Chagres on December 27, 1848. She
was followed two days later by the *John Benson,* which had left
New York on December 11, 1848. By the time the *California*
arrived at Panama on January 17, 1849, five more vessels had
arrived at Chagres, loaded with potential prospectors. When the
California was ready to sail northward along the Pacific the following month, some ten additional vessels had arrived at Chagres.
These seventeen ships had brought in a total of 726 passengers.
This great number of Argonauts created a problem for the *California,* which only had been built to carry 250 passengers. To
make matters worse, when the *California* arrived at Panama,
there were some seventy Peruvians on board. The Americans in
Panama were infuriated over the fact that Peruvians were taking
up space that they thought was "rightfully" theirs, and they
were determined to put them ashore. However, the whole affair
was finally settled when extra berths were constructed outside
in the open space for the South Americans. When the ship finally
sailed for the gold fields, she carried some 365 passengers plus a
crew of thirty-six. Over 400 people sailed on a ship that originally had been built for only 250. The *California* was not the
only ship to face this problem. Throughout the first few years
of the Gold Rush there existed a shortage of ships on the Pacific
Coast.[8]

Meanwhile, on the Caribbean side of the Isthmus of Panama, after an average sea voyage from the East Coast of eight days, ship after ship arrived, filled with anxious, impatient gold-seekers usually wearing red shirts and slouch hats, and carrying bowie knives and revolvers. Ever since Porto Bello on the Atlantic (east of the present-day canal) had been closed toward the end of the colonial period, ships on the Caribbean anchored at sea about one mile from the town of Chagres. This was necessary because the water over a sand bar at the mouth of the Chagres River had a depth of only thirteen feet. Passengers had to disembark into small native boats which carried them to the town of Chagres located near the mouth of the river on the south side.[9]

CHAGRES

In 1848 according to the travelers, Chagres was a dirty, smelly hole with a few mud huts with thatched roofs. Daniel A. Horn, a traveler from Alabama to California via Panama in 1850, in a letter to his sisters and mother, wrote the following description:

> The houses are only hovels that, in the States, would not even do for Negro quarters or even for a respectable cow house. The whole town does not look near so well as the quarters on a Southern plantation. They are built by planting four posts in the ground, about 10 feet high, for the corners: rafters [are] made of cane or bamboo, forming a very steep roof and covered with cocoa or palm leaves, though when properly put on they make a very tight roof, but do not last probably more than a very few years. Many of them are not enclosed at all at the sides, and those that are have only cane put upright and daubed with mud. . . . They are filled with filth, have no beds, but [the occupants] either sleep in hammocks or have cowhides on the ground. They have no tables or chairs, and the only cooking utensil I could see was an earthen jar something in the shape of a pot, in which they cooked their food. They had no dishes, forks, or spoons, and only a butcher's knife and a shell . . . for a spoon.[10]

The impression of North Americans traveling across the Isthmus at that time was probably the same as Horn's. Some insurance companies considered Chagres "the most unhealthy place in Christendom," for which reason many travelers had to forfeit their insurance policies when they stayed overnight at the town. The life-expectancy of the natives was 20 years; the situation was aggravated by the cholera brought in from New Orleans and New York only to flourish in the heat of the tropics. The first outbreak killed one-fourth of the native population.[11]

To make matters worse, between 1852 and 1855, chaos ruled in Panama. The Isthmians, led by Justo Arosemena and General Tomás Herrera, were trying to get approval from the central government for statehood. This would enable them to be part of Colombia while still tending to their own local problems with more autonomy and power. These negotiations, rebellion against the reforms of the Constitution of 1853, and political tensions, with their sequel of violence, brought upon the Isthmus the curse of instability and innumerable governors—some for a few days only—which together with old and continual economic problems, some of whose roots went as far back as the fight for independence from Spain, created an intense air of insecurity, poverty and chaos.[12] These manifestations of total disintegration had much bearing on the unfavorable opinions of many a Forty-Niner in Panama.

Horn, in describing Chagres in 1850, said that about half of the natives in Chagres were full-blooded Negroes. The remainder of the population was made up of Indians, Spaniards and a mixture of all three. The natives spoke a combination of Spanish and African dialects which made it difficult for travelers, even those who spoke Spanish, to understand them. Their appearance, according to Horn, was not as respectable as that of Negroes in his home state of Alabama. Their dress, Horn wrote, except for a few cases, would be termed indecent in the United States. However, the women dressed better than the men. They were fond of gaudy laces and other types of ornaments, but lacked "taste" in the way they dressed. In all, according to Horn, the natives were a little better off than savages.[13]

The climate of Chagres, according to some, caused the natives to be lethargic. It also made the Americans, especially those who were in a hurry to get to California, angry and, in some cases, brutal. As soon as the impatient travelers got off the ships, they would ask the natives how to get to Panama City. The natives would point to banana boats on the river which they called bungos. These boats were hollowed out from single logs and were about twenty-five feet in length and about three feet in width. They were covered with palm-thatched roofs to protect bananas from the sun. The Americans would then ask to be taken to Panama City immediately. Of course, "immediately" was too soon for the natives, who would answer, "Mañana." The Americans would reply, "Manyana hell. We vamoose right now." The travelers would then drag the natives toward the bungos, shouting and threatening them with bodily injury.[14]

However, with the beginning of emigration to California, the area around the Chagres River underwent a change. In January, 1849 when the Orus, the first steamer to go up the Chagres River, arrived, the need for some kind of wharf became apparent. An agent of the company which ran the Orus had a wharf built on the opposite bank from the native town of Chagres. The agent also arranged to have a small building of Georgia pine constructed behind the wharf to serve as an office. As the number of travelers and traffic on the Chagres River increased, additional wharves were built. The heavy tropical foliage was cut back to make room for shanty buildings to be used primarily by Americans, some Frenchmen and a few others. Several companies with various methods of river communications established themselves in the new town.[15] An American, Captain Abraham Buncher, who at one time worked for the New York Herald, organized a river transportation system. Buncher's system, known as the Isthmus Transportation Company, employed some forty small boats to carry freight and passengers up the river.[16]

Except for the terrain and for the lack of hitching posts, the new town of Chagres looked like the mining camps of the West.

It was a wild, roaring, American-run frontier town, populated at times with thousands of Forty-Niners. The Americans who were on their way to California remained at Chagres long enough to find transportation to Panama City. However, like most boom towns, Chagres had a permanent population of steamboat crews and mechanics, express agents, bartenders, innkeepers, gamblers, waiters, barbers, cooks and prostitutes.

Between 1849 and 1851 at least three dozen guidebooks for traveling to the gold fields appeared in the United States. One of the better guidebooks for the Panama route was written by George Alexander Thompson in 1849. Thompson included material from official reports written by United States agents. He also described conditions to be found along the Isthmian route. But probably the best of the guidebooks was the one written by Joseph W. Gregory, owner of an express company operating between California and the Atlantic coast. Gregory had made the trip across the Isthmus several times.[17]

By the end of 1849 the new Chagres had four frame hotels. The two main hotels were the Crescent City and the Californian. They were two-story wooden buildings, with porches around each floor. The rooms of these hotels were huge barrack-styled chambers, filled with cots which were rented at $4.00 per night. When the hotels were overcrowded, hammocks were swung between posts and rented out for $2.00 a night. The hotels usually reserved one room for women travelers. But again, if the hotels were pressed for space, women were placed in the same rooms, separated from the men by only a screen made of palm leaves, blankets or sheets.[18] Some hotels were merely tents at first; furthermore, they were crowded tents. One Chagres inn lacked a coffee grinder, as one goldrusher discovered when he ordered coffee. He was asked to wait while a fresh supply was prepared. Presently, he glanced out the window only to see a native girl squatting on the ground, chewing coffee beans and spitting them into a pot. The traveler decided not to have any coffee after all.[19]

Since refrigeration was impossible, the menus of the hotel dining-rooms and the Eagle Cafe and Restaurant in town included dried meat, bread, beans, fruits and coffee. The price for meals at these establishments was much more reasonable than the prices for sleeping quarters. Because of the Black Swamp, which was located behind the town, the eating places were usually filled with cockroaches.[20]

Besides the bars of the four main hotels, there were also many others, including the Silver Dollar Saloon. Liquid refreshments at these bars cost anywhere from one dollar up. They were about seven times as expensive as drinks were in New York. But the high cost of liquor did not discourage the adventurers or the returning prospectors who had gold in their pockets.

The only real discouragement that erased some of the great enthusiasm of the travelers to California was death from yellow fever, malaria, typhoid, cholera or gunshot wounds. Because there were no law-enforcement officers the number of deaths from gunshot wounds was unusually high. Since there was no cemetery, the dead were dropped into the Chagres River with no questions asked.

Travelers who were fortunate enough to stay alive had many places to spend their money. Almost everyone who came to Chagres had money. Travelers who came from the East had their grubstakes, and those who came from the West had gold because the miners that had gone broke either stayed in California or made their way back East across the overland routes. Travelers could spend their cash at gambling houses such as the Emporium or the Monte Carlo Casino. The latter did the most business. Games included roulette, blackjack, casino, poker, faro, craps, and *trente et quarante.*

Women took advantage of the Forty-Niners. The dance hostesses, charging two dollars for a dance, were but one type of woman in business. When these hostesses were offered a drink, which cost a dollar (the house kept fifty cents and the girl the other fifty), they ordered a Blue Moon, which was only colored water. Other money-making women were employed as prostitutes. There was even a House of All Nations run by a French couple who backed the name of the establishment by having an assortment of black, white and brown blends of Panamanian women. There were also some Americans, mostly *mademoiselles* from New Orleans, and a few second-rate girls from Paris.

Since there were no banks, the women changed the money received for their services into large-quantity bills. These in turn they kept where women of that type usually put things for safe-keeping. Also, since there was no law enforcement, the girls carried guns even while entertaining men. One Briton commented that this practice was "disconcerting as hell. All the time she kept one hand on her blasted six-shooter."[21]

The selling of pleasure by women seems to have been a successful business, for there were over two hundred prostitutes at Chagres during the Gold Rush days.[22] However, not much is known about them, since, unfortunately for historians, none ever published memoirs. What is known, however, and ably expressed by Panamanian historians, is the moral corruption bred by adventurers that seemed to interminably plague that isthmus, not only in Chagres, but everywhere along the route. Bonifacio Pereira Jiménez, a contemporary historian from Panama, bitterly comments on the moral pains, the silent consequences of those wild and wooly days:

> Nobody respected anyone. Adventurers and North American soldiers arrived in Panama thinking and believing that here neither life nor property need be respected. . . . He who was strong imposed himself, he who carried a revolver or a rifle. They raped the damsels with impunity, and they abused the elderly; they trespassed into the homes of the people with unpardonable cynicism. Brothels and bars were like mines planted in the middle of the city. Joints for gambling and for vices of the lowest kind. The dance of gold stepped parallel to the macabre dance of crime. The people . . . suffer the depravations of irresponsible evil-doers and hoodlums . . . assimilate pains which begin to leave scars in the abdomen . . . hide their sadness. . . .[23]

Chagres, with all its wild pleasures and hardships, was short-lived. By November, 1851, the Panama Railroad had built about ten miles of track inland from Aspinwall (later called Colón) and east of Chagres. This advantage was discovered accidentally by the ship *Georgia* that had been prevented from docking at

Chagres because of a storm. After that, travelers on their way to California would go to Aspinwall and then ride the train inland as far as possible. All the money extractors followed the travelers to Aspinwall and Chagres died.[24]

THE ROUTE FROM CHAGRES

The original fees charged for going up the Chagres had risen, before the Aspinwall "discovery," from ten dollars per passenger to forty and fifty dollars, but then declined by 1852 to about four dollars per passenger. Even before the new facilities were available, natives at Chagres had discovered that the Americans were not to be so easily cheated, for by 1851 they had learned how not to be swindled.[25]

During the dry season, from December until April, the traveler's destination from Chagres was Gorgona, a small village some forty miles from Chagres and about twenty miles from Panama City. During the remainder of the year, the rainy season, Forty-Niners could go as far as Cruces, another village located about five miles up the Chagres River from Gorgona, and some fifteen miles from Panama City. The boat trip from Chagres to Gorgona took about three days. This, of course, depended upon how skillful the native boatmen were and also upon the swiftness of the river current. During the rainy season, native boats would usually travel at night, between the hours of midnight and sunrise, because it usually rained in the daytime, making the current of the river too swift. Layovers during the trip were ordinarily at native villages along the river. During the dry season, travelers would hang up hammocks, if they had any, for the night. Some of the natives of the villages would rent out space under roofs and sell food to the travelers at outrageous prices. Then at Gorgona and Cruces, native towns of some five hundred inhabitants, there were some hotels and saloons operated by Americans.[26]

From Gorgona or Cruces, the Forty-Niners would hire mules and horses for the one-day trip to Panama City. Baggage and other personal affects were usually carried by the natives on their backs. Some persons even rode in chairs that were strapped to the heads of Negroes and Indians. For women, the journey to Panama City presented problems. In order to escape male abuses, many women wore trousers and dressed like men. Some women, however, wore long skirts which made it difficult to ride the horses or mules along the narrow, washed-out, muddy trail.

As the number of travelers using the Panama route increased, various companies were formed to handle the transportation of freight across the Isthmus. One such company was Wells Fargo, famous freight company of the West.[27]

PANAMA CITY

After about a one-day ride, or two-day walk, and after being exposed to cholera and other diseases, the gold-seeker would arrive in Panama, which had a population of about ten to twelve thousand. Panama City, according to an English vice-consul there, was not a bad looking city in 1856; and the inner walled area was actually rather elegant. The *arrabal* or outer city was populated by colored peoples and animated by bustling daily activities and colorful sights and smells—some not so pleasant.[28] There were few hotels in Panama at first, but facilities continued to increase. Panama became more and more American in its ways as immigrants filled the city. A newspaper, founded by an American in 1859, advertised the American Hotel, the French Hotel and the Oregon Hotel, as well as bars and restaurants, which were owned primarily by Americans. In the spacious dining hall of the American Hotel, Protestant religious services were held each Sunday. Some social functions, as well, were enjoyed by both cultural groups on the Isthmus, the Panamanians and the Americans. Good relations existed between businessmen of both groups, and advertising in the paper was done in both languages.[29]

After the long trip across the Isthmus, at an average cost of $380, the travelers expected to leave immediately for California. However, in Panama they were usually faced with a delay, sometimes as long as two months. This meant spending additional money on food and lodging. Some travelers had bought through tickets for the trip to California before they had left New York, but many had to wait in Panama for their ship to arrive. Others arrived on the Isthmus with no tickets to California and had to depend on their luck for accommodations. Many of them were at the mercy of speculators who would buy up the tickets and then resell them at huge profits.[30]

These long delays in Panama City caused many problems. Riots and near-riots were not uncommon in the city during the long periods of waiting. Even after the railroad was temporarily completed in 1855, chaotic revolutionary activities in Bogotá regarding the final stages of General Melo's revolt and the death of Tomás Herrera had forced the garrison stationed in Panama to march to Cartagena. The governor of Panama, José María Urrutia Añino was spending much of this period with his family in Natá. His lack of responsibility in this regard and the absence of an effective police force resulted in the even greater insecurity of the town. For these reasons, the Railroad Company and navigation enterprises had to depend on the "Isthmian Guard" under the direction of Ran Runnels, for which even the Panamanians were grateful.[31] Nevertheless, ill-feeling, brought on by boredom, impatience and the hot climate, caused much trouble between emigrants and Panamanians. Other causes of trouble between the two groups were the landing tax of two dollars charged by the local government and the unhealthful environment in Panama. Malaria and epidemics of cholera, which threatened to wipe out the Isthmian population in 1849 and 1850, caused the death of many a Forty-Niner.

Cholera had been brought to the Isthmus on the *Falcon* and had spread voraciously over all the Isthmus. The coincidental presence of General José Domingo Espinar (see Chapter I), who was a military doctor, was a blessing, for he risked his life and sacrificed his pay in trying to combat this epidemic. The cholera was wiped out finally in August of 1850. So desperate were the travelers because of their lamentable situation in Panama that some would set out for California even in canoes.[32]

The Panama route, during the period between 1848 and 1869, saw the transit of some 375,000 persons. About one-fifth of the total number of emigrants to the gold fields between 1849 and 1859 went across Panama. From 1859 until 1869, nearly half the emigrants used the Isthmian way. Generals, naval officers, financiers and judges, gamblers and women of ill-repute—all types of persons bound for the new country—used the Panama route. The travelers via Panama were very significant in developing materially the region of the Pacific Coast, and Panama, with its narrow isthmus, once more proved to be the roadway for gold, for bustling activity and for commerce—the Crossroads of the World.[33]

Yet its potential, positive development and wealth remained at the mercy of external forces—mainly Colombia and the United States. Unfortunately, these two powers did not often stop to take into consideration in their treatment of Panama, the internal turmoil of the Isthmus caused by the sudden influx of men and bustling life and its needs, the use of its resources and of its peoples. The Isthmians continued to suspect that Colombia was using the Isthmus as a colonial source of wealth for the national government; these suspicions arose from the favoritism shown the United States on every issue (see Chapter II) and the fear of Colombia to take a stand in favor of Panama lest it should lose financial benefits it could reap by "selling" the Isthmians to the powerful commercial nation of the north. The sacrifices made by most Panamanians were not sufficiently recompensed; they were not the masters of their destiny, even though there was a sense of unity, a feeling of belonging apart from the rest of Colombia. It continued to appear that Isthmian sacrifices were for the benefit of two foreign nations—Colombia and the United States.

NOTES

1. Kemble, *The Panama Route*, 33; Steward Edward White, *The Forty-Niners: A Chronicle of the California Trail and El Dorado* (New Haven, 1918), 55.

2. Octavius Thorndike Howe, *Argonauts of '49: History and Adventures of the Emigrant Companies from Massachusetts, 1849-1850* (Cambridge, 1923), 901; Julius H. Pratt, "To California by Panama in '49," *The Century Illustrated Monthly Magazine*, XLI (1891), 901; White, *The Forty-Niners*, 63.

3. Kemble, *The Panama Route*, 33; White, *The Forty-Niners*, 96.

4. Mack, *The Land Divided*, 136.

5. Castillero R., *Historia de Panamá*, 96; John Haskell Kemble, "The Gold Rush by Panama, 1848-1851," *The Pacific Historical Review*, XVIII (1949), 45; Mack, *The Land Divided*, 136; William D. McCain, *The United States and the Republic of Panama* (Durham, 1937), 8-9.

6. John Haskell Kemble, "Pacific Mail Service Between Panama and San Francisco, 1849-1851," *The Pacific Historical Review*, II (1933), 407; Kemble, *The Panama Route*, 27; Mack, *The Land Divided*, 138; Minter, *The Chagres*, 198; White, *The Forty Niners*, 97.

7. Howe, *Argonauts of '49*, 17; Kemble, *The Panama Route*, 33; Mack, *The Land Divided*, 138-139. Meanwhile, the *California*'s two sister ships, the *Panama* and the *Oregon* had left New York. The *Panama* left New York on December 1, 1848, but was forced to return to port because of engine trouble. She again set sail, this time on February 17, 1849. The *Oregon* sailed on December 9, 1848, arriving in Panama on February 23, 1849.

8. Kemble, *The Panama Route*, 33-35; Mack, *The Land Divided*, 138-140; Minter, *The Chagres*, 202. Bonifacio Pereira Jiménez suggests that Minter's work authentically describes the Chagres of the Gold Rush. See his *Biografía del Río Chagres*, (Panama, 1964), 89.

9. "A Yankee Trader in the Gold Rush: Letters of Walter Gardner, 1851-1857," ed. John Walton Caughey, *Pacific Historical Review*, XVII (1948), 416; White, *The Forty-Niners*, 97.

10. "Across the Isthmus in 1850: The Journey of Daniel A. Horn," ed. James P. Jones and William Warren Rogers, *The Hispanic American Historical Review*, XLI (1961), 534-535.

11. George W. Groh, *Gold Fever* (New York, 1966), 36; Kemble, *The Panama Route*, 167.

12. Alba, *Cronología*, 176-180.

13. "Across the Isthmus in 1850: The Journey of Daniel A. Horn," 535; Bayard Taylor, *Eldorado or Adventures in the Path of Empire* (New York, 1856), 11. Actually, the natives probably dressed in appropriate style for the climate of Chagres which was considered to be the most unhealthful and uncomfortable on the Isthmus.

14. Minter, *The Chagres*, 202.

15. *Ibid.*, 237.

16. Kemble, *The Panama Route*, 171.
17. Kemble, "The Gold Rush by Panama," 47, 49; Minter, *The Chagres*, 236-237.
18. Minter, *The Chagres*, 238.
19. Groh, *Gold Fever*, 33, 34.
20. "Across the Isthmus in 1850: The Journey of Daniel A. Horn," 535-536; Minter, *The Chagres*, 239.
21. Minter, *The Chagres*, 239, 242, 243.
22. *Ibid.*, 237.
23. Pereira, *Historia de Panamá*, 265-266.
24. Minter, *The Chagres*, 243, 266; Russel, *Improvement of Communication*, 60.
25. "Across the Isthmus in 1840: The Journey of Daniel A. Horn," 536; Joseph Henry Jackson, *Gold Rush Album* (New York, 1959), 111; Kemble, *The Panama Route*, 169; Taylor, *Eldorado*, 12.
26. "Across the Isthmus in 1850: The Journey of Daniel A. Horn," 538; Kemble, "The Gold Rush by Panama," 51-52; Kemble, *The Panama Route*, 169-172; Minter, *The Chagres*, 223-229; Pratt, "To California by Panama in '49," 901; Taylor, *Eldorado*, 12-19.
27. Jackson, *Gold Rush Album*, 116-117; Kemble, *The Panama Route*, 171-172; Minter, *The Chagres*, 244; Taylor, *Eldorado*, 19-20.
28. Angel Rubio, *La ciudad de Panamá* (Panama, 1950), 55.
29. Eugene R. Huck and Edward H. Moseley, "The Forty-Niners in Panama: Canal Prelude," *Militarists. Merchants and Missionaries* (Univ. of Alabama, 1970), 59; Kemble, "The Gold Rush by Panama," 53. The first press to arrive in America's new western territory, which stands today on display in the office of the *Independent*, in Independence, Inyo County, California, passed through Panama. It was brought by Judson Ames of Baton Rouge, who arrived at Chagres in January of 1850. He formed the *Panama Herald* to keep other Americans who were delayed in Panama informed. He later sold his paper to the *Panama Star* and later the two names were united to form the Panama *Star & Herald* which today is Panama's leading newspaper (and also has a Spanish edition). See: Minter, *The Chagres*, 214.
30. Jackson, *Gold Rush Album*, 118-119; Kemble, "The Gold Rush by Panama," 54-57; Minter, *The Chagres*, 208; Taylor, *Eldorado*, 24.
31. See Chapter II.
32. Alba, *Cronología*, 178-179; Castillero R., *Historia de Panamá*, 96-97; Jackson, *Gold Rush Album*, 119; Kemble, "The Gold Rush by Panama," 53-55; Mack, *The Land Divided*, 146-148.
33. Kemble, *The Panama Route*, 206-207. One of Panama's mottos is: *Puente del Mundo, Corazón del Universo,* which means, Bridge of the World, Heart of the Universe.

CHAPTER V

Transition, Turbulence, and Turmoil: 1855-1898

From the completion of the railroad and the establishment of the Federal State of Panama in 1854 until independence in 1903, the Isthmus was plagued by international, national and internal problems. Rapid political change stemming from the clashes of Liberals and Conservatives in Colombia, the withdrawal of powers of local self-government by a centralist Colombia, violence associated with those changes and with racial and economic problems on the Isthmus, and inflammatory rhetoric, all intensified local grievances. One estimate summarized this turmoil as forty different administrations, some fifty riots and rebellions, five attempts to secede from Colombia, and at least thirteen interventions by the United States. Nothing seemed to bring internal peace, not political change, not foreign intervention, not even the optimism engendered by the French Canal project. But one certainty did emerge in the minds of Panama's leaders: they became more certain than ever that Panama's interests required the attainment of local self-government. In 1898 they believed that this might be possible within a Colombia ruled by the Liberal Party. By 1903 they had decided to seek independence in name as well as fact. The second half of the nineteenth century is thus the story of how Colombia drove Panama to seek an independence toward which her internal political and economic development had long pointed and in which international forces, especially the United States, had vested interests.[1]

ORGANIZATION OF THE FEDERAL STATE

Justo Arosemena handled the organization of the Federal State from July to September of 1855 with vigor, logic and dedication, inspiring new attitudes and the confidence that great things could be accomplished. He adapted laws which his experience in the National Government and abroad had shown were useful, and refused to let reactionary forces implant obsolete and even cruel laws (as for example, a bill to revive debtor's prison). Nevertheless, some of his serious suggestions, like the establishment of an income tax, were considered so radical that when they did get written into law they were hardly enforced.

Despite his great energy and the amount of work which Arosemena did in organizing the wheels of government, he only remained two-and-a-half months (July to September of 1855) as head of State. His resignation came about under a personal mood of deception and some bitterness. A critical issue which helped create Arosemena's feelings dealt with the fees which the state hoped to collect for itself and which were relentlessly attacked by foreign commercial enterprises, including the Railroad Company, and by some members of the Isthmian community. Arosemena felt that such laws were fair. In the past he had argued that a trans-isthmian route which would go straight through would not enrich or even stimulate greatly the economy of the Isthmians. Apparently he supported the tonnage fees as a means of insuring that Panama would profit from its position as an isthmian and commercial entity and get some good from having the railroad exist in its midst. However, pressure was brought to bear on Arosemena when opposing elements not only published criticisms in the *Star and Herald,* but also appealed to the Bogotá Government to annul the laws regarding tonnage. This the Bogotá Government did, although not until after Arosemena had resigned.

Arosemena had foreseen this response of the Bogotá Government, because he knew full well the great pressure exerted by the railroad interests. He had promoted a law to mitigate such conflicts of authority and to make it possible for the Isthmian government to retain some semblance of dignity when faced with similar dilemmas and conflicts. Arosemena's law was essentially a provision that the execution of any state law could be suspended by the governor in the event that conflict over it arose between the national and the state authorities. Thus, absolute showdowns could be more gracefully resolved than otherwise would have been possible.[2]

The leaders of Panama were already aware, then, at this early stage following the completion of the railroad, that their relationship with the United States was potentially dangerous, and that the advantages their geographical blessings promised were illusory and disappointing. Economic interventions, supported by strong military threats, were foreseen as frequent events by men like Justo Arosemena; the realization of such probabilities also made its bitterness felt among other Panamanians who, like Don Justo, had hoped for far greater benefits for their country.

Francisco de Fábrega, the vice-governor, replaced Justo Arosemena as governor. Fábrega named a conservative like himself, Bartolomé Calvo, to the post of Secretary of State, an important ministry at this time because it was during Fábrega's administration that the infamous Watermelon War took place. The riot (as it essentially was) was the culmination and the focus of many problems facing both North Americans and Panamanians during the epoch during and after the construction of the railroad. The incidents leading up to the riot and its *denouement* are particularly important in attempting to show to what depths communication and mutual respect between the two groups had degenerated within such few years. As typical (though on a larger scale) of action stemming from attitudes which had been developing on the Isthmus, the Watermelon War deserves to be examined closely. Furthermore, a detailed account is essential in any effort to familiarize the historian with the spirit of those times in Panama.

THE WATERMELON WAR

The events that began the afternoon of April 15, 1856 were consequences of attitudes and reactions which had been building up since the arrival of the Forty-Niners. As we have already seen in Chapter IV, a great number of these Americans were of undesirable character. Many of them were brash, rude, and topped their faults with an air of arrogance which was difficult for the natives to ignore. Such insults to the local culture as the Forty-Niners lighting their cigars with the candles in the churches were taken as evidence of the disdain which the Americans felt for everything that did not pertain to their own culture and beliefs. Since many people carried firearms and knives with which to protect themselves from abuse, it was inevitable that clashes would occur. One such clash was the racial-cultural riot which is known as the Watermelon War, which ended in the death of sixteen to eighteen persons and the wounding of several others, Americans and Panamanians.

The riot began near the railroad station or terminal building in Panama City near a district which had been built by American businessmen to cater primarily to the Americans who were stopping in Panama before going across or who had just crossed the Isthmus and were waiting for their ocean vessels. By the mid 1850s, American-run businesses had almost all disappeared from the inner city, and passengers usually went no farther than those hotels, saloons and brothels owned by Americans and other whites, which had sprung up along the beach between the railroad and the walled city. The railroad terminal itself was situated along the beach, three-eighths of a mile north of the walled city of Panama. The station building was a split-level structure of plain pine boards. The lower floor, seven feet off the ground, was primarily a freight room, with a baggage room and a railroad and ticket office at the eastern, or beach, end of the building. On the second floor on that end were three more offices and a telegraph room. There was no waiting room. The ticket office opened onto a wide platform on the north side of the building where passengers filed past to buy their tickets.[3]

On Tuesday, April 15, 1856 at about 5:30 p.m., a drunk California-bound traveler, Jack Oliver, and some companions left a saloon some two hundred yards from the railroad station. Oliver decided he wanted a piece of watermelon which was being sold by a mulatto fruit vendor—José Manuel Luna. Oliver took the piece of watermelon, ate part of it but refused to pay. Luna followed the drunk demanding his money. Oliver became insulting with a "Don't bother me. Kiss my arse."[4] Luna warned him that they were not in the United States—to pay and get it done with. Oliver drew his pistol, saying that that was his payment. Luna drew his knife. Friends of each tried to intervene. One of Oliver's companions offered to pay but was ignored. Probably things would have settled down if a light-colored Peruvian Negro, Miguel Abraham, had not snatched Oliver's pistol which went off but did not hurt anyone. Oliver and his friends gave chase, threatening to kill the Peruvian. Abraham was able to lose them, and the Americans brazenly continued to a saloon to celebrate and boast about the incident. News of the disturbance spread, and distorted the incident out of proportion. Suddenly, the bells of the Church of Santa Ana began to peal, followed by another round closer to the area involved.[5] Crowds began to surge from the city through the Ciénega (a crowded slum of shanties between Santa Ana and the railroad station, stretching beachward as far as the saloons and hotels). The mob was after Oliver. It entered the American business sector, breaking things, looting and demanding Oliver, but Oliver had already left. Those Americans in the sector who could sought refuge in the railroad station, where they found danger, not security.

About 950 persons, more than one-half of them women and children, had arrived earlier in the day from Colón to board the *John L. Stephens* which was anchored in the bay. Some had already boarded the *Taboga,* which was to take them to the *Stephens,* but since it was low tide the *Taboga* was temporarily stranded in the mud at the foot of the railroad wharf. By six o'clock in the evening, about 600 people had been processed and most of them had boarded the *Taboga.* However, there still were more than 300 to be processed. Another crowd in the yard

consisted mainly of passengers who had arrived from the West
Coast and were to take the train to Colón. As the riot continued
in the American business sector close by, the travelers inside the
station became almost desperate with fear, for they lacked an
adequate number of firearms and ammunition. Railroad officials
tried to reassure the crowds of passengers with reminders that
the power of the railroad was held in awe by the natives and that a
message for protection had been sent to the police chief. A group
decided to leave the station and go to one of the hotels to rescue
some stranded women and children from the terror of the natives. However, they were driven back and then fired upon from
within the compound. The danger of the situation became more
and more apparent to the passengers at the station and the superintendent of the railroad handed out the last few weapons left.[6]

Meanwhile, the United States consul, Colonel Thomas Ward,
who was actually not too popular with the American residents
of Panama because of his outspoken and blunt manner, sent his
secretary to fetch Governor Francisco Fábrega, who had by this
time arrived at La Ciénega to try to calm things down. Fábrega
found, however, that the riot had taken a new direction and was
aimed at destroying all whites, not only Americans. Being white
himself and representing socially the white native element of
the population, Fábrega was afraid that action to curb the riot
against the Americans might further drive the rioters against
white Panamanians.[7] Furthermore, Fábrega so resented the arrogance of the consul in sending for him, the *Governor*, that he
refused to meet with him until arrangements were made to meet
each other half-way. But Ward and the Governor missed each
other; the Governor got fired at instead in the very area where
they were supposed to meet. A bullet went through his hat.
Ward's secretary, who was with the Governor, was wounded.
The Governor then ordered the police to take the railroad station; mob and police both wanted to control the railroad terminal, and the Americans resisted, but the mob finally overran the
station, attacking men and women, looting and destroying.

Outside the immediate circle of the turmoil, Ward and some railroad officials[8] found the Governor and reminded him that the United States would no doubt send a warship, and who could answer for what might follow? Though the Governor felt he could not control the looting and destruction, he was able to prevent the blacks from shooting a cannon at the *Taboga*. Governor Fábrega reminded them that there were two Panamanian women aboard the vessel and that they would be killing their own people. By thus appealing to the reason of some of the more influential men among the Negro populace, he was able to avert further destruction and loss of life. Passengers were allowed to leave the station and board the *Taboga*. The police chief and railroad officials had their hands full trying to keep the natives from shooting and the police from bayonetting the passengers. The riot was over. About sixteen passengers had been killed, and some mutilated; about sixteen were injured. The natives lost one or two lives and had some fifteen injured.[9]

There was an official inquiry, headed by Amos Corwine, a former United States consul. The finding of this group was that the riot was the result of Abraham's "rashness." Corwine recommended that the United States take over and occupy Panama. This option, and this version of the situation, were popular in the United States.[10]

A few months after the Watermelon incident, Pablo Arosemena (nephew or cousin of Don Justo) published an analysis of the investigations held by the North Americans. Among other things, he discredited through logical arguments the accusations of a certain consul that the affair was premeditated. In doing so, Arosemena showed the many faults in the gathering of testimony (such as the language barrier between investigators and witnesses) and such careless assumptions on the part of some witnesses as that of stating that the church bell of La Ciénega (where there was not one church) might have been a signal to others. He also referred to the lack of cooperation of the American consul when the Panamanian public interpreter was sent by the Governor of

Panama at the request of the consul himself to copy the testimonies of the North Americans.[11]

In spite of these protests, the United States demanded compensation. After long negotiations and armed intervention, the North Americans received about $400,000 in gold.[12] This payment was made with great reluctance, for the Colombian Government felt that the United States had no legal claim to any payment whatsoever. The Colombian Government conceded that the police force was not present in sufficient proportion to humanly control the riot. Nevertheless, it did not agree with the claims of the United States that the Colombian Government should pay in this case any more than the United States had paid in common criminal cases of brutality perpetrated continually by American passengers of the lower class upon the Panamanians; that is to say, nothing. In the view of the Colombians this outrage was similar to those perpetrated on Panamanians except that it had reached notorious proportions. As to the claims that foreigners should have the rights of protection from the Government of the host country, the Colombian Ministry of Foreign Affairs was in complete accord. However, this principle was argued further, qualifying the rights as well as the obligations of foreigners everywhere to abide by the laws of the host country:[13]

> The foreigner cannot have nor expect greater protection for himself than that which is offered to the citizens: the foreigner also has the duty to obey the laws of the State where he resides; and if with his contempt of the authorities of the country, and with his continual acts of brutality against the natives he provokes disorder and revenge, he has no right to blame either the country or its Government, but should blame only himself.[14]

Several conclusions were reached concerning the causes of the worst racial riot of Panama up to that time, among them the following:

(1) Importation of Negro labor during the construction of the Panama Railroad had added a disorderly element to the population;

(2) Many immigrants, passengers, and some undoubtedly

desperate characters, were a disturbing factor, for many had strong convictions concerning the place the Negro should occupy in society, and their consequent air of superiority could only lead to confrontations between the two groups;

(3) Deep political suspicions had been engendered in the minds of officials and the people by the operations of the filibusters and William Walker in Nicaragua and by the annexation resulting from the Mexican War (1845-1848). The popularity in the United States press of the idea of taking over the Isthmus justified the fears of the Panamanians.[15]

Justo Arosemena, though not directly involved in this disaster, had strong feelings about it and explained the roots of the tragedy as follows:

> The United States excite their citizens to covet eagerly . . . and the result is that for some time, the men of the Yankee race who pass through the Isthmus or establish themselves upon it, put themselves out to cause difficulties of all kinds, in order to make impossible in the State all government emanating from the natives. Thus they prepare and justify, slowly, a movement to lead one day to the absorption of the Isthmus by the United States.[16]

Arosemena's opinion probably had been encouraged by the pressures he himself had had to resist when he was trying to organize the Federal State and was defeated by the power of the United States Government operating on behalf of the railroad.

More recent opinions tend to see in the Watermelon War the results of economic pressures felt by the masses after the end of the construction of the railroad, aggravated by the already common superior attitudes of Americans and long years of oppression of the colored peoples many of whom had only recently been freed from legal slavery.[17]

INTERNAL PROBLEMS AND THE FEDERAL STATE

The Isthmus was beset by other problems besides the race riots, but while enemies of the Federal State were blaming it for the fiscal troubles of the Isthmus (which were actually inherited from previous mismanagement and expenses), and while many criticized its policies as supportive of oligarchical groups[18] the wheels of government kept turning.

The first regular elections for Governor of the State and for *diputados* to the *asamblea* under the Constitution of 1855 were held early in 1856. Many candidates for Governor were proposed, among them Justo Arosemena, Bartolomé Calvo (Secretary of State under Fábrega), Manuel María Díaz, Rafael Núñez, Tomás Cipriano de Mosquera, Salvador Camacho Roldán and Pedro Alcántara Herrán. However, for many reasons, the first three remained candidates as long as Arosemena did. Arosemena had resigned from the governorship under such circumstances as to lead the public to believe that he no longer wanted to govern. His family was opposed to his candidacy. His father feared that if Justo won the election the prestigious postions which many members of the family held would be jeopardized.[19] Don Justo himself wrote the following with regard to this situation:

> I belong to an extensive family, many of whose members serve or will later serve in very important posts; and any government whose executive head is closely related to persons serving under him or who head other branches of government would without doubt deserve the description of oligarchical. Our conscience could be and would be actually clear, if we simply undertook to carry out our duties faithfully; but the people, jealous of their liberty whose value is priceless, would look with justified distrust upon such a state of affairs.[20]

The Conservative Bartolomé Calvo won the election, but the Liberal Party was able to capture a majority of the seats of the *asamblea*. Calvo was not a native of the Isthmus, but he had the support of even some Liberals like Pablo Arosemena and Gil Colunje whose prestige was already on the rise. He also had the support of Fábrega, under whom Calvo was Secretary of State. This led some commentators to the opinion that Fábrega was merely ruling through Calvo. Passionate but petty rivalries in the *asamblea* resulted in such spiteful actions by Calvo's opponents as boycotting the *asamblea* and not forming a quorum in order to prevent certification of the new governor-elect. Inflammatory newspapers and other pressures finally led Fábrega to arrest and deport two *diputados* considered to be the most vocal and ardent members of the Liberal Party, José María Goytía and Pedro Goytía. Fábrega was hard-pressed to justify or explain this arbitrary action (*diputados* enjoyed immunity) but it did restore some calm to the state congressional activities, and it prevented a rebellion called for by members of the Liberal Party.[21]

Perhaps more conducive to the stifling of the rebellion were the two warships, the *Independence* and the *St. Mary's*, which the United States sent to the area. Commodore William Mervine landed about 160 men and occupied the railroad station on September 19, 1856, because of the danger of civil war posed by the political arguments between Liberals and Conservatives in the *asamblea*. The United States was ill-disposed to allow the recurrence of Watermelon War deaths because of inadequate forces.[22] In order to offset the effects of negative propaganda, Calvo secured favorable conditions for foreigners and was successful in demonstrating the ability of the Isthmian government to guarantee security of the transit area. He was able to restore the treasury (which was and had been constantly under the strain of foreign debt) in two years, through wise and well-administered fiscal policies. A sales tax was levied, certain properties or holdings of the government were sold, more care was exercised in the effectiveness of the tax collecting system, certain taxes were moderately raised and others were more fairly and evenly distributed; and finally all government employees, from the governor to the last public employee, suffered salary decreases.

When Calvo resigned in 1858 to accept the post of *Procurador General de la Nación,* the second in command, Don Ramón Gamboa took over until new elections, which were won by José de Obaldía. Some Liberals resented Obaldía; many held that his lack of vigorous campaigning in the national elections campaign of 1854, during which he had run as a vice-presidential candidate, had allowed the victory to fall into the hands of the Conservatives. In spite of that resentment, in the 1858 gubernatorial

elections on the Isthmus, he was again launched as a Liberal candidate. This time he won, and the *asamblea* unanimously elected
Doctor Rafael Núñez as vice-governor.[23]

TENSION IN THE CENTRAL GOVERNMENT
AFFECTS PANAMA

Because the Liberals in Colombia were again split, the elections of 1857 brought a Conservative triumph in congress and in
the presidency, to which Doctor Mariano Ospina Rodríguez was
elected. The statehood of Panama of 1855 was followed by similar legal arrangements to form seven other states (Antioquia,
Santander, Bolívar, Boyacá, Cundinamarca, Cauca and Magdalena) in 1858; statehood was safe from abolishment in spite of
the Conservative victory, for it was no longer the Liberals who
were ardently advocating the formation of these states. The Conservatives were upholding Federalism, not from principle but for
convenience, in the hope that they could gain local autonomy
in certain states where they could consider their beliefs safe from
outside interference. The Liberals, on the other hand, felt that
only through some stronger voice in the federal government
could they hope to regain the power they had lost in so many
states. Consequently, they chose not to intensify support of the
sovereignty of the states, the majority of which were in the
hands of the Conservatives.[24]

In 1859 trouble again flared in Colombia. The Conservatives,
with a majority in congress, passed several laws. One reducing
the size of the standing army infuriated not only the army but
also the moderate Liberals, groups which had been supporting
each other for years. (Possibly the desire on the part of the Liberals to gain back control of the government made them prefer
to have at least the allegiance of available Federal forces in the
event of insurrections from Conservative states.) Another law
increased the government's control of the states' militias. The

law that most enraged the Liberals gave the government great powers of intervention in state elections. Since Conservatives were in power in the federal government, such intervention would tend to be in favor of the Conservatives. One important and very irritating law dealt with the special post of *Intendente* created to defend the territory of Panama and to assure the safety of foreigners and their interests in accord with international agreements. The law later was extended to other states, in spite of protests from the Isthmus that the *Intendente* was abusing his extensive powers. The wide range of powers which the new *Intendentes* had created conflicts with the powers of the various governments of Cauca, Magdalena and Santander and led to the civil war which followed. In Magdalena, furthermore, where elections had been won by extreme Liberals (Radicals), Conservatives revolted but were crushed. However, the President of the Republic (Ospina) gave important positions within the federal government to the leaders of this revolt, and they in turn accused the Liberals of being anarchists, immoral and tyrants. The Liberals in Magdalena were indignant. Realizing the danger they faced, they made an alliance with the state of Santander in order to defend their sovereignty and political existence. The Conservatives, however, actually had some reason to criticize the state of Santander, for such extreme laws were promulgated there that even Liberals were not pleased with some of them.[25]

The atmosphere of tension created by all these laws and the subsequent distrust and disagreements between the two parties led to Conservative as well as Liberal revolts throughout Colombia. General Mosquera was made "Supreme Director of the War" by the Liberals in 1860. Although a Liberal, the Governor of Panama, José de Obaldía, refused to implicate Panama in the war; and his successor, Santiago de la Guardia, a Conservative chosen through popular election for the term 1860 to 1862, also maintained the neutrality of the Isthmus. These leaders felt that it behooved Panama to verbally support the legitimate forces of Colombia whenever such forces respected its statehood and its sovereignty over certain jurisdictions. Since the Conservatives were losing, however, the Isthmians under the leadership of de la Guardia, declared themselves separate from the Colombian government the 31st of March, 1861. Once the war was practically won by the Liberals (1861) and peaceful restoration seemed in order, Colombia proposed that Panama join what the new government chose to call the United States of Nueva Granada. Panama signed the *Convenio de Colón* of September 6, 1861 in which Colombia agreed to continue to support its statehood, and in which Panama agreed to again be part of Colombia.[26] However, this new annexation was not completely formalized until after a confrontation between the new federal government and the legitimate state government of Santiago de la Guardia.

As has been noted, Obaldía and then de la Guardia had prevailed on the Isthmians to refuse aid to the non-legitimate forces of Mosquera. This state of neutrality and then of independence on the Isthmus while the Federation was in the midst of war and chaos had serious repercussions. When Mosquera won, he was not at all eager to please the Panamanians.

Mosquera suspected that Panamanians wanted independence. Though as a whole his suspicions were unfounded, he felt that de la Guardia might have been moving in that direction.[27] Thus, he did not heed the *Convenio de Colón*. He felt he was strong enough to get the type of agreement he wanted without consideration for the wishes of the Panamanians.[28] To that end he sent Colonel Peregrino Santacoloma with troops to Panama in June of 1862. In two letters dated the 9th and the 23rd of June, 1862 on behalf of Governor de la Guardia, Pablo Arosemena (who during his career was representative and senator in the Federal Congress, *diputado* in the State *asamblea* and President of the State of Panama) voiced the suspicions which this military intervention had aroused in Government circles in Panama. The fact that no previous notice, formal or informal, had been given to Panamanian officials by Mosquera's government concerning the landing of troops on the Isthmus, had fanned these suspicions.

Santacoloma "explained" the arrival of the troops to Pablo Aro-semena, but the reasons given seemed very weak to the Panama-nians who felt that their sovereignty was at stake.[29]

In the meantime, Justo Arosemena had been sent to Bogotá to try to enforce the *Convenio de Colón*. He failed to convince Mosquera or to counterbalance Mosquera's suspicions regarding desires for total independence on the Isthmus. When de la Guardia was killed in Panama on July 25, 1862 fighting against the forces of Mosquera under Santacoloma in defense of state sovereignty, Arosemena was blamed for de la Guardia's death.[30]

THE CONVENTION OF RIO NEGRO AND ITS REPERCUSSIONS

The vengeful mood of the Liberal national government's ac-tivities in 1861 only helped to widen the gap between Liberals and Conservatives on the Isthmus. Delegates for the Constitu-tional Convention at Río Negro were elected without the partici-pation of Conservatives at all. The Convention met in February of 1863 and by the 8th of May proclaimed the new Constitution for Colombia.

Although the aims of the Liberals in general stemmed from the highest motives and desires, the Constitution's authors did not clearly foresee some weaknesses which were later to cause many conflicts. The description by Justo Arosemena of the Con-stitution five years after it had been proclaimed, shows that this man, who had actively participated in the formation of the document, had by then realized why it was failing in carrying out the justice which the delegates felt they had made possible in 1863:

> The section regarding civil rights was copious and scrupulous, but it omitted the means to realize these rights, and thus, al-though it decreed many rights, it gave, actually, no guarantees. When it conferred sectional rights (state rights) it actually au-

thorized perpetual sedition and the means by which the states
could constantly menace each other, and one or all of them
could menace the general Government. By organizing the individual national powers, as if they were simply guests in the constitutional mansion, it took away their essence and their real
strengths and made them useless to the union and almost in-
compatible amongst themselves. Finally, it planted without a
plan, doctrines as brilliant for their novelty as they were dangerous for their reach, especially because of the strange interpretations they have received.

This is the Constitution of 1863, whose minor defect is perhaps that it was sanctioned by one party without the partici-
pation of representatives from the opposing party, and even if
it could be bettered by complementary laws and explanations,
it would always have against it the ill-will of its adversaries
whose defeat gave it birth.[31]

The earlier antipathy of Mosquera toward the Panamanians,
which had led to the death of de la Guardia and to a sense of loss
on the Isthmus, accentuated the criticism Mosquera received because of his arbitrary interpretations of the Constitution of 1863
which he had sponsored. The writings of Pablo Arosemena clearly
show the resentment which even Liberals in Panama felt against
Mosquera. Though Mosquera was limited by the Constitution as
to interference in state activities of Panama, he circumvented
many laws to keep greater control. Men like Santacoloma, who
had his moral support, abused the rights and the treasury of Panama, events which led to Isthmian uprisings and *coups d'état* in
the years following the adoption of the new Constitution of
1863.[32]

For the next twenty-five years, similar political actions, attempts by governors and presidents of the state (the title of the
governor had changed) to dissolve the *asamblea,* revolutionary
activities, *coups d'état* and conspiracies characterized politics
on the Isthmus. The state of constant turmoil of the Isthmus aggravated the poverty of the country by increasing excessively
the costs of the government. This in turn forced taxation of
business enterprises on the Isthmus. During the administration
of Gil Colunje (1865-1866), for example, the treasury was so

depleted that many public schools had to be closed for a while; only enough money was left to barely maintain civil law and order for the safety of the citizens.[33]

One of the most serious "revolutions" occurred during the state administration of the Liberal Fernando Ponce. General Buenaventura Correoso, who had put him in power with military force on July 5, 1868, again had to defend this administration because of a very serious uprising spearheaded by Chiricanos, Conservatives of Chiriquí. They intended to launch Amador Guerrero as their candidate in the next elections, but at this point they proclaimed Santiago Agnew as provisional President of the State, and Juan N. Venero as Secretary of State. The movement spread into Veraguas where the main Conservative strength lay. General Correoso defeated the rebels, who were under the command of Aristides Obaldía, on October 21, and attacked the Conservatives in Hatillo, near Santiago, on November 12. Here the government troops defeated the Conservatives and took Amador Guerrero prisoner.

This revolution, thus far the most bloody among the Isthmians, left a deep schism between the political parties.[34] Subsequently, hardly one President of the State was elected, or took over, before a challenge was heard from the other side. In addition, large scale revolutions in Colombia like the one in 1876 affected Panamanians, many of whom fought in them. (Small interferences from Colombia also had their effects.[35]) At Las Chancas, in Colombia, Panamanian volunteers headed by General Correoso were involved; victory there for the Liberal forces allowed Correoso to be President of the State of Panama, a typical reward for military prowess at this time, and an example of the arbitrary powers which the Bogotá government claimed for itself.

So violent was the situation on the Isthmus that not even the transactions which took place in 1878 regarding the French Canal project were vigorous enough to wipe out the plague of insurrection and revolt which had invaded the Isthmus and the rest of Colombia.[36] The political chaos in Panama reached the point where there were two Presidents of the State in 1884, each supported by his own party group—Dámaso Cervera and General Benjamín Ruiz. The latter was eventually defeated and Cervera was placed in the presidency by National troops. In July of 1884 elections were held for President of the State. Rafael Núñez, now President of Colombia, was blamed for Justo Arosemena's loss of the election. Juan Manuel Lambert, candidate of the Independents (moderate Liberals), won. But Lambert was not "approved" by Núñez and instead José María Vives León was named by the *asamblea* to head the government until elections could be held for the Constitutional Convention of 1886.[37]

THE LIBERAL REVOLUTION OF 1885

In 1875 there had developed another split in the party ranks of the Liberals. The moderate Liberals formed a party of their own known as the Independent Party.[38] These Independents developed a program which called for amendments to the Constitution of 1863 (Río Negro) in order to correct some of the evils which they felt were extant in it.

Fortunately for the Independents' program, Rafael Núñez was finally elected President in 1883. The Núñez administration has been named "Regeneration." Núñez attempted to unite the Liberals and the Conservatives. His policy was one of moderation and tolerance. To avoid an open war with the Radicals, he appointed Eusorgio Salgar and Santos Acosta, both Radicals and personal friends, to his cabinet. To obtain the support of the Conservatives, he likewise appointed members of that party to his government. Núñez wanted to amend the Constitution of 1863 in order to bring peace and prosperity to Colombia, perhaps by centralizing powers in such a way that they could no longer be arbitary, and by making more clear and specific some of the principles which the 1863 constitution merely outlined or generalized and which even many Liberals wanted amended. (A provision which contrasts the two constitutions concerns the Church in Colombia. One of the specific provisions of the new charter sponsored by Núñez recognized the Apostolic Roman

Catholic religion as that of the nation; public powers were to protect it and cause it to be respected as an essential element of social order, but the Church was not to be official and was to preserve its independence.) However, Núñez's immediate plans were not known.[39]

Rafael Núñez had taken over the presidency of the republic at a very delicate moment in the history of Colombia. The financial state of the union was totally out of control; hatred between the main parties had reached unbelievable depths; and the Radicals thought only of ways to make unbearable the government which Núñez was heading. Since they had not been able to prevent his rise to power, they hoped to dislodge him with such tactics. Failing all other means, the Radicals declared war in 1884. This civil war first broke out in the state of Santander. In order to meet the emergency, Núñez united both the Independents and the Conservatives into the National Party. This action led to more violence, which Núñez finally put down by declaring a state of siege and assuming special powers. The fighting ended on August 26, 1885.[40]

PEDRO PRESTAN AND THE BURNING OF COLÓN

On the Isthmus, the most serious consequences of the Liberal revolts of 1884-1885 were felt in the city of Colón in March of 1885. The city had been drained of protective guards when the national troops under General Carlos A. Gónima left on March 16 to help squelch a Liberal revolt in Panama City led by General Rafael Aizpuru. The following day, Pedro Prestán, a mulatto Liberal, announced a revolt in Colón. He was able to gather about 200 poorly-armed individuals; the majority being foreign men of dubious reputations, they failed to inspire confidence among the populace.

Prestán had ordered arms from the United States. They arrived on March 30. The agent of the steamship company (John M. Dow), following the orders of Gónima, refused to allow Prestán to have them. Prestán, an active and defiant Liberal, did not passively tolerate this decision of the agent; he kidnapped him, another employee of the company, the United States consul and two officers of the United States warship *Galena*. He informed the commander of the ship that he would not free the prisoners until the arms were delivered, and that he would fire upon any ship that attempted to land troops. For any aggression from the navy against the city, he would make reprisals on American residents. The consul ordered the arms turned over to gain liberty for himself and the other hostages. But the captain of the *Galena* took possession of the vessels with the arms in the name of the Government of the United States. Prestán then had the hostages transferred to Monkey Hill where the revolutionary forces had their advance front.

In the meantime, Gónima was able to turn his attention to the activities of Prestán and dispatched 160 men by train as far as Mindí, from where they marched to the rebel camp. The rebels withdrew into the city of Colón and fought against the government troops that attacked the city. They managed to withstand the attack for about eight hours. By four o'clock in the afternoon of March 31, 1885 the rebels were almost defeated. Suddenly, a fire broke out and spread wildly throughout the city, completely destroying Colón. Close to 10,000 people were left homeless and without provisions. The cost of the fire was over six million dollars and, to make matters worse, the Insurance Company refused to pay. Sometime later, on May 6, the Haitian Antonio Pautrizelle and the Jamaican George Davis (Coco-bolo), were tried by the War Council (Panamanian Conservatives) for setting fire to Colón. They were convicted and hanged.

Meanwhile, Prestán had managed to escape to the state of Bolívar and attempted to join the revolutionary army near Cartagena. However, the leaders of this movement refused to permit Prestán to join their group until he could prove his innocence with regard to the fire in Colón which had caused a deep feeling of repulsion and horror everywhere. Prestán remained a sort of prisoner in the camp of General Ricardo Gaitán Obeso until the latter was defeated while trying to capture Cartagena. Prestán, now alone, fell into the hands of Government troops in Santa

Marta and was taken to Colón where he was court-martialled for instigating the fire of Colón. The validity of the trial remains clouded with uncertainty and doubt, for among the witnesses and the jury there were personal enemies of Prestán. The council condemned him to be hanged on August 18, 1885. Up to the last minute, Prestán protested his innocence, but also declared that he forgave his enemies.[41]

In the meantime, while government troops were being deployed against Prestán, the Liberal Rafael Aizpuru took possession of arms destined for Central America at the railroad station. He attacked the headquarters of the military in Panama and succeeded in gaining control of the city. However, his attempts to establish any kind of government were futile. On April 8 at the request of the Colombian minister in Washington, United States Naval forces disembarked 1000 men in Colón. The purpose was to protect lives and prevent the atrocities of fighting within the city which could result, as it had at Colón, in great tragedy. Aizpuru was imprisoned and freed only after he promised not to fight within the immediate radius of the city. With this, the foreign troops returned to their headquarters at the railroad station.

The Liberals were all but crushed by this time. Mishaps and insufficient strength, in addition to the superior United States forces and the power of persuasion which they exerted, had reduced the troops to less than one half, through desertions and loss of lives. Aizpuru surrendered unconditionally to Colonel Rafael Reyes who landed April 28 with more than 850 men with instructions to sustain Colonel Miguel Montoya as Civil and Military Chief of the State while the national reconstruction of the Government of the entire nation began.[42]

THE CONSTITUTION OF 1886

Núñez's overall victory in Colombia cemented his power as head of the National Party and of the government. He knew the time was ripe for writing a new constitution. Thus, in Septem-

ber of 1885 he called for a constitutional assembly to meet in
Bogotá on November 11 to draw up a constitution for what was
to be called the Republic of Colombia. The eight states each sent
two delegates to the assembly, and Núñez advised these sixteen
Conservatives and Independents that they should draw up a constitution that did not have the evils of previous documents which
had caused political and economic chaos.[43] Unfortunately, the
1886 Constitution, like that of 1863, was written on the heel
of bitter contentions, and resentment was to be expected from
the losing party. In spite of that, however, the 1886 Constitution, though amended almost beyond recognition, is still the
Constitution of Colombia.[44]

The Constitution of 1886 formed a centralized republic,
with the states being reduced to departments. However, since
Colombians resented having a totally unitary form of government, provisions were made in the Constitution to give the
departments some local option. The peculiar interests and geographic position of Panama required special provisions for Panama which made it more dependent than other departments on
the executive branch of the Republic, almost as if it were a national territory. The head of each department was to be a governor, appointed and removed by the president. All anti-Catholic
measures found in the Constitution of 1863 were annulled. The
new Constitution recognized the Catholic religion as that of the
nation, and all public officials were to protect it and "cause it
to be respected as an essential element of social order."[45] However, the Catholic Church was not to be the established church
and no one was forced to support or contribute to it. Individuals
were allowed freedom of choice. The government, on the other
hand, was to protect the Church, its property, services and clergy
from indignities. As further protection for the Church, the Constitution provided that it should control public education and
that it should run its own internal affairs. The Constitution of
1886 also abolished unlimited freedom of the press, although a
"free" press was permitted. It further provided that political
prisoners would henceforth neither be under international law
nor have the right to possess arms; it also re-established the

death penalty for political crimes. In fact, this constitution abolished all Liberal and Radical provisions found in the Constitution of 1863.[46]

THE ISTHMUS BEFORE THE REVOLUTION OF 1895

Immediately after the enforcement of the new Constitution of 1886, the Isthmus achieved some stability. Two governors had long terms: General Juan V. Aycardi lasted five and one-half years until August of 1893, and Ricardo Arango was governor from 1893 to 1898. During the term of Aycardi, because of the enthusiasm of a few natives like his Secretary General, Santiago McKay, many advances were begun in Panama. Telegraph service between the capital and some interior towns was inaugurated. Electric lights were installed in Panama and Colón. Various public buildings were constructed.[47] Such improvements probably were the result of the new economic activities revolving about the French Canal,[48] even though work on the canal was suspended temporarily in 1889 by the Canal Company. The cessation of work on the canal soon produced grievous results in the economy of the Isthmus, which reached its greatest economic decline in 1893.[49]

A better governor for the Panamanians was the next one, Don Ricardo Arango. He was a native of Panama and tried to place more Panamanians in positions of power. The economic problems which he inherited were combatted with vigor. He was very progressive in trying to encourage agriculture and industry. He succeeded in raising educational levels by placing efficient and dedicated men in that branch of public affairs.[50]

Fortunately for the alleviation of the depression in which the Isthmus was submerged, a new Canal Company was organized with enough capital to continue the work on the canal for a few more years.[51] Perhaps this new, though relative, prosperity was the reason for the lack of Isthmian participation in the Liberal Revolution of 1895.

THE REVOLUTION OF 1895

The revolt of 1895 had been in the making for a long time. When Núñez retired temporarily from government in 1888, before his term was concluded, Carlos Holguín had succeeded him as President. During his term of office there developed a split in the Conservative Party which was aggravated during the election of 1892. At that time, Núñez was again a candidate for President and won the elections. The Liberals, in opposition to Núñez and taking advantage of the Conservative split, once again began to cause trouble. In order to remedy the Conservative split and the attacks by the Liberals, Miguel Antonio Caro, the Vice-President who was actually running affairs while Núñez remained most of the time on his farm, initiated strong press censorship and imprisonment and the banishment of important opposition leaders.

Núñez himself had previously ruled with a strong hand and had increased the strength of the Church. He had been with the Liberals at first and then switched to the Conservative side to become an ultra-Conservative.[52] Financial scandals and inflation characterized his government. Taxation had more than doubled; duties were made oppressive; and the foreign debt had not been paid. Elections were controlled by the soldiers who guaranteed the success of the Conservatives. Liberals charged that the government, through misrule, was leading the country backwards.[53] A great share of the blame was placed by Liberals on the Constitution of 1886. Many of the objections which the radical Liberals had to that Constitution were voiced by Justo Arosemena who wrote the following interpretation of it:

> It rigorously centralizes the government of the Republic, suppressing the federal states with the same rights it might have to subjugate the entire nation to the position of a colony of Germany or Russia, the states having had no representation, and not having renounced their autonomy, if such autonomy can be renounced. It synthesizes its character in the Executive Power, given to a President called *the Government,* for a period of six years and with his having hardly any responsibility. It places completely under his power those governors or chiefs of the new sections or dissolved states, renovating thus the tyr-

anny of the old regime of Colombia. It gives him powers of all kinds in case of war, either external or internal, turmoils which are so easy to invent or to promote on purpose. With the approval of Congress, it gives him certain extraordinary powers even in times of peace, for reasons of public convenience. He has the right to appoint justices of the supreme court and of the superior courts, who for the first time in the constitutional history of the Republic, receive their appointments for life. Those in the employment of the Executive are permitted to run for Congress, which together with the power of the veto, more efficient now than before, give the Executive overwhelming influence on legislative activity. It reestablishes, finally, the partnership of Church and State, and gives again (Article 41) religious education to the youth.

Certainly, it did not fail to declare and define guarantees, going back somewhat upon the road taken toward individual autonomy, as for example when it reestablishes capital punishment which maintains its essence of barbarism and its resulting crimes, or when it subjects the press once again to the whims of incompetent authorities or judges, thus drowning the only sure voice of opinion. . . . But it would be enough to mention only the censorship imposed upon the newspapers that do not praise the Government, and the deportation, without trial, of important citizens who are dissident, to qualify as mere mockery the so-called *Regeneration* of Colombia.[54]

Such suspicions and resentments toward the new Constitution were also felt by other Liberals who demonstrated their great and violent disapproval of it first in 1895 and finally in 1899. On the Isthmus the revolt of 1895 was hardly felt for it merely involved a Liberal attack on the police and military headquarters of Bocas del Toro, the 8th of March, 1895. Though the police surrendered without resistance, the fifty soldiers under the command of Captain Alejandro Ortiz finally defeated the attackers. The chiefs of the Liberals died along with five of their companions. The Government lost nine men and had several wounded.[55] A similar outcome occurred in other provinces where the Liberals revolted.

The causes of the Revolution of 1895 were in no way mitigated by the elections of 1898. Manuel A. Sanclemente was elected President with José M. Marroquín as Vice-President.

The elderly Sanclemente, however, was forced to leave Bogotá for reasons of health, and Marroquín took over the reins of government. Though Marroquín was a tolerant and conciliatory man and initiated several progressive laws, when Sanclemente returned to Bogotá to take over his government he did not approve of the reforms that his Vice-President had undertaken, and he made it clear that he would change the policies that had been begun by Marroquín. Sanclemente's poor health and the financial troubles in which the government found itself led the Liberals to prepare a revolution. Thus, the cruelest and longest struggle that Colombia had known since Independence began in the department of Santander in 1899.[56] Though the revolution of 1895 had not affected the Isthmus very seriously in terms of bloodshed and ruin, the basic currents which had provoked the uprising elsewhere were still vital elements influencing what was to come to the Isthmus. Sensing that rumors of an invasion of Panama by revolting Liberals might become a reality, a military Governor, General J.M. Campo Serrano, was named by the Central Government in January of 1900 to replace Doctor Facundo Mutis Durán who had been named by Marroquín in October of 1899.[57]

PRELUDE TO THE THOUSAND DAYS' WAR

As already mentioned, and supported by the opinions of Justo Arosemena, conditions leading to the revolt of the Liberals in 1899 were many indeed. Until 1880 gold and silver had been the medium of exchange. The government withdrew this supply and replaced it with almost worthless paper money. Commerce and industry suffered because of this depreciated money. Colombia's treasury was empty.[58]

In addition, prior to 1899 Liberals had been imprisoned for opposing the Conservative government. At Panopticon, the state prison in Bogotá, some three thousand political prisoners were

being held. Here and in other prisons throughout Colombia tor-
ture was freely used. Government troops almost daily committed
atrocities against the Liberals. According to one eye-witness, he
saw "women sawn in halves by rawhide ropes because they refused to tell where their revolutionist husbands were hidden. I
have seen children tortured and flogged to death, and wounded
men killed mercilessly on the field of battle." [59]

Added to these abuses, the Liberal press had been confis-
cated.[60] But perhaps the condition that contributed most to
the Liberal revolution was the gain and abuse of power by the
Church. Primary education and the establishment of a public
school system adopted by the Liberals had been abolished, and
the few remaining schools were under the control of the Church.
The Church not only became involved in education, but by sid-
ing with the Conservatives, it also became involved in government. At election time the polls were usually guarded by "soldiers with fixed bayonets, and other bands of soldiers paraded
the town, terrorizing the people. Several priests watched over
the booths, too, and whenever a Liberal came up to register his
vote, they ordered the soldiers to drive him away, which was
done at the point of the bayonet."[61]

The causes of the Liberal revolt in Colombia were felt on
the Isthmus of Panama. Besides the national economic problems,
the Isthmus of Panama, which had been a free zone, was now
burdened by taxes that were increased along with duties.[62]

The past decades had repeatedly witnessed similar scenes
which had led the Isthmus to experience numerous riots or rebellions. A sense of mistrust pervaded the relations of the Panamanians and the Colombians, whom many Isthmians felt treated
Panama as only a colony instead of as an integral part of the Colombian nation. These economic and political sufferings added
intensity to the various political opinions brought on by the im-
pending revolution. Understood thusly, it is not surprising that
one of the strongest and most bitter struggles during the Thousand Days' War took place in Panama.

NOTES

1. Castillero, *Historia de Panamá*, 76-130; Parks, *Colombia and the United States*, 219.
2. Pablo Arosemena, *Escritos*, ed. Nicolás Victoria J. (Panama, 1930), I, 264; Chong, *Historia de Panamá*, 174; Moscote and Arce, *Justo Arosemena*, 116-117, 250-255.
3. John C. Kennedy, "Incident on the Isthmus," *American Heritage*, XIX, No. 4 (June, 1968), 66.
4. *Ibid.*, 67.
5. Apparently someone had heard "Fire!" and even though Mass was being celebrated, the church bells of Santa Ana (not too near the Ciénega) rang as was the custom. See: Clifford A. Hauberg, "Economic and Social Developments in Panama, 1849-1880" (Ph.D. dissertation, University of Minnesota, 1950), 207; Parks, *Colombia and the United States*, 219.
6. Kennedy, "Incident on the Isthmus," 66, 67, 68, 69; Sosa and Arce, *Compendio*, 240-241. Actually, the only weapons left were a double-barreled shotgun, a pair of pistols, a sabre, and a rusty fourteen-year-old Flintlock musket.
7. Kennedy, "Incident on the Isthmus," 69; Sosa and Arce, *Compendio*, 241. The mob ran down the streets crying: "Mueran los blancos!" Hubert H. Bancroft, *History of Central America*, Vol. 3 (San Francisco, 1887), 520.
8. Kennedy, "Incident on the Isthmus," 70; Sosa and Arce, *Compendio*, 241-242. The officials were Captain Allan McLane, the Pacific Mail agent; Alexander Center, Superintendent; and William Nelson, railroad employee. The Police Chief was colored.
9. Bancroft, *History of Central America*, 521; Kennedy, "Incident on the Isthmus," 72; Sosa and Arce, *Compendio*, 242.
10. Corwine relied on the testimony of four employees of the railroad who had been near the scene of the actions which started the riot. They said the incident concerning the watermelon occurred at 6:30; that Luna spoke English and was using bad language, cursing; that Luna followed Oliver with a knife; that Oliver then drew his pistol, but put it back at the request of passengers near by; at that moment a light-colored Negro grabbed it, fired it, missed Oliver but hit Dennis Shannon (one of the four witnesses); that no shots were fired by the passengers at the natives but that Luna and Abraham left for the Ciénega and returned with three other natives armed with machetes and threatening the Americans. Then the mob that had welled attacked the hotels and bars looking for Oliver. See: Hauberg, "Economic and Social Developments in Panama, 1849-1880," 204-205.

11. Pablo Arosemena, *Escritos,* Vol. I, 159-210.
12. Correa, *Apuntes de Historia Patria,* 138; Sosa and Arce, *Compendio,* 242. In Kennedy, "Incident on the Isthmus," 72, the sum is said to be $160,000. Alba, *Cronología,* 184, says the sum paid was 584,603 *pesos oro.*
13. Arosemena, *op. cit.,* 219-223; Alba, *Cronología,* 184, feels that the United States claims were unfair considering the culpability of Jack Oliver and other Americans through the years.
14. Arosemena, *op. cit.,* 222.
15. Alba, *Cronología,* 185; Hauberg, "Economic and Social Developments in Panama, 1849-1880," 202; Rippy, *The Capitalists and Colombia* (New York, 1931), 45. On the matter of fear of war between Colombia and the United States over Panama, see: Arosemena, *op cit.,* 230-236.
16. Quoted in Chong, *Historia de Panamá,* 175.
17. See: Kennedy, "Incident on the Isthmus," 66; Alba, *Cronología,* 184; Chong, *Historia de Panamá,* 175.
    Slaves were freed in 1852. Justo Arosemena had been a chief promulgator of that law. See: Pereira, *Historia de Panamá,* 274.
    Perhaps if Justo Arosemena had still been governor, his public reputation for racial compassion might have enabled him to mitigate the riot by influencing the rioters. By that time, however, he had left the country for the United States where his children studied. (He eventually remarried a North American lady after being a widower.)
18. According to the biographers of Justo Arosemena, his father Mariano did take advantage of his son's prestigious positions to try and enhance his own personal situation. It was difficult for people to make distinctions between close members of a well-known family group. That is why Don Justo was also included in criticisms such as this situation incited. See: Moscote and Arce, *Justo Arosemena,* 258-260.
    It should be noted that Don Mariano had previously considered that the oligarchy would take advantage of power in a federal system, but had considered that the oligarchy was composed of families like the Fábregas and not his own. See: Miró, *Mariano Arosemena,* 21. However, for whatever reasons (probably due in part to scarcity of competently trained administrators) Fábregas and especially Arosemenas held many important posts in the government.
19. Alba, *Cronología,* 181; Moscote and Arce, *Justo Arosemena,* 264-267; Sosa and Arce, *Compendio,* 242-244.
20. Moscote and Arce, *Justo Arosemena,* 266.
21. *Ibid.,* 267; Sosa and Arce, *Compendio,* 267.
22. Parks, *Colombia and the United States,* 224.
23. Alba, *Cronología,* 185-186; Sosa and Arce, *Compendio,* 245-247.

24. Gibson, *The Constitutions of Colombia*, 217-221, 247-249; Henao and Arrubla, *History of Colombia*, 467-472; Moscote and Arce, *Justo Arosemena*, 276-277.
25. Gibson, *The Constitutions of Colombia*, 247-249; Henao and Arrubla, *History of Colombia*, 467-472; Moscote and Arce, *Justo Arosemena*, 281-288; Sosa and Arce, *Compendio*, 247. Some of the Radical laws were: Only civil marriage was considered valid, and could be dissolved by either partner; a man and woman were to be considered married if they had lived under the same roof for over one year; illegitimate children were to be admitted into the same home, at the same table and to equal inheritance rights with legitimate children; violation of women over twelve years of age was not to be considered a crime [the author believes this may refer to statutory rape]; persons instigating or taking part in the violent overthrow of the government were not to be punished, and the government only had the right to resist. See: Moscote and Arce, *Justo Arosemena*, 285-286.
26. Alba, *Cronología*, 190.
27. Justo Arosemena later wrote about de la Guardia: "The personal adhesion of a few friends was interpreted [by de la Guardia] as support by all the Isthmians, without regard to political shades of difference. But his deepest motivation, of which I am sure he was not aware (and this happens frequently to all men) was independence." Quoted in Soler, *Pensamiento panameño y concepción de la nacionalidad durante el Siglo XIX*, 110. Ricaurte Soler believes that many Panamanians, subconsciously at least, were groping for independence. *Ibid.*, 109-111.
28. *Ibid.*, 105-110.
29. Arosemena, *op. cit.*, 270-280.
30. Soler, *Pensamiento panameño y concepción de la nacionalidad durante el Siglo XIX*, 109. Even in some contemporary opinions, Justo Arosemena is criticized. Ricaurte Soler compares Arosemena and de la Guardia in the following way: "Two opposing solutions were found by Isthmian statesmen involved in the affair. Arosemena opted for the provisional acceptance of the violation of sovereignty, as he foresaw a denouement imposed by arms. It is the logical decision of his cold temperament and his utilitarian mentality. De la Guardia turned to force and perished in the action of Mata-Palo [where he was killed, in the interior of Panama] at the age of 33. It is the psychological decision of a passionate spirit who sacrifices his life to his 'duty and dignity, the sovereignty of the State and the legality of his Government'." Nevertheless, Arosemena defended himself after the death of de la Guardia, showing the reasons why he had failed in an article entitled "El Convenio de Colón." This *Convenio* had made Panama a part of the *Estados Unidos de Nueva Granada* during a period of war in Colombia. When Mosquera's victory was certain enough to establish

a more permanent *Estados Unidos de Colombia,* Panama, according to Mosquera, was incorporated under different stipulations and with less sovereignty than provided for in the *Convenio de Colón.* Mosquera's legal argument was sound, according to Arosemena. Moreover, the fact that Mosquera felt that he could enforce his will regardless of Panamanian wishes, led to the failure of Justo Arosemena's attempts to have the *Convenio* accepted by Mosoquera's government. Justo Arosemena, "El convenio de Colón," *Teoría de la nacionalidad* (Panama, 1968), especially 47-50; Chong, *Historia de Panamá,* 178-181; Moscote and Arce, *Justo Arosemena,* 292-295.

31. Moscote and Arce, *Justo Arosemena,* 314-315.

32. See, for example, pages 64-130, of the *Escritos* of Pablo Arosemena in which he dissects with logic and flourish the decisions of Mosquera, showing how many of them were outright violations of the Constitution of 1863. See also: Sosa and Arce, *Compendio,* 251-254.

33. Alba, *Cronología,* 199.

34. Moscote and Arce, *Justo Arosemena,* 297; Sosa and Arce, *Compendio,* 250-259. See also: Gibson, *The Constitutions of Colombia,* 291; Henao and Arrubla, *History of Colombia,* 487; "The Struggle in Colombia," *The Saturday Review,* XCII (September 14, 1901). 327.

35. One such occasion was the overthrow of the President of the State, Gabriel Neira, on April 5, 1873 when the Supreme Court named Dámaso Cervera as State President. However, when Manuel Murillo Toro, President of Colombia, found out that Cervera did not sympathize with the candidacy of Santiago Pérez for President, he ordered a counter-revolution. After a short, bloody encounter in the streets of Panama City, Neira was reinstated. The many participations of the Colombian army in the revolts of Panama for the political interests of Presidents of Colombia, which disrupted interoceanic traffic, gave a motive to the United States to land naval forces. See: Sosa and Arce, *Compendio,* 261-262. The President of the United States, Theodore Roosevelt, in his State of the Union Message the 7th of December, 1903, listed at least 48 moments of tension, revolt or violence related to the Isthmus or to Colombia which did or might have affected transit across the Isthmus. See: Alba, *Cronología,* 208-210 for the list.

36. By 1878, the engineers Napoleon Bonaparte Wyse, Armando Reclus, and Pedro J. Sosa, had formulated the canal project which was finally accepted. The project was supposed to be completed in less than ten years. On December 31, 1878, Ferdinand de Lesseps, the hero of the Suez Canal and president of the Interoceanic Canal Company, arrived in Colón. By the 10th of January, 1880, the first shovel-full of dirt was taken at the mouth of the Río Grande, which was to be the Pacific entrance to the Canal.

The author feels that this particular canal endeavor has had so much publicity—positive and negative—in so many qualified books written or translated into English and easily available, that he will merely make comments here which might reveal the attitudes of Panamanians toward the French and their attempt to build the canal. Supporting this decision to omit the physical and business workings of the project during the nineteenth century is the fact that the canal was not finished by the French, and that the sale of the company to the United States did not occur until the twentieth century. However, the author recommends certain books which deal in depth with these transactions, the scandal that invaded the workings of the company, and the attitudes of various nations before the problem of continuing the digging of the canal. Among these books are: Maron J. Simon, *The Panama Affair* (New York, 1971); Gerstle Mack, *The Land Divided* (New York, 1944); José C. Rodrigues, *The Panama Canal: Its History, Its Political Aspects, and Financial Difficulties* (New York, 1885); Wolfred Nelson, *Five Years at Panama* (New York, 1889); Alicia Alzamora, "La participación de los franceses en la construcción del Canal Interoceánico," Thesis, University of Panama, 1952.

37. Moscote and Arce, *Justo Arosemena,* 413; Sosa and Arce, *Compendio,* 270-271.

38. Pablo Arosemena felt that the Liberal Party was split not so much because of differences in philosophies or principles, but rather by personal hatreds and competitions. He also felt that the Independents should either unite with other Liberals or simply categorize themselves as members of the Conservative Party. See: Arosemena, *op. cit.,* 139-140.

39. Gibson, *The Constitutions of Colombia,* 305; Henao and Arrubla, *History of Colombia,* 501-506.

40. Alba, *Cronología,* 213; Gibson, *The Constitutions of Colombia,* 305, 353; Henao and Arrubla, *History of Colombia,* 502-503; Jones, *An Introduction to Hispanic American History,* 363; Kirkpatrick, *Latin America,* 261; Moscote and Arce, *Justo Arosemena,* 414.

41. Sosa and Arce, *Compendio,* 277-279; 282. The story of Prestán has been dramatized in several novels of contemporary Panamanian writers, especially in *Pueblos perdidos* (Panama, 1962) of Gil Blas Tejeira; in this novel Prestán is actually the protagonist of the first third of the narration. The author presents him as a man of high ideals but of little patience. Here, Prestán feels great bitterness because of the disdain he senses is felt for him because of his race, both by Americans and other whites. In the novel, Prestán is framed by foreign witnesses and the Conservative military court, whose prejudiced remarks condemn him to the gallows.

42. Alba, *Cronología*, 214, 215; *New York Times*, August 8, 1901; Sosa and Arce, *Compendio*, 279, 280.

43. Gibson, *The Constitutions of Colombia*, 305-306; Henao and Arrubla, *History of Colombia*, 504-505.

44. Moscote and Arce, *Justo Arosemena*, 415-418.

45. Gibson, *The Constitutions of Colombia*, 320; Sosa and Arce, *Compendio*, 285-286.

46. Gibson, *The Constitutions of Colombia*, 311-347; Henao and Arrubla, *History of Colombia*, 506-507; Jones, *An Introduction to Hispanic American History*, 363; Kirkpatrick, *Latin America*, 261; *New York Times*, October 28, 1894; *New York Times*, September 26, 1899.

47. Sosa and Arce. *Compendio*, 286-288.

48. John and Mavis Biesanz, in their study of the sociological structure and the relationships among all the peoples who have populated Panama through the years, describe the scenes in Panama during the French construction and mention the nostalgia of the Panamanians when they considered the French era: " 'The time of the French' was a time of free-flowing money and wine, of roulette and elegance. Paris ruled fashions in social events, language, and clothing. The French introduced sidewalk *cafés* and the promenade. Latin in culture like the Panamanians, the French celebrated each milestone of the enterprise with grandiloquent ceremony, symbolic acts, flowery words, and copious draughts of champagne. Their lavish gestures were greatly admired by the Panamanians, who were at a loss to understand the matter-of-fact lack of ceremony of the successors to the French on the job." John and Mavis Biesanz, *The People of Panama* (New York, 1955), 40.

49. Sosa and Arce, *Compendio*, 290.

50. One unfortunate mishap during the administration of Arango was the terrible fire which broke out in Panama City in June of 1894. 125 houses were burned to the ground. The Fire Department, which had been in existence for six years, was not able to control the fire, and the value of property lost was calculated to be four million dollars. See: Alba, *Cronología*, 227-231; Sosa and Arce, *Compendio*, 289-291.

51. *Ibid.*

52. Pablo Arosemena bitterly resented Núñez's conversion to a Conservative role: he accused him of betraying the friends who had supported his candidacy in 1874 when he had just returned from a long residency in Europe (where, it was rumored, Núñez had changed his views about government). If at that time he had disavowed the ideals of the Liberals, Arosemena felt, he should have made it known rather than pretending to continue embracing their cause in order to get their support. See: Arosemena, *op. cit.*, 142-143.

53. Gibson, *The Constitutions of Colombia,* 353-354; Henao and Arrubla, *History of Colombia,* 515-516; S.F. Massey, "The Late Revolution in Colombia," *Journal of the Military Service Institution,* XXII (July-December, 1897), 288-311; *New York Times,* June 10, 1894; *New York Times,* October 28, 1894.
54. Moscote and Arce, *Justo Arosemena,* 419-420.
55. Sosa and Arce, *Compendio,* 292-293.
56. Gibson, *The Constitutions of Colombia,* 353-354. Henao and Arrubla, *History of Colombia,* 516-519; Kirkpatrick, *Latin America,* 261-262.
57. Sosa and Arce, *Compendio,* 294.
58. R.B. Cunningham Graham to *Saturday Review,* October 5, 1901, 430; "The Struggle in Colombia," 327; *The New York Times,* September 26, 1899.
59. Thomas S. Alexander, "The Truth About Colombia," *The Outlook,* LXXV (December, 1903), 994.
60. Cunningham Graham to *Saturday Review,* 430; "The Struggle in Colombia," 327.
61. Alexander, "The Truth About Colombia," 993-996.
62. Castillero R., *Historia de Panama,* 76-130; *Colombia and the United States,* 219.

CHAPTER VI

The Thousand Days' Civil War
on the Isthmus

PRELIMINARY BATTLES IN PANAMA

As the year 1898 was coming to a close, the Colombian Liberal Party was completing plans to commence another armed revolt against the hated Conservatives. This revolt proved to be the longest and most devastating civil war every experienced by Colombia in more than eighty years of independence.[1] The main plan called for the revolt to erupt spontaneously throughout the whole of Colombia, including the distant and always-neglected department of Panama. Panama was of great importance to the Liberal plan because it was geographically isolated and accessible only by sea. The Liberals' strategy also called for tactics that would divert attention from the main battle areas in Colombia proper. Liberals in Panama could prevent the soldiers garrisoned there from being deployed to Colombia and vice-versa. This, in essence, was the proposal presented by General Rafael Uribe Uribe, a leading member of the Liberal hierarchy in Colombia, to his comrades on the Isthmus towards the end of 1898.[2]

The revolutionary movement began on the Isthmus in Natá on October 27, 1899. Amateurish, it did not forecast the terrible bloodshed in which the peaceful interior of Panama was to be involved in the years to come.[3] While these minor revolutionary attempts were taking place in Panama, Doctor Belisario

Porras, a leading member of the Panamanian Liberal Party was in voluntary exile in Central America.[4] With moral support from two members of the Liberal hierarchy in Colombia, Rafael Uribe Uribe and Simón Restrepo, Porras was finally able to enlist the aid of President José Santos Zelaya ("the blackest of all the dictators in Nicaragua's history,"[5]) and of General Eloy Alfaro, President of Ecuador.[6]

Porras launched his forces at Punta Burica in the Province of Chiriquí on March 31, 1900; here he immediately proclaimed himself Military and Civil Chief of the Department. This was the same title that President Rafael Núñez had given his agents on the Isthmus. Completing the revolutionary directive, Porras gave to General Emiliano J. Herrera the title of Chief of Military Operations. As one of the conditions for helping the Liberals, Zelaya had insisted that Porras choose as his Chief of Military Operations either Herrera or Abraham Acevedo. Although Porras had originally planned to name a Panamanian, Rafael Aispuru, he chose Herrera instead in order to comply with Zelaya's wishes.

Notwithstanding evidence of Herrera's immediate disdain for Porras and of signs of disobedience, Liberals took the city in Chiriquí. This caused alarm in many quarters, particularly among diplomats and military representatives of the United States.[7] From David, Porras, Herrera and the revolutionary committee planned their steps on their way to Panama City. The campaign through the interior of Panama was not militarily difficult except that the Liberals found it hard to hold some of the towns that the Conservatives easily abandoned to them, and to organize local governments in these places.[8]

The confusion during some phases of this campaign sprang from internal strife among the Liberals spurred mainly by personal antagonisms between Herrera and Porras.[9] Their disagreements, so apparently petty at times, were to characterize the entire first campaign of the Liberals on the Isthmus. These constant personal antagonisms were affecting the Conservatives favorably, but in spite of them the Liberals were able to defeat the Conservatives near Bejuco, in an area known as La Negra Vieja.

The victory of the battle of La Negra Vieja, which lasted some eight hours, was a great psychological boost to the Liberals. The armaments that the Liberals had received from Zelaya were obsolete and rusty and in some cases did not even function. These arms—Remington, Lebel, Remington Lee, Winchester— were the ones that Zelaya had in his deposit from previous campaigns. They were of no use to the Nicaraguan dictator. This accumulation of various types of arms led to a mixture of bullets of different caliber. With these mixed weapons and ammunition, the Liberals were able to defeat an army well-equipped with uniform weapons.[10] With the news of Porras' victory at La Negra Vieja, volunteers began to flock to the Liberal movement; supplies began to arrive from surrounding areas and even from Panama City.[11] However, Porras spent the whole month of June waiting for the arrival of Doctor Eusebio A. Morales (his Secretary of the Treasury) with aid from Nicaragua and Ecuador.[12]

Finally, on July 4, 1900 Morales arrived at Porras' camp in Chame, accompanied by General Simón Chaux, Military and Civil Chief of the Pacific Coast in Colombia, and many other Liberals. These men brought with them, in addition to the arms Morales had acquired, some 300 Mausers and 40,000 rounds. Chaux and his followers also brought with them a plan to attack the capital from Chepo with part of the revolutionary army. Herrera, with most of the Liberal troops, marched to join this group in La Chorrera. He left Porras with only about eighty men in Bejuco.[13]

The Liberals anticipated bloodshed and a hard fight in their attempt to take Panama, and therefore notified the various consuls in the capital of their intended attack. They also informed them that they would guarantee free transit of the railroad.[14] Meanwhile, on July 14, 1900 when Porras was preparing to leave the Chame area for La Chorrera, he received word that Eusebio Morales (who had gone again to Nicaragua to get arms) was arriving in San Carlos. Morales was bringing 600 Remington rifles, 100,000 rounds and one Krupp cannon. But the captain of the vessel *Momotombo* that was bringing the arms refused to go to La Chorrera and insisted on landing at San Carlos. How were the Liberals going to transport these arms sixty miles to La Chorrera? They immediately thought of Victoriano Lorenzo, the leader of the Indians of La Trinidad, Las Churuquitas, Cacao, La Pintada and Sorá, for transporting these arms. Lorenzo, with 200 men, arrived at Bejuco to see Porras. The two men made a pact to deliver the armaments by way of the mountains in exchange for certain favors, among which was the assurance that tithes still imposed upon the Indians by the Government would be abolished if the Liberals should win. The arrangements concluded, Porras now left from La Chorrera on July 16, 1900.[15]

There, after many plans for attacking Panama City had been discussed, at times passionately, the majority of the officers accepted Porras's plan to attack from the hills of Cangrejo, Bella Vista and Perry's Hill.[16] In spite of preliminary serious lack of communication, errors in judgement, and orders that were disobeyed, once the campaign got under way, Emiliano Herrera was able to turn the Conservative forces back from Corozal.[17] Instead of pushing their advantage, the Liberals sent a 24-hour surrender ultimatum to Albán. Herrera gave as his reason for not following up his success the fact that Porras was a very jealous man, a man who could not tolerate having anyone else taste the glory which he thought was rightfully his. Herrera also claimed that his honor was at stake, since he had given Porras his word that both would enter the city together. However, bitterness between the two leaders continued. Herrera knew that the "Kaiser" (Porras was called by his enemies *"El Kaiser de Las Tablas"*) had not carried out his part of the plan to attack Panama; that is, Porras had not arrived in La Boca as scheduled.

On July 22, 1900 Herrera sent word to Porras notifying him of the victory at Corozal, asking him for an additional 200 men and informing him that he would attack Panama within 24 hours. The "Kaiser" was furious. He felt that his rights as Supreme Chief of the Revolution had been violated by the surrender ultimatum Herrera had sent Albán. He thus sent his own peace terms to the Governor of Panama and, through pure dislike for Herrera, informed Albán of the disloyalty and lack of morale among the Liberals. This action was a God-send to the Conservatives, for now they were aware of ill-feeling and disunity among the leaders of the Liberal army. It further served to strengthen their own low morale. At the same time, Porras sent a message to Herrera congratulating him on his victory. Fearing that Herrera wanted the troops to form one army under his command, Porras advised Herrera that he would need his own troops because he would take La Boca the 23rd, no matter what the cost.[18] Later, several causes prompted Porras to abandon the attack on La Boca, so he sent Herrera the troops he had requested and turned over his command to General Chaux.[19]

At the same time, Government forces were working day and night building up their defensive position which extended from La Boca to the bridge over the railroad entrance to Panama City at Calidonia, where the Government placed fortifications and barriers, and on to Trujillo beach.[20] Finally, on July 22, 1900, Albán replied to Herrera's ultimatum. His answer read:

> Panama, July 22, 1900.—General Emiliano J. Herrera. Unfortunately, the conditions contained in your note of today are unacceptable to me. We remain cordially yours, Carlos Albán.[21]

There were several reasons for Albán's refusal. Campo Serrano was due back any moment with troops from Colombia and by now Albán felt that the city was well-fortified.[22] An English traveler at the time described the scene of preparations:

> There, upon the railway bridge, stood about a hundred of the Government troops, who held it against a strong attacking force of the Revolutionists. The position of the Government troops was a strong one, and they held it easily. Their trenches extended to the left of the bridge for some four hundred or five hundred yards, while two Hotchkiss guns commanded the bridge, and a third commanded a hill behind the trenches. The guns on the bridge, I learned, were worked by an American artillery-man in the pay of the Government, who had been through a good deal of the Cuban campaign, and who had fought well at Santiago. He it was who had conducted the Government

retreat from Corozal; and he it was who, together with General Carlos Albán, had been instrumental in throwing up these trenches; so that by the time Revolutionary forces had advanced from Corozal the defenses had been long completed.[23]

On July 22, 1900, in preparation for the assault, Herrera withdrew his rear guard from Corozal and thus removed his only route of escape. He set up his headquarters on Perry's Hill. The rest of the Liberal troops were to occupy the surrounding hills. Two of his divisions were to attack by way of the beaches Peña Prieta, Trujullo and Marañón. Two divisions were to attack by way of San Miguel. The center, consisting of five divisions under the command of General Simón Chaux, was to make a direct assault on the bridge at Calidonia.

On July 24, 1900 the Liberals began their attack on the bridge. This was one of the bloodiest battles of the revolution, for the Liberals fell at each wave of attack. When Porras heard the gunfire from Farfán, he thought the Liberals were victorious and left for Herrera's headquarters on Perry's Hill. Landing at Boca la Caja, Porras met some Liberals who had escaped the battle and who informed him that all was lost. Porras arrived at Perry's Hill to find an army completely destroyed, depleted and without hope. What he had feared (and expressed during one of the military meetings before the attempt to capture Panama) had happened. Panama would not be taken by way of the bridge.[24]

On July 25, 1900 through the mediations of the consuls of the United States, Great Britain and France, a 24-hour truce was called, so that the ambulances of the British might enter and pick up the wounded and the dead. The conditions at that time were best described by an eye-witness:

> The dead were uncared for for many days, and animals in all stages of putrefaction were scattered over the road, in the trench and the bush. It is remarkable that Panama escaped a pestilence. When the people finally realized the danger from such a situation, after three or four days, the bodies of men and animals were burned with kerosene in the wreckage of the native huts in the vicinity of the battlefield.[25]

Herrera's strategy of attacking Panama had left the Liberals isolated on Perry's Hill. The road to Corozal was in the hands of the Conservatives. Since the Liberals lacked ships, the only way out was by way of Chepo. This route, however, was out of the question, for the remaining rebel forces were too hungry and fatigued to march seventy-five miles to Chepo. To aggravate matters, on the 25th, José María Campo Serrano arrived in Colón with 1,250 men. The Government gunboat *La Boyacá* was also due to arrive soon. The situation of the Liberals was completely hopeless.[26] Herrera turned over his command to Carlos A. Mendoza with instructions to sign the peace treaty. At 3:00 p.m. on July 26, 1900 the hostilities in the first Liberal invasion of Panama were concluded.[27]

It is likely that the invasion of Panama at this time would have succeeded had it not been for the personal differences between Herrera and Porras. The fault lay with both individuals; they had created an amateur and unadmirable example for the lesser officers and had come to disregard party unity in order to think more of their own personal gain and glory.

GUERRILLA ACTIVITIES AND THE INVASION OF DOMINGO DIAZ

From the confusion there arose guerrilla warfare, led by several individuals, including the picturesque Indian *cacique,* Victoriano Lorenzo.[28] According to the surrender terms of July 26, 1900 after the Battle of Calidonia, the Liberals were to cease all resistance on the Isthmus. Most of the participants in the civil war left the area, but those who stayed, including Victoriano Lorenzo, were expected to give up their arms according to the terms of the surrender pact. The *Cholos* had given up the idea of fighting and were returning contentedly to the mountains to hunt deer with their new rifles. However, an enemy of Lorenzo told the Conservatives where the Indian chief had supposedly hidden the arms. Colonel Pedro Sotomayor, ordered by Albán to pursue and capture Lorenzo, burned huts and committed

atrocities against Lorenzo's family and friends in his attempt to
locate the arms. When the news of these happenings reached Lorenzo in Gatún, he decided to take arms against the Conservatives. The Indian's cry of war echoed through the mountains.
The *Cholos*, like the rest of the oppressed and working classes,
had felt some attraction to the Liberal movement, not because
they understood the theory behind the movement, but because
they understood the Liberal revolution as a war of the poor
against the rich.[29]

Rebellion flared among the rest of the Liberals when the
Government imprisoned some Liberal soldiers and sympathizers
without benefit of trial or *habeas corpus*. Sometimes government
officials freed Liberals upon payment of a ransom, but more frequently they imprisoned them in Las Bóvedas, one of the most
notorious prisons in Panama. In addition, the Liberals were required to make monthly donations for war expenses. All of these
acts by the Conservatives served only to rekindle the fire of rebellion in the Liberals, many of whom had planned to continue
fighting anyway.[30]

While the *Cholos* were waging guerrilla warfare in the mountains of Coclé, other guerrillas led by Colonel Manuel Patiño began warfare in the areas surrounding Chepo and Corozal. At
their headquarters in Corozal, the Liberals now proclaimed General Domingo Díaz as Civil and Military Chief of the Army. Domingo Díaz was a strong personality and enjoyed the sympathy
of many residents of Panama City, especially among the masses.
His attraction was further enhanced by the heroic deeds of his
son, Temístocles, who had died at the Battle of Calidonia. Díaz
left Patiño and General Manuel Antonio Noriega in charge of
continuing warfare while he went to Nicaragua to equip an army
consisting of exiled Panamanians and Colombian Liberals.[31]

Meanwhile, Belisario Porras was in Costa Rica attempting to
form a strong invasion force. On July 8, 1901 he was confirmed
as Civil and Military Chief of the Department of Panama by
General Benjamín Herrera, Director of the War for Cauca and
Panama. Thereupon, Porras tried unsuccessfully to persuade Domingo Díaz, who was in Nicaragua, to resign his claims as the

leader in Panama.[32] Porras arrived at Penonomé toward the end of August, 1901. He and his aides were extremely disappointed to find that almost all of the *Cholos* had gone to till the soil and visit their families. However, Victoriano immediately sent emissaries to the mountains to call his Indians to reunite. In a few days, *Cholos* from all over the mountains of Coclé, armed with rifles, shotguns, machetes and the will to fight, presented themselves to Porras.[33]

At about the same time, on September 16, 1901 and in spite of lack of cooperation from Porras, Díaz landed at San Carlos with an invasion force transported from Nicaragua aboard the *Momotombo*.[34] On September 29, 1901 he arrived at La Chorrera where he set up temporary headquarters.[35] Meanwhile, Patiño was not idle, and his raids along the Panama Railroad continued. The rebels raided Gatún, Bohío, Basobispo, and Matachín, taking quantities of powder and dynamite which belonged to the railroad. The United States, pressured by its consul and the president of the Panama Railroad Company, Edward Simmons, prepared gunboats to be sent to Panama in case they should be needed.[36] Expressing the United States position in regard to the Isthmus, *The New York Times* editorialized as follows:

> The United States cannot interfere in the Colombian rebellion except to keep traffic open on the isthmus, and then only in case the Colombian Government requests it. It is Colombia, and not the United States, which has guaranteed the open isthmus. But, in return, the United States has guaranteed the neutrality of the isthmus and the sovereignty of the Colombian Government there. The moment these are threatened, the United States can and will interfere.[37]

Nevertheless, Patiño did not relent, and when the Conservative Governor Albán withdrew troops from Colón for use elsewhere, Patiño was ordered to capture the city. It was not long before Albán was informed of the capture of Colón. He returned and was successful in weakening the defenses of the Liberals, especially in Buenavista, very near Colón proper. Simultaneously, the commander of the Colombian gunboat *Próspero Pinzón* threatened to bombard the city of Colón if the Liberals did not surrender. Fortunately for the citizens of the city, this threat was not carried out because of the mediation of several American, British and French commanders of ships anchored nearby.[38]

The Liberal commander in Colón, now General Domingo S. de la Rosa (Patiño had drowned crossing the Fox River during the capture of Colón), received yet another threat from Captain Thomas Perry of the Gunboat *Iowa*, stating that the United States would land troops if any interruption of railroad traffic were made. Perry further declared that Colombia had formally asked for United States intervention, because Colombia felt at that moment that it could no longer guarantee free transit across the isthmus. To strengthen further Perry's position, the United States consul in Panama, Mr. Hezekiah A. Gudger, received on November 20, 1901 a cable from the Assistant Secretary of State, David J. Hill, which read as follows:

> Notify all parties molesting or interfering with free transit across the Isthmus that such interference must cease and that the United States will prevent the interruption of traffic upon the railroad. Consult with Captain of *Iowa* who will be instructed to land Marines if necessary tor the protection of the railroad in accordance with the treaty rights and obligations of the United States. Desirable to avoid bloodshed if possible.[39]

About 100 marines from the *Machias* did land at Colón to take possession of the railroad station.[40]

Faced with the defeat at Buenavista and then with threats from the Government to the north, the Liberals agreed to the surrender terms proposed by Albán. On November 28, 1901, General de la Rosa signed the surrender document in the presence of Commanders Thomas Perry (*Iowa*), P. Lebrisse (*Le Suchet*), A. Galloway (H.M.S. *Tribune*), Francis Delano (*Marietta*), Henry McCrea (*Machias*), and Carlos Albán.[41]

With the surrender of the Liberals at Colón, the Conservatives were now free to pursue Porras and Lorenzo in the province of Coclé. From his camp at La Negrita, Porras desperately wrote to the Colombian general, Benjamín Herrera, asking him to send arms and artillery and inviting him to join the Liberal campaign in Panama. At the same time, Victoriano Lorenzo, who had sent his men home, called them back. Some 700 men presented themselves before Porras to report for duty.[42] All of this activity was in preparation for the next campaign, the most united and successful, which was to be led personally by General Benjamín Herrera.[43]

THE LAST LIBERAL INVASION

On December 24, 1901 the last Liberal invasion of the Isthmus of Panama took place when 1,500 well-disciplined veterans of battles in Colombia arrived at the port of Tonosí. They were led by General Benjamín Herrera who was designated Director of the War for Cauca and Panama by Gabriel Vargas Santos, Supreme Director of the War and Provisional President of Colombia.[44] Herrera was accompanied by an able general staff.[45] Liberal command of three ships along Panama's Pacific Coast further enhanced the self-assurance of the Liberals.[46]

After a decisive naval victory on January 20, 1902 in which the Conservative ship *Lautaro,* with General Albán on board, was sunk, Herrera advanced his troops towards his main objectives, Panama and Colón. As Liberal forces approached the cities, however, they were informed that United States marines, summoned by the Colombian Government, were blocking the entrance of the cities and were stationed along the railroad terminals of both Panama and Colón. Herrera was infuriated and frustrated by the fact that a foreign power was preventing the success of his campaigns.[47]

In order to control the interior more definitely and thus be in a better position to bargain with the United States, Herrera established a stronghold at Aguadulce. There, he decisively defeated the Conservatives.[48] In order to spare the citizens of the city the horrors of fighting within it, on February 24, 1902 the Conservatives signed an act of capitulation in which they agreed to surrender all of their arms.[49]

In the city of Panama the Conservative leaders soon received news of their defeats both in Aguadulce and in David, where the Liberals had extended their interior campaign. Fortunately for them, the new Conservative Civil and Military Chief of the Department of Panama, General Victor Manuel Salazar, arrived at the capital. Salazar had been Chief of Staff under General Albán at the time of the battle at the Puente de Calidonia during the first large invasion of Panama. Knowing the precarious situation of the Conservative army, the most Salazar could expect to do was defend the city of Panama and await naval reinforcements to combat the Liberals' ship, the *Padilla,* and regain control of those ports and the interior now held by the Liberals.[50]

The Liberals, on the other hand, did not remain inactive. Herrera was informed that the Colombian Government was preparing a large force to invade Panama. To give the impression of being weaker than he was, he retreated to David, where he expected the enemy would attack him.[51] Arriving in David on March 12, 1902 Herrera, who had not heard from General Manuel Quintero, in charge of the David expedition, was surprised to find that he had defeated the Conservatives and was in possession of the city. Against the advice of Quintero, Herrera decided to send troops to Almirante on the Atlantic seaboard in order to gain some control on that side of the Isthmus. Thus, about 1,250 men departed for Bocas del Toro and suffered many discomforts and hardships as they crossed the rain-drenched mountains. When they finally arrived at the island of Bocas del Toro on April 18, 1902 the Liberals defeated the Government forces stationed there after a short, but violent, encounter.[52]

When Salazar found out what had happened it was not difficult for him to recognize the tactical error made by the revolutionaries in establishing their stronghold on an island which could be assailed from all sides. With ease, Salazar's naval forces from Colón trapped the Liberals, who surrendered almost immediately. Surprisingly, they were allowed to return to Chiriquí completely armed.[53] According to Salazar, it was the intervention of Captain McLean of the U.S.S. *Machias,* who acted as intermediary at the surrender, which pressured the Conservative leader to give such generous terms to the Liberals,[54] perhaps the only intervention at this time which favored the Liberals.

While the Liberals were having internal problems, the Conservatives were concentrating the largest available force to crush Herrera once and for all. More than 5,000 veterans of battles in Colombia and in Panama were to be led by Salazar and General Pompilio Gutierrez, who had been sent to Panama to help him.[55]

Herrera was aware of all the Conservative moves through the efficient telegraph service he maintained between Aguadulce and David. His maneuvers and tactics, which included a second victory over Aguadulce (this time a bloody one), brought success to the Liberals once more. When it was all over, four divisions of the best Conservative soldiers had been defeated. Thirteen generals, 500 officers, and more than 3,600 men were made prisoners. The booty was so great that in Aguadulce the revolutionaries obtained more armed power than they had had in two years of combat—one warship, one supply ship, almost 4000 rifles, 600,000 bullets, 5 cannons, a machine gun, 100 tents, and numerous materials usable for fortification.[56]

The siege of Aguadulce, which lasted about four weeks, proved to be the best-planned military operation of the war. The Liberal General Herrera demonstrated there his natural ability to plan military strategy. Without any academic degree, his mind not filled with inapplicable theories, Herrera was rapidly becoming one of the finest generals of Colombia. In Aguadulce, there had been no surprises for Herrera. Every detail had been foreseen. Behind ditches and wire, the Conservatives had been trapped.[57]

Meanwhile, in Panama, General Salazar, who had not heard from General Luis Morales Berti (the Conservative in charge of Aguadulce) since the latter part of July, remained doubtful and worried about the activities in the interior. All contact, including telegraph service between Panama and Aguadulce, had been interrupted since July by Victoriano Lorenzo. The *cacique* had been ordered to force the retreat to the capital of any Conservative troops remaining in the area from Panama to La Chorrera and also to prevent any Government reinforcements from reaching Berti.[58] Salazar knew that if Herrera won, he could make an almost unopposed march to Panama.

With the surrender of Berti, Herrera planned an attack on Panama and Colón. In order to prepare for this final assault, Herrera gave instructions to Quintero to march to La Chorrera and wait for General Julio Plaza who was to cross the Continental Divide and join forces with him. Meanwhile, another force was to disembark at a port close to Panama and await for more exact orders.[59]

Even before the Liberal troops left Aguadulce, Herrera received a note from the United States Consul, H.A. Gudger, reminding him that his country still would not allow fighting within the cities of Panama and Colón or along the railroad line. Herrera did not know what to do. Even though he controlled the whole interior with an army of about 9,000 men, he feared the consequences of confronting the United States. He therefore submitted the consul's note to a general staff meeting for consideration. The majority of the generals, led by Sergio Pérez, Inspector General of the Army, voted stubbornly to continue the plans of attack against Panama and Colón.[60] While this meeting was in process, Herrera received the following letter, dated September 19, 1902 from Rear Admiral Silas Casey of the United States gunboat *Wisconsin,* reaffirming the Consul General's position with regard to United States intervention:

> General Benjamín Herrera.—Dear Sir: I have the honor of informing you that the armed forces of the United States are guarding the railroad line and the line of transit across the Isthmus from one sea to the other, and that no person will be authorized to molest or bar in any form the circulation of traffic and obstruct the route of transit. No other troops but those of the United States may occupy or use the line. All this with the greatest impartiality and without any desire to intervene in the internal struggles of the Colombians.—[61]

Herrera, faced with the threat of United States intervention could do little more than stimulate confidence and keep his forces occupied.[62] At length, on the advice of General Quintero,

Herrera began to exchange letters with Salazar with regard to a possible peace settlement. These negotiations were unsuccessful because Herrera was in complete control of the Isthmus of Panama (with the exception of the terminal cities) and wanted peace on his own terms.[63]

The final blow to Herrera's tenacity was dealt when he received a letter from General Rafael Uribe Uribe in which the latter advised him to end the war. Uribe Uribe had lost at La Ciénaga in Colombia and had signed the peace treaty of Nerlandia after that battle on October 28, 1902. He now realized that no amount of help to Herrera could overcome American intervention.[64] He wrote as follows:

> ... finally, knowing your situation, caused practically entirely by American intervention, we realized here that nothing we could or could not do would in any way affect, for better or for worse, the state of your problem.[65]

A few weeks earlier, around September 19, Admiral Casey had placed marines aboard the trains for the protection of passengers,[66] and forbade Colombian military officers, troops, arms or ammunitions to be transported across the Isthmus by rail unless special permission had been granted. Conservative General Salazar had decided to stop the trains for inspection as they approached Panama and Colón in order to prevent the rebels from boarding and surprising the cities.[67] As long as this policing did not interrupt traffic and since arrangements had been made with the railroad company, Salazar felt that the Bidlack Treaty would not in any way be violated by Colombia.[68] Furthermore, the treaty assured the sovereignty of Colombia, for according to its contents the United States could intervene when Colombia requested that it do so.[69] Salazar protested that not only were the actions of Admiral Casey in direct violation of the passes issued by the railroad company, but they were also violations of the Bidlack Treaty of 1846. Salazar accused Casey of immorally and unjustly attacking Colombia's rights of sovereignty and property over the Isthmus. At the same time, Salazar made it

clear that the Liberals were not to be considered under the protection of the treaty, as they were not the defenders of the laws
of the nation.[70]

After this confrontation, Casey received from the Secretary
of the Navy[71] a message ordering him to abide by the treaty as
it had been interpreted by Salazar.[72] Following orders, Casey allowed the Government to use the railroad again, but excluded
the Liberals. This exclusion was in keeping with the Bidlack
Treaty, a treaty respected by the United States and upheld
against the Liberals only so long as it was convenient to the
United States.[73] The exclusion of the Liberals from the applica-
tion of the treaty left them no choice but to accept the suggestion of Admiral Casey to make peaceful arrangements. Herrera
reluctantly agreed to surrender and meet with the Government
representatives.[74]

On November 19 the legations met on board the *Wisconsin.*
Herrera brought with him from Aguadulce his Chief of Staff,
Lucas Caballero and his Secretary of Treasury, Doctor Eusebio A.
Morales. Salazar, General Alfredo Vásquez Cobo and Nicolás
Perdomo represented the Government. Within a quarter of an
hour, discussions were underway on the celebrated Treaty of
Wisconsin.[75]

The treaty dealt mainly with peace, arms and amnesty. Article seven stated that once peace had been declared, the Colombian congress was to decide what to do about the Panama Canal,
the elections, and questions involving paper money.[76] All of
these factors had caused the war. Bitterly, Herrera signed the
peace treaty, reflecting that the observations of his friend and
fellow-officer, Lucas Caballero, were true: that the sovereignty
of Colombia hung precariously at the mercy of American intervention, which impeded the peoples from deciding their own
destinies in their own territories.[77]

With the signing of the treaty, all hostilities ended; and Panama, which had had a certain relative degree of prosperity maintained by commerce, agriculture and cattle-raising at the on-
slaught of the war, now lay in complete ruins, in spite of the
new air of tranquility.[78]

RESULTS OF INTERVENTION IN THE
THOUSAND DAYS' WAR

American intervention in Panama had been foreseen by many Liberal and Conservative leaders since the beginning of the revolution. Porras, for one, had been idealistic and felt that the *estados poderosos,* as he called the powerful states to the north, would feel sympathy for the democratic (i.e. Liberal) cause, especially if the rebels proved themselves brave and honorable. As to the failure of the United States to rally to this cause, the suspicion may arise that the United States foresaw greater cooperation from the Conservatives in the matter of the future Canal Treaty. A crucial factor which can lead to this suspicion is that when the United States did support the Panamanian independence movement in 1903 in order to make the Canal Treaty a reality, the officials of the new republic were Conservatives.

Unfortunately for the Liberal ideals, the government as well as the people of the United States were misinformed about the real motives behind the revolt. Public lack of interest and incorrect reporting led the Americans and even their representatives abroad to regard the whole affair with scorn and misunderstanding.[79] Perhaps because of this gap between the government of the United States and the peoples of Colombia, many of the lesser representatives, including consuls and navy commanders, were given a certain amount of freedom in their relationships with the rebels. This may very well explain why United States naval forces did not intervene substantially during the first campaign of Porras.[80]

There is no doubt, however, that as interest in a canal across the Isthmus increased in the United States, it became more and more convenient for the Americans to intervene repeatedly in the internal affairs of Colombia. The Bidlack Treaty of 1846 provided the perfect pretext for many of the aggressive actions (such as the confrontation between Admiral Casey and General Salazar) which humiliated the governments of Colombia and Panama,[81] and which prevented the Isthmians from determining their own political and economic future. It became more and more apparent that the power of the United States was truly to be taken into account on every important Isthmian issue. Once again, the geographical advantages on which the Panamanians had hoped to capitalize turned instead into a lure for foreign intervention.

NOTES

1. Castillero R., *Historia de Panamá*, 131.
2. Rubén D. Carles, *Horror y paz en el Istmo, 1899-1902* (Panama, 1950), 7; Domingo S. de la Rosa, *Recuerdos de la Guerra de 1899 a 1902: Cauca y Panamá* (Barranquilla, n.d.), 7-8; Fernando Galvis Salazar, *Uribe Uribe* (Medellin, 1962), 90-96; Manuel Octavio Sisnett, *Belisario Porras o la vocación de la nacionalidad* (Panama, 1959), 80.
3. Armando Aizpurua, *Biografía del General Manuel Quintero V.* (Panama, 1956), 35; de la Rosa, *Recuerdos de la Guerra*, 10-11; Sisnett, *Belisario Porras*, 80; Carles, *Horror y paz*, 11-12.
4. Sisnett, *Belisario Porras*, 69-70.
5. Harold Lavine, *Central America* (New York, 1964), 60; Sisnett, *Belisario Porras*, 70.
6. Colon *Starlet*, October 21, 1899; The Panama *Star and Herald*, October 20, 1899; Victor M. Salazar, *Memorias de la Guerra (1899-1902)* (Bogotá, 1943), 39; Belisario Porras, *Memorias de las Campañas del Istmo, 1900* (Panama, 1922), 30-35; "The Trouble in South America," *The Outlook*, LXVIII (August 24, 1901), 941-942; Conversation with Ricardo J. Alfaro, ex-president of Panama, Panama, July 12, 1966.
7. Hezekiah A. Gudger to David J. Hill, Assistant Secretary of State, April 3, 10, and 24, 1900. Department of State, Consular Dispatches, microfilm, National Archives [hereafter cited as Diplomatic Dispatches]; W.W. Cobbs, Consul at Colón, to State Department, January 14, 1897; June 29, 1900; April 16, 1900. Aizpurua, *General Manuel Quintero V.*, 45-46; Juan Arosemena Q., *La Guerra de los Mil Días* (Panama, 1964), 15; Carles, *Horror y paz*, 16; Porras, *Memorias*, 89-100; Salazar, *Memorias de la Guerra*, 36-44; Sisnett, *Belisario Porras*, 82, 88; *Star and Herald*, April 11, 1900 (From then on nothing relating to this phase of the war on the Isthmus was found by the author in the Panama *Star and Herald*.); *The New York Times*, July 26, 1900.

The United States citizens had a considerable amount of investment in and around David. So much so, that President Alfaro of Ecuador, along with others, did not think it was wise for Porras to choose Chiriquí as the place to begin the revolution. They feared that the United States might intervene. See: Aizpurua, *General Manuel Quintero V.*, 37, 44.

8. Arosemena, *La Guerra de los Mil Días*, 15; Carles, *Horror y paz*, 16-18; Porras, *Memorias*, 179; Sisnett, *Belisario Porras*, 11, 91, 93-94, 95; Aizpurua, *General Manuel Quintero V.*, 50-55. For example, David was retaken with ease by the Governor of Panama. See: Aizpurua, *General Manuel Quintero V.*, 36-57; Carles, *Horror y paz*, 19-20; Diplomatic Dispatches, May 1, 1900.

9. For examples of these encounters, see: Arosemena, *La Guerra de los Mil Días*, 19-24; Carles, *Horror y paz*, 20-22; Sisnett, *Belisario Porras*, 10, 97-102; Porras, *Memorias*, 206-209, 219, 227-231; Aizpurua, *General Manuel Quintero V.*, 56-57.

10. Mateo F. Araúz, *Relatos sobre la "Guerra de los Mil Días" y otros artículos* (Panama, 1951), 39-43; hereafter cited as Araúz, *Relatos sobre la guerra*.

11. Some of them were sent by Rodolfo Chiari, future president of Panama. After the battle of La Negra Vieja, General José María Campo Serrano, who was the Governor, left for Colombia to seek more troops. In his place, after the resignation of his secretary Tomás Arias, Carlos Albán took over. See: Aizpurua, *General Manuel Quintero V.*, 59; Salazar, *Memorias de la Guerra*, 45.

12. Araúz, *Relatos sobre la guerra*, 45; Porras, *Memorias*, 257, 259; Sisnett, *Belisario Porras*, 105-107. According to *The New York Times*, June 13, 1900, not only were Nicaragua and Ecuador aiding the rebels, but also Venezuela. In a Diplomatic Disptach, June 18, 1900, Gudger stated that a gunboat had left Guayaquil, Ecuador with men, arms and ammunition to join the Liberals. Gudger presumed that in the event of fighting which would interrupt railroad service, the United States would interfere.

13. Carles, *Horror y paz*, 26-27; Castillero, *Historia de Panama*, 132; de la Rosa, *Recuerdos de la guerra*, 60-67; Porras, *Memorias*, 259-275; Salazar, *Memorias de la Guerra*, 48; Sisnett, *Belisario Porras*, 105-107.

14. Carlos S. Mendoza, secretary to Porras, to the various consulates in Panama, dated Chame, July 14, 1900; Porras, *Memorias*, 280-296; Salazar, *Memorias de la Guerra*, 49-50; Sisnett, *Belisario Porras*, 107; Diplomatic Dispatch, July 19, 1900, stated that the Liberals had notified their intentions of attacking.

15. Aizpurua, *General Manuel Quintero V.*, 59; Araúz, *Relatos sobre la guerra*, 44-52; Carles, *Horror y paz*, 27; de la Rosa, *Recuerdos de la guerra*, 66-67; Porras, *Memorias*, 290; Sisnett, *Belisario Porras*, 108. These arms never got to Porras. They were to be used by Lorenzo in a future campaign. See: Aizpurua, *General Manuel Quintero V.*, 109-111.

16. Aizpurua, *General Manuel Quintero V.*, 60-61; Arosemena, *La Guerra de los Mil Días*, 27-28; Carles, *Horror y paz*, 27-28; Rubén Carles, *Victoriano Lorenzo, el guerrillero de la tierra de los cholos* (Panama, 1966), 25-26; Porras, *Memorias*, 291-296; Sisnett, *Belisario Porras*, 109-110.

17. Aizpurua, *General Manuel Quintero V.*, 66-68; Araúz, *Relatos sobre la guerra*, 55-57; G. Kennedy Chrystie, "Personal Experiences of a Colombian Revolution," *The Living Age*, VIII (November 16, 1901), 419-420; Carles, *Horror y paz*, 29; Castillero, *Historia de Panamá*, 132; de la Rosa, *Recuerdos de la guerra*, 68-69; E. A. Hackett, "A Central-American Revolution," *Harper's Weekly*, XLIV (December 1, 1900), 1134-1135; Porras, *Memorias*, 320; Sisnett, *Belisario Porras*, 110-111; in a Diplomatic Dispatch dated July 21, 1900, Gudger advised of the Government's defeat; Diplomatic Dispatch, July 27, 1900.

18. Aizpurua, *General Manuel Quintero V.*, 75-81; Arosemena, *La Guerra de los Mil Días*, 28; Araúz, *Relatos sobre la guerra*, 56; Carles, *Horror y paz*, 28-29; de la Rosa, *Recuerdos de la guerra*, 70; Diplomatic Dispatch, July 21, 1900; Porras, *Memorias*, 320-321; Sisnett, *Belisario Porras*, 113 [this last source contains opinions about Porras' actions that deviate somewhat from other sources].

19. Aizpurua, *General Manuel Quintero V.*, 82-83; Araúz, *Relatos sobre la guerra*, 56; Sisnett, *Belisario Porras*, 113-114. Among the reasons that prompted Porras' change of mind, was the warning by General Chaux that if Herrera failed on the 24th to take Panama, only he would be to blame. See: Sisnett, *Belisario Porras*, 114.

20. Salazar, *Memorias de la Guerra*, 58-59; Sisnett, *Belisario Porras*, 114.

21. Aizpurua, *General Manuel Quintero V.*, 87.

22. *Idem*, 87-88; Salazar, *Memorias de la Guerra*, 58; Sisnett, *Belisario Porras*, 114-115.

23. G. Kennedy Chrystie, "Personal Experiences of a Colombian Revolution," 420.

24. Aizpurua, *General Manuel Quintero V.*, 89-92; Arosemena, *La Guerra de los Mil Días*, 29; Carles, *Horror y paz*, 30-31; de la Rosa, *Recuerdos de la guerra*, 81; Salazar, *Memorias de la Guerra*, 58; Sisnett, *Belisario Porras*, 115. Emiliano Herrera, known by a friend of the eyewitness, was said to be a keen, hard-hearted soldier of fortune to whom personal danger was an unknown quality and a man quick to avail himself of any advantage. *The New York Times*, August 26, 1900.

25. Hackett, "A Central American Revolution," 1135.

26. Aizpurua, *General Manuel Quintero V.*, 92; Salazar, *Memorias de la Guerra*, 60; Sisnett, *Belisario Porras*, 116.

27. Aizpurua, *General Manuel Quintero V.*, 94; Diplomatic Dispatch, July 27, 1900; Sisnett, *Belisario Porras*, 117. For an excellent eyewitness account of the battle of Calidonia, see *The New York Times*,

August 26, 1900. Generals Emiliano J. Herrera and Chaux, and José A. Ramírez were allowed to leave with all those wishing to do so. They were also allowed to take with them 1000 rifles, 100,000 shots, 3000 to 5000 pesos, two cannons and bank drafts to the value of 4,500 pesos given to them by Mauricio Halphen, a businessman of David. See: Sisnett, *Belisario Porras*, 119. Herrera left on July 30, 1900, aboard the English warship *Leander* to Ecuador. See: Aizpurua, *General Manuel Quintero V.*, 94. Casualties were estimated by Gudger to be about fifty percent. See: Diplomatic Dispatch, July 27, 1900. Six hundred died or were wounded out of a force of 1,200 men. See: de la Rosa, *Recuerdos de la Guerra*, 84; Salazar, *Memorias de la Guerra*, 60; "The Rebellion in Colombia," *The Outlook*, LXV (August 4, 1900), 760, corroborates these figures.

28. In Porras' first campaign, Lorenzo's attitude toward the revolutionists was one of sympathy; he and his men served Porras' army as cargo bearers and guided them through the mountains. Afterward, when Porras promised the Indians liberty and justice if he won, the *Cholos* participated more actively. They recognized Porras as the only Liberal chief. See: Carles, *Horror y paz*, 36-37. Lorenzo was thinking of sending a delegation to England to ask Queen Victoria for help in attaining their liberty. See: Carles, *Victoriano Lorenzo*, 35.

29. Aizpurua, *General Manuel Quintero V.*, 111; Carles, *Victoriano Lorenzo*, 36; Carles, *Horror y paz*, 36.

30. Aizpurua, *General Manuel Quintero V.*, 95-102; Carles, *Horror y paz*, 37; Diplomatic Dispatch, September 8, 1900; Benjamin Latorre, *Recuerdos de Campaña (1900-1902)* (Usaquén, Colombia, 1939), 60-63; Sisnett, *Belisario Porras*, 120.

31. Carles, *Horror y paz*, 53; de la Rosa, *Recuerdos de la guerra*, 97; Sisnett, *Belisario Porras*, 123.

32. Aizpurua, *General Manuel Quintero V.*, 112-116; Sisnett, *Belisario Porras*, 122-124. On December 16, 1900 Porras had been appointed to this position by Gabriel Vargas Santos, the Supreme Director of the war and provisional President of Colombia. See: Jorge Martínez Landínez, *Historia militar de Colombia* (Bogotá, 1956), 278; Salazar, *Uribe Uribe*, 151-152; Sisnett, *Belisario Porras*, 124.

33. Carles, *Horror y paz*, 51-52.

34. de la Rosa, *Recuerdos de la guerra*, 107; Diplomatic Dispatches, September 23, 1901 and September 30, 1901. The armament that Díaz was bringing with him from Nicaragua consisted of some 300 Remington rifles. With him came many generals, including Domingo S. de la Rosa. See: de la Rosa, *Recuerdos de la guerra*, 104-105.

35. There were ill feelings among many of Díaz's higher officers, which, as could be expected, resulted in a weakening of the army. The second in command, General Paulo Emilio Obregón, finally withdrew and joined

forces with Porras in the mountains. See: Carles, *Horror y paz*, 55; de la Rosa, *Recuerdos de la guerra*, 109-110.

36. Diplomatic Dispatches dated July 29, August 3 and 26, 1901; *The New York Times* dated August 2, 6-9, and 13, 1901. In a Diplomatic Dispatch dated August 26, 1901 Gudger stated that the news of a U.S. ship being sent to Panama had had a good effect. He said that the Liberals had been ordered not to damage the railroad or interfere with the transit.

37. *The New York Times*, August 8, 1901.

38. Carles, *Horror y paz*, 58; de la Rosa, *Recuerdos de la guerra*, 121-127. The British were present because their consul in Bocas del Toro had requested protection from his Government for its citizens who were in danger. See: *The New York Times*, October 19, 1901. The French were concerned over their canal interests. See: *The New York Times*, August 26, 1900.

39. Diplomatic Dispatches, November 30, 1901 and November 21, 1901.

40. de la Rosa, *Recuerdos de la guerra*, 129-132; *The New York Times*, November 21, 1901.

41. de la Rosa, *Recuerdos de la guerra*, 135-136, 137; Diplomatic Dispatch, December 2, 1901; "On the Isthmus," *The Outlook*, LXIX (December 7, 1901), 861; *The New York Times*, November 20, 1901. Marines landed from the *Iowa*, the *Marietta* and the *Machias* to take over the Liberals' arms. Marines from the *Suchet* landed on property of the French Canal Company. See: *The New York Times*, November 30, 1901. On December 5, 1901 Domingo Díaz surrendered at Gorgona. See: *The New York Times*, December 6, 1901.

42. Sisnett, *Belisario Porras*, 127.

43. Benjamín Herrera is not to be confused with Emiliano Herrera who participated with Porras in the first campaign against Panama City.

44. Lucas Caballero, *Memorias de la Guerra de los Mil Días* (Bogota, 1939), 138-139; *The New York Times*, December 31, 1901.

45. Included in his staff were Sergio Pérez and Paulo E. Bustamante, heroes of the battles of Tumaco and Barbacoas in Colombia proper. See: Sofonias Yacup, *Litoral Recóndito* (Bogota, 1934), 213.

46. Araúz, *Relatos sobre la guerra*, 63; Caballero, *Memorias de la Guerra*, 153-154, 158; Castillero, *Historia de Panamá*, 133-134; Latorre, *Recuerdos de Campaña*, 64-65, 68. Herrera's three ships consisted of one cruiser, *El Almirante Padilla*, and two gunboats, *El Cauca*, and *El Panamá*. See: Caballero, *Memorias de la Guerra*, 133.

47. Arosemena, *La Guerra de los Mil Días*, 39; Caballero, *Memorias de la Guerra*, 185-187; Sisnett, *Belisario Porras*, 129.

48. Arosemena, *La Guerra de los Mil Días*, 39; Caballero, *Memorias de la Guerra*, 200-201; Salazar, *Memorias de la Guerra*, 164.

49. Aizpurua, *General Manuel Quintero V.*, 146-149; Arosemena, *La Guerra de los Mil Días*, 40-42; Caballero, *Memorias de la Guerra*, 207-224; Carles, *Horror y paz*, 72-75; Latorre, *Recuerdos de Campaña*, 73-76; Salazar, *Uribe Uribe*, 186-189; Sisnett, *Belisario Porras*, 129. On their way to Aguadulce, Herrera and his army camped in the plains of El Limón. This was adjacent to the farm of Marcos Robles, grandfather of ex-President Marcos A. Robles of Panama. See: Arosemena, *La Guerra de los Mil Días*, 39; Caballero, *Memorias de la Guerra*, 211. One of the Liberal generals leading the attack on Aguadulce was the able General Sergio Pérez. See: *Idem.*, 216-217.

50. Carles, *Horror y paz*, 77-78; Salazar, *Memorias de la Guerra*, 182.

51. Aizpurua, *General Manuel Quintero V.*, 150; Caballero, *Memorias de la Guerra*, 225-227.

52. Aizpurua, *General Manuel Quintero V.*, 170; Carles, *Horror y paz*, 78-80; Latorre, *Recuerdos de Campaña*, 81-83. It seems that Zelaya encouraged Herrera to occupy a port on the Atlantic side. This would enable Zelaya to help the Liberals in Bolivar and Magdalena (Colombia) and also Cipriano Castro of Venezuela. Colombia was furious at the continued aid Zelaya was giving the Liberals. On June 20, Salazar authorized an expedition to Blue Fields, Nicaragua, to stop the aid of the Liberals and at the same time to help a Conservative revolutionary expedition that was being organized on the Isthmus by a group of Nicaraguan conservatives. Salazar sent the *Pinzón* and 400 men. However, the expedition was driven back by bad weather which damaged the *Pinzón*. See: Carles, *Horror y paz*, 80; Salazar, *Memorias de la Guerra*, 207-219. Colombia continued its demands that Nicaragua stop aiding the rebels and again threatened war. Nicaragua sent diplomatic notes to the various Central American nations asking them for assistance in the event that Colombia did declare war. See: *The New York Times*, August 30 and 31, 1902. It was felt by the Colombian and U.S. governments, that Zelaya was helping Liberals in Panama to keep up the war so that the United States would choose Nicaragua for the canal site instead of Panama. See: Thomas S. Alexander, "The Truth about Colombia," *The Outlook*, LXX (December 26, 1903), 993-996.

53. Aizpurua, *General Manuel Quintero V.*, 170-171; Arosemena, *La Guerra de los Mil Días*, 232-238; Carles, *Horror y paz*, 79-80; Salazar, *Memorias de la Guerra*, 190-198. The surrender of Bocas was the only one by the Liberals under the command of Herrera up to that time. See: Caballero, *Memorias de la Guerra*, 234. While in Chiriquí Province, Herrera seized coffee crops, some of which belonged to Americans. H.A. Gudger wrote Herrera demanding satisfaction. When he did not receive a reply, Gudger ordered the U.S. warship *Ranger* to David to "take such measures, drastic or otherwise, as its captain [might] find

necessary." "The Colombian Revolution near Panama," *Harper's Weekly*, XLVI (August 23, 1902), 1156.

54. Salazar, *Memorias de la Guerra*, 195-196.

55. Caballero, *Memorias de la Guerra*, 239-240; Carles, *Horror y paz*, 91.

56. Caballero, *Memorias de la Guerra*, 292; Joaquín Tamayo, *La Revolución de 1899* (Bogotá, 1940), 240.

57. Aizpurua, *General Manuel Quintero V.*, 184; Arosemena, *La Guerra de los Mil Días*, 43; Bogotá *El Tiempo*, November 21, 1952; Caballero, *Memorias de la Guerra*, 293-294; Carles, *Horror y paz*, 98; Latorre, *Recuerdos de Campaña*, 91; "Revolutionary Disturbances in Venezuela, Colombia and Hayti," *The Outlook*, LXXI (August 9, 1902), 901. Herrera had the ability to analyze an enemy position and think of the right plan. See: Salazar, *Memorias de la Guerra*, 248-250.

58. Aizpurua, *General Manuel Quintero V.*, 182-183; Arosemena, *La Guerra de los Mil Días*, 44-46; Caballero, *Memorias de la Guerra*, 288, 290-291; Castillero, *Historia de Panamá*, 134; Salazar, *Memorias de la Guerra*, 246-247. For a copy of the surrender document, see: Caballero, *Memorias de la Guerra*, 295-299. Salazar kept hearing rumors about Berti throughout the month of August. On August 4, Salazar received a telegraph from San Carlos which claimed that some of Herrera's officers were in retreat. See: Panama *Star and Herald*, August 4, 1902. The telegram for the telegraph inspector at San Carlos confirmed the defeat of the rebels at Aguadulce. This report was based on reports of two Government soldiers who had escaped from the rebels. These soldiers also reported that many of the revolutionists were being forced to fight, and that this was encouraging desertion. *The New York Times*, August 5, 1902 and August 7, 1902. All these rumors were false. The news of the surrender at Aguadulce did not appear in *The New York Times*, until September 10, 1902. On September 11, 1902, the Navy Department received a telegram from Commander Potter of the *Ranger* stating that Aguadulce had surrendered.

59. Aizpurua, *General Manuel Quintero V.*, 185; Latorre, *Recuerdos de Campaña*, 105-106; "The Crisis at Colon," *The Outlook*, LXXII (September 20, 1902), 148.

60. Aizpurua, *General Manuel Quintero V.*, 186; Carles, *Horror y paz*, 101; Velasco, *La Guerra en el Istmo*, 224. Typical of many zealous Liberal families, not only General Sergio Pérez, but also his sons Alejandro and Eladio fought for the Liberal cause. See: Araúz, *Relatos sobre la guerra*, 65, 70; Caballero, *Memorias de la Guerra*, 324, 326, 334; Latorre, *Recuerdos de Campaña*, 101.

61. Caballero, *Memorias de la Guerra*, 186. "Señor General Benjamín Herrera.—Estimado Señor: Tengo el honor de informarle que las fuerzas armadas de los Estados Unidos vigilan las vías del ferrocarril y la

línea de tránsito a través del Istmo de Panamá de un mar al otro y que ninguna persona será autorizada para molestar or estorbar en ninguna forma la circulación de los tránsitos y obstruir la ruta de tránsito. No hay más tropas que las de los Estados Unidos que puedan ocupar o utilizar la linea. Todo ello con la mayor imparcialidad y sin ningún deseo de intervenir en luchas intestinas de los colombianos.–"

62. Carles, *Horror y paz*, 102.
63. Aizpurua, *General Manuel Quintero V.*, 187; "The Colombia Insurgents Defeated," *The Outlook*, LXX (April 12, 1902), 898; Salazar, *Memorias de la Guerra*, 275-298. Salazar stated in his memoirs that the Government was soon to be reinforced by an additional 10,000 troops from Colombia. See: Salazar, *Memorias de la Guerra*, 284.
64. Caballero, *Memorias de la Guerra*, 288, 314-315, 347-350; Carles, *Horror y paz*, 103; *The New York Times*, October 13, 29 and November 8, 1902; Salazar, *Memorias de la Guerra*, 284-298; Galvis Salazar, *Uribe Uribe*, 217-228. The *Bogotá*, formerly the *Jessie Banning*, was commanded by Captain Henry Marmaduke, who had served on the *Merrimac* and the Confederate commerce destroyer *Alabama*. The *Bogotá* was manned by an American crew. When Salazar took the ship to the coast of Aguadulce to demonstrate its power to the enemy, it was fired upon by a few rebels from the shore. Consequently, an American, Richard Kane, was killed. See: *The New York Times*, August 28, September 12 and November 13, 1902; Salazar, *Memorias de la Guerra*, 284. The *Bogotá* was not the only Conservative ship which had Americans as part of the crew. The *Chucuito* had George B. Parker, H.L. Goodling, and George Cross aboard as gunners. See: *The New York Times*, September 28, 1902.
65. Carles, *Horror y paz*, 103; Salazar, *Memorias de la Guerra*, 296.
66. *The New York Times*, September 19 and 20, 1902.
67. *The New York Times*, September 19 and 20, 1902.
68. *Idem*, September 17 and 19, 1902.
69. *Idem*, August 8, 1901 and September 27, 1902 [give views on the treaty as applied in 1885].
70. *Idem*, October 6, 1902.
71. The Secretary of the Navy at that time was William H. Moody.
72. *The New York Times*, October 7 and 15, 1902.
73. It was disregarded in 1903 when it was not a convenient treaty, but by then it was too late for the Liberals.
74. Carles, *Horror y paz*, 104; Castillero, *Historia de Panama*, 134-135; Salazar, *Memorias de la Guerra*, 283-284, 295-296, 306-326.
75. Aizpurua, *General Manuel Quintero V.*, 188; Bogotá *El Tiempo*, November 21, 1952; Latorre, *Recuerdos de Campaña*, 111; *The New York Times*, November 22, 1902; November 23, 1902; November 24, 1902;

December 14, 1902; Salazar, *Memorias de la Guerra*, 327-331; Panama *Star and Herald*, November 23, 1902.

76. For a copy of the treaty, see: Caballero, *Memorias de la Guerra*, 355-360; Salazar, *Memorias de la Guerra*, 331-333.

77. Caballero, *Memorias de la Guerra*, 353-354.

78. Carles, *Horror y paz*, 91. For an excellent conclusion and remarks about the aftermath of the Thousand Days' War, which actually lasted 1,130 days, from October 18, 1899 to November 21, 1902, see: Caballero, *Memorias de la Guerra*, 370-391.

79. Carles, *Horror y paz*, 109-110; Porras, *Memorias*, 82-84. Examples of the attitude toward the war are best illustrated by the following articles: "The Revolution in Colombia," *The Outlook*, LXV (May 5, 1900), 8; "The Rebellion in Colombia," *The Outlook*, LXV (August 4, 1900), 760; "A Double Revolution," *The Outlook*, LXVI (November 10, 1900), 627-628. One article stated that the Liberal party was anti-clerical, one of the reasons for the disturbances. It further stated that no one was really interested in establishing a constitutional form of government. See: "The Trouble in South America," *The Outlook*, LXVIII (August 24, 1901), 941-942. Commander Mead of the *Philadelphia* showed his ignorance of the causes of the war when he met with Porras on April 15, 1900. See: Porras, *Memorias*, 143-144. Rear Admiral Casey stated he detected no difference in the principles upheld by either of the Colombian parties, except in matters relative to the Church. See: "Admiral Casey and the Colombian Situation," *The Outlook*, LXXII (October 18, 1902), 384-385; *The New York Times*, October 11, 1902. It was not until later during the war that the true motives became known in articles in the United States. Some of these articles were: "The Struggle in Colombia," *The Saturday Review*, XCII (September 14, 1901), 326-327; R.B. Cunningham Graham to *The Saturday Review*, XCII (October 5, 1901), 430-431; Harold Martin, "Venezuela and Colombia," *The Independent*, LII (October 26, 1901), 2527-2532; "Some Inside Panama History," *The Outlook*, LXXV (December 12, 1903), 890-893; Henry Loomis Nelson, "The Revolution and War in South America," *Harper's Weekly*, XLV (October 12, 1901), 1040-1041.

80. Carles, *Horror y paz*, 110-111; *The New York Times*, October 6, 1902.

81. Caballero, *Memorias de la Guerra*, 193; Salazar, *Memorias de la Guerra*, 157; *The New York Times*, October 7, 1902; "The Truth about Colombia," 993-996.

CHAPTER VII

Conclusions

Even before its independence from Spain, Panama had been developing what later intellectuals were to call a "transit" personality, for Panamanians realized that their most obvious resource was their geographic advantage as an isthmus in the center of the New World.[1] Whether this way of looking at themselves together with the desire of Panamanians to capitalize on their location has enhanced or handicapped their way of life is a question which has been and still is debated by many. Whatever the philosophical answer, the Isthmus has prospered materially (though perhaps not spiritually) when it has been able to exploit its possibilities as a route of transit. The tragedy of the economic life of the Isthmus has been that while providing the resource, it has reaped only crumbs of the wealth that the Isthmians expected would flow from such accomplishments as the railroad; gains have been meager in comparison with the political and spiritual consequences they have suffered in terms of respect from both Colombia and the United States.

Early in the history of the Isthmus as an appendage of Nueva Granada, the people of Panama (through leaders like Tomás Herrera) by trial and error fumbled in finding a way to exploit their advantage as an isthmus. Various opinions regarding the level of independence from Nueva Granada which would be needed for them to run their own affairs as a commercial nation finally led to the relatively stable political reality of the Isthmus as a state within a union. The successful completion of the railroad by foreigners (who were inspired by the dreams of Aspin-wall and New York capitalists) seemed a promise of success to come. Justo Arosemena and others in search of a national iden-tity as free men tried to raise the level of culture and education as well as the level of economic prosperity. For some Panamanian enterprises at least, the railroad created material wealth, but it also created racial and cultural clashes between Panamanians and North Americans; and, at the invitation of the Bogotá gov-ernment, many interventions by the United States. Panamanians felt that they had been sacrificed, that the price they had paid was too great.

The many so-called "revolutions" in Colombia in the second half of the nineteenth century made revolutions in Panama more numerous and complex because of continuous Colombian inter-ference and resulted in the cultural desolation of Panama. These revolutions made Panamanians want to cut themselves off com-pletely from the horrors of Colombia's civil wars, which wreaked havoc where such wars had no business to be—namely, on the Isthmus. Whenever there was an uprising in any part of Colom-bia, the new president would send a new governor with troops and war material, for which Panamanians had to pay the bill.

Panamanians continued to consider themselves as Justo Aro-semena had seen them, as a people apart. It is true that they had some goals and traditions in common with the rest of Colombia, but not enough to justify their dependency on Bogotá and their involvement with her wars. Panamanians as a whole preferred at this time to be as neutral as possible. Rafael Núñez, the Liberal-turned-Conservative, dealt a death-blow to the sovereignty of Panama as a state within a federation when he reduced Panama to a suppressed dependency whose governors were appointed from Bogotá. Thus crippled, Panama suffered during fatal clashes between Liberals and Conservatives through the period of French canal construction and the bloody Thousand Days' Civil War.

Added to the humiliations that any civil war brings, was the knowledge that Isthmians—and even Colombians—could not forge the destiny of their own land without interference from the United States. A "Black Legend" to the effect that it would have been impossible for Panama to gain its independence from Colombia without the aid of the United States sprang up in Panama and the United States in 1903 and has survived for many years; yet the opposite had been true toward the end of the Thousand Days' War on the Isthmus. If the United States had not intervened, the independence that many men of the Liberal Party were dreaming about would have been possible, indeed probable.[2] The philosophies that formed the very foundations of Liberalism, though they may have become dim, faded, or confused by the end of the nineteenth century, had surely not disappeared altogether. Sincere Liberal leaders like Benjamín Herrera would have been the last to turn against the Isthmians in the event that they should wish independence. If Liberal leaders hindered such a move, they would have been contradicting their entire political philosophy. Liberals on the Isthmus did attain an unquestionably secure military position under General Benjamín Herrera during the Thousand Days' War, and American interference at a crucial moment in their campaign squelched any possibility of final success for the Liberals. Many Liberals were already hinting and talking about a movement for Independence from Colombia which would establish "La República Andina" and which would also include the Cauca area of Colombia, another Liberal stronghold.[3] Notwithstanding the lack of greater documentary evidence readily available relating to this desired secession from the rest of Colombia, the history of Panama supports this possibility. From its first rather emotional attachment to Nueva Granada under the banner of the hero, Bolívar, until its final independence in 1903, Panama has struggled to identify and proclaim itself an entity with its own set of problems, peoples, and even culture. The disputes that prompted Justo Arosemena to publish his *Estado Federal de Panamá* (1855) were often related to this particular desire to verify what Panamanians sensed was their own peculiarly Isthmian way of life and philosophy.[4]

It is quite possible that history might have recorded a different story if the civil war in Colombia had remained only domestic and had not created international effects. Whatever the outcome, the Thousand Days' War left a financial and spiritual scar on the Isthmus. The waste and loss which remained at the end of this bitter war were to further affect the search of Isthmians for peace and prosperity in the promise of a canal treaty with the United States. This new illusion, in turn, would lead to the final rupture of the Isthmus from Colombia with the support of United States military power. Independent Panama has not escaped its heritage of suffering. It continues to suffer deeply in the twentieth century as it did in the nineteenth.[5]

NOTES

1. One of the results of this view of themselves is that, in the opinion of the author, Panamanians have in the past developed or maintained a "mentality of a mistress" in addition to the "mentality of a place in transit" and the "mentality of people looking out from a balcony" (expressions attributed to or coined by Octavio Méndez Pereira and by Rogelio Sinán respectively). In their desire to exploit for themselves what they sensed was their principal resource, they became increasingly dependent on foreign elements for their sense of economic security, in spite of believing that they were actually being exploited by those elements.

   Only recently have Panamanians begun to exhibit real confidence in their own ability to handle technical and commercial activity as well as Americans or other foreigners. See: Daniel Goldrich, *Radical Nationalism: the Political Orientations of Panamanian Law Students* (Michigan State University, 1962), 8.

2. In the past, research in this area had not been very scholarly, not documented sufficiently, and therefore the credibility of such contentions was sparse in certain Isthmian circles.

3. Conversation with his father, Dr. Alejandro Pérez Rivas (son of General Sergio Pérez) by Dr. Alejandro Pérez Venero Sr. as told to Alex Pérez-Venero, Jr.; letters from his father and conversations with him by Senator Avelino Pérez of Colombia's Liberal faction; interview with Senator Pérez, August, 1966.

4. See: Soler, *Teoría de la nacionalidad*, 18-19, which deals here with similar ideas related to mid-nineteenth-century political views and philosophies.

5. For a well-written and passionate interpretation of the effects of Panama's historical patterns on its people, see: Juan Materno Vásquez, *Sobre el hombre cultural panameño* (Panama, 1971), especially pp. 1-6.

Bibliography

MANUSCRIPTS

Alzamora, Jacobo, "Reminiscencias históricas de la Guerra de los Mil Días," Penonomé, 1900-1902, ms., National Archives of Panama.

U. S. DOCUMENTS

Malloy, William M., ed., *Treaties, Conventions, International Acts, Protocols and Agreements Between the United States of America and Other Powers*, Washington, 1910.

Manning, William R., ed., *Arbitration Treaties among the American Nations, to the Close of the Year 1910*, New York, 1924.

Manning, William R., ed., *Diplomatic Correspondence of the United States Concerning the Independence of the Latin Republics*, 3 vols., New York, 1925.

Manning, William R., ed., *Diplomatic Correspondence of the United States: Inter-American Affairs, 1831-1860*, 12 vols., Washington, 1932-1939.

Miller, Hunter, ed., *Treaties and Other International Acts of the United States*, 8 vols., Washington, 1931-1948.

Sullivan, G.H. and W.N. Cromwell, ed., *Compilation of Executive Documents and Diplomatic Correspondence Relative to a Trans-Isthmian Canal in Central America*, 3 vols., New York, 1903.

U.S. Congress, House Committee on Foreign Affairs, *The Story of Panama: Hearings on the Rainey Resolution*. 62nd Cong., 2nd Sess., January 26-February 20, 1912.

U.S. *Congressional Globe*. 30 Cong., 2 Sess., 1849.

U.S. Department of State, *Dispatches from United States Consuls in Colón* (Aspinwall), 1899-1902. Microfilm, National Archives, Washington.

U.S. Department of State, *Dispatches from United States Consuls in Panama, 1899-1902.* Microfilm. National Archives, Washington.

U.S. Department of State, *Treaty Series,* Nos. 431, 624 and 661.

U.S. House of Representatives, Executive Document No. 1, Serial 1594, 43rd Cong., 1st Sess., 1873.

U.S. House of Representatives, *Chiriquí Commission* Executive Document No. 41, Serial No. 1097, 36th Cong., 2nd Sess., January 1861.

U.S. House of Representatives, *Chiriquí Grants,* Executive Document No. 46, 47th Cong., 1st Sess., 1882.

U.S. House of Representatives, Executive Document No. 228, 25th Cong., 2nd Sess.

U.S. House of Representatives, Report No., 26, 42, 30th Cong., 2nd Sess.

U.S. House of Representatives, *Canal or Railroad Between the Atlantic and Pacific Oceans,* Report No. 145, Serial 546, 30th Cong., 2nd Sess., February 20, 1849.

U.S. House of Representatives, *Canal—Atlantic to Pacific* (Mercer Report), Report No. 322, Serial No. 352, 25th Cong., 3rd Sess., 1839.

U.S. Senate, Executive Document No. 1, 34th Cong., 1st Sess., 1855-1856.

U.S. Senate, *The Executive Proceedings of the Senate of the United States on the Subject of the Mission to the Congress at Panama together with the Messages and Documents Relating thereto,* Document No. 68, Serial No. 127, 19th Cong., 1st Sess., March 22, 1826.

U.S. Senate, *Report of Joseph L. Bristow,* Document No. 429, Serial 4919, 59th Cong., 1st Sess., 1906.

U.S. Senate, *Diplomatic History of the Panama Canal,* Document No. 474, 63rd Cong., 2nd Sess., 1914.

U.S. Senate, *Memorial of Wm. H. Aspinwall, John L. Stephens, and Henry Chauncy, In Reference to the Construction of a Railroad across the Isthmus of Panama,* Misc. Doc. No. 1, Serial No. 533, 30th Cong., 2nd Sess., 1848.

FOREIGN DOCUMENTS

Arosemena, G., Diógenes A., *Documentary Diplomatic History of the Panama Canal,* Panama, 1961.

Panama. *Documentos básicos de la política exterior del Gobierno Revolucionario; resumen documental,* Panama, 1971.

Panama. *Documentos fundamentales para la historia de la nación Panameña,* Panama, 1953.

Panama. *Registro municipal número especial: dedicado a la conmemoración del primer centenario de la independencia del Istmo, de la Corona Española,* Panama, 1921.

Panama. *Relaciones diplomáticas y consulares entre Panamá-Estados Unidos*, 2 vols., Panama, 1966.
Venezuela. *Venezuela en el centenario del Congreso de Panamá*, Caracas, 1962.

INTERVIEWS

Alfaro, Don Ricardo J., Ex-President, Republic of Panamá, Panama, July 12, 1966.
Carles, Don Rubén D., Panama, summers 1966 and 1971.
Claire, Don Horacio, member *Academia Panameña de la Historia*, Panama, summers 1966 and 1968.
de Leon, Don Gerardo, District Attorney, Panama, summers 1966 and 1969.
Lleras Restrepo, Don Carlos, President of Colombia, Republic of Colombia. Bogotá and Panama, summer 1966.
Pérez Chávez, Don Lizardo, Lieutenant Colonel, Colombian Army, Bogotá, Colombia, August, 1966.
Pérez, Don Luis Avelino, Senator, Colombian Senate, Bogotá, Colombia, August, 1966.
Robles, Don Marcos A., President of Panama, Republic of Panama, August 29, 1966.
Informal conversations with Panamanian diplomats, politicians, professors, novelists and businessmen.

BOOKS

Abbot, Henry L., *Problems of the Panama Canal*, New York, 1907.
Abbott, Willis J., *Panama and the Canal*, New York, 1914.
Abert, S.T., *Is a Ship Canal Practicable?* Cincinnati, 1870.
Acosta, Joaquín, *Compendio histórico del descubrimiento y colonización de la Nueva Granada en el siglo décimo sexto*, Paris, 1848.
Aguilera, Rodolfo, *50 millas de heroicidad*, 6 ed., Panama, 1961.
Aguilera, Rodolfo, *Historia de una vida vulgar*, Panama, n.d.
Aguilera, Rodolfo, *Rosca, S. A.*, Panama, 1963.
Aizpurua, Armando, *Biografía del General Manuel Quintero V.*, Panama, 1956.
Akers, Charles Edmond, *A History of South America, 1854-1904*, London, 1912.
Alba C., Manuel María, *Cronología de los Gobernantes de Panama 1510-1967*, Panama, 1967.

Alemán, Roberto R., *The Panama Canal Treaty: A Study in the Field of International Relations (Text of lecture delivered at Louisiana State University Law School on April 21, 1959)*, Panama, 1959.

Alfaro, Ricardo J., et. al., *Los canales internacionales*, Panama, 1957.

Alfaro, Ricardo J., *Medio siglo de relaciones entre Panamá y los Estados Unidos*, Panama, 1959.

Alfaro, Ricardo J., *Panorama Internacional de América*, Cambridge, Massachusetts, 1938.

Allen, Gina, *Gold!*, New York, 1964.

Los amigos de la Verdad, *Sucinto Examen: y refutación que los amigos de la verdad hacen de un cuaderno que el Coronel Francisco Urdaneta ha publicado para vindicar su conducta en los días 11 y 12 del último Septiembre, y acriminar a los habitantes de Medellín*, Medellín, 1829.

Ammen, Daniel, *The American Interoceanic Ship Canal Question*, Philadelphia, 1880.

Ammen, Daniel, *The Errors and Fallacies of the Interoceanic Canal Question*, New York, 1886.

Anderson, C.L.G., *Old Panama and Castilla del Oro*, Washington, 1911.

Anderson, Robert, *An Artillery Officer in the Mexican War, 1846-1847*, New York and London, 1911.

Arango, José Agustín, *Datos para la historia de la independencia del istmo*, Panama, 1922.

Araúz, Mateo F., *Relatos sobre la "Guerra de los Mil Días" y otros artículos*, Panama, 1951.

Arias, Harmodio, *El Canal de Panamá, un estudio en derecho internacional y diplomacia*, translated by Diógenes A. Arosemena, Panama, 1957.

Arosemena, Carlos C., and Nicanor A. de Obarrio, *Datos históricos acerca de los movimientos iniciales de la independencia, relatados por los próceres*, Panama, 1937.

Arosemena, Juan Q., *La Guerra de los Mil Días*, Panama, 1964.

Arosemena, Justo and Gil Colunje, *Teoría de la nacionalidad*, ed., Ricuarte Soler, Panama, 1968.

Arosemena, Justo, *El Estado Federal de Panamá*, Panama, 1965.

Arosemena, Justo, *Examen sobre la franca comunicación entre los dos océanos*, Bogotá, 1846

Arosemena, Justo, *The Panama Canal in the Light of American Interests*, Washington, D.C., 1880.

Arosemena, Mariano, *Apuntamientos históricos (1801-1840)*, Panama, 1949.

Arosemena, Mariano, *Historia y nacionalidad (testimonios éditos e inéditos)*, ed. Argelia Tello de Ugarte, Panama, 1971.

Arosemena, Mariano, *Independencia del istmo*, Panama, 1959.

Arosemena, Pablo, *Escritos*, 2 vols., Panama, 1930.

Arrocha Graell, Catalino, *Historia de la independencia de Panama, 1821-1903*, Panama, 1933.

Autenrieth, E.L., *A Topographical Map of the Isthmus of Panama, Together with a Separate and Enlarged Map of the Lines of Travel, and a Map of the City of Panama, with a Few Accompanying Remarks for the Use of Travelers*, New York, 1851.

Avila, Eneida, *Looking into Panama*, Panama, 1963.

Ayala, Victoriano, ed., *Derecho administrativo*, Panama, 1922. [Lectures given by Dr. Belisario Porras while professor in 1902, 1903 and part of 1904 in the Law School, Salvador.]

Bakenhus, Reuben, Harry Knapp, and Emory Johnson, *The Panama Canal*, New York, 1915.

Bancroft, Hubert H., *California Inter Pocula*, San Francisco, 1888.

Bancroft, Hubert Howe, *History of Central America*, vol. 3, San Francisco, 1887.

Barra, E.I., *Tale of Two Oceans*, San Francisco, 1893.

Bates, Lindon W., *The Panama Canal: Systems and Projects of Lindon W. Bates*, New York, 1905.

Batista Ballesteros, Isaias, *El Drama de Panamá y América, nuestras relaciones con los E.E.U.U.*, Panama, 1961.

Beale, Howard K., *Theodore Roosevelt and the Rise of America to World Power*, Baltimore, 1956.

Beatty, Charles, *De Lesseps of Suez, the Man and His Times*, New York, 1956.

Beleño C., Joaquín, *Curundú*, Panama, 1963.

Beleño C., Joaquín, *Gamboa Road Gang*, Panama, 1960.

Beleño C., Joaquín, *Luna Verde*, 2nd ed., Panama, 1961.

Beluche M., Isidro A., *Independencia y secesión de Panama*, Panama, 1965.

Benedetti, Eloy, *Tres ensayos sobre el Canal de Panamá*, Panama, 1965.

Bennett, Ira E., *History of the Panama Canal: Its Construction and Builders*, Washington, 1915.

Bertaut, Jules, *Paris, 1870-1935*, New York, 1936.

Berthold, Victor M., *The Pioneer Steamer California*, Boston, 1932.

Bibliografía Panameña existente en la biblioteca de la Universidad, 1903-1953, Panama, 1953.

Biddle, Charles John, *Comunicaciones, entre el Señor Carlos Biddle, coronel de los Estados Unidos del Norte, i la sociedad amigos del país*, Panama, 1836.

Bidwell, Charles Toll, *The Isthmus of Panama*, London, 1865.

Biesanz, John and Mavis, *The People of Panama*, New York, 1955.

Bishop, Joseph B. and Farnham, *Goethals, Genius of the Panama Canal*, New York, 1930.

Bishop, Joseph Bucklin, *The Panama Gateway*, New York, 1913.

Blanksten, George I., *Ecuador: Constitution and Caudillos*, Berkeley and Los Angeles, 1951.

Bolívar, Simón, *Conciudadanos!* Bogotá, 1830. [Speech by Simón Bolívar, bound in book form in the library of Louisiana State University].

Bolívar, Simón, *Selected Writings of Bolívar,* ed. Harold A. Bierck, trans. Lewis Bertrand, 2 vols., New York, 1951.

Borthwick, J.C., *Three Years in California,* Edinburgh, 1857.

Bourson, Alexander, *Le Scandal du Panama,* Paris, 1931.

Boyd, Federico, *Exposición histórica acerca de los motivos que causaron la separación de Panama de la República de Colombia,* Panama, 1911.

Brandon, William, *The Men and the Mountain: Fremont's Fourth Expedition,* New York, 1955.

Bunau Varilla, Philippe, *Historia auténtica de la escandalosa negociación del tratado del Canal de Panamá,* eds., Juan Rivera Reyes and Manuel A. Díaz E., Panama, 1964.

Bunau Varilla, Philippe, *Panama, the Creation, Destruction and Resurrection,* London, 1913.

Bunau Varilla, Philippe, *From Panama to Verdum: My Fight for France,* Philadelphia, 1940.

Bushnell, David, *The Santander Regime in Gran Colombia,* Newark, 1954.

Caballero, Lucas, *Memorias de la Guerra de los Mil Días,* Bogotá, 1939.

Cajar C., Leonidas, *25 años de labor en el desarrollo del folklore nacional,* Panama, 1961.

Callejas B., Santander, *Resumen político de la administración del doctor Manuel Amador Guerrero,* Panama, 1933.

Cameron, Ian, *The Impossible Dream: The Building of the Panama Canal,* New York, 1972.

Campbell, David N. E., *Searchlight on the Panama Canal,* Baltimore, 1909.

Campos, Germán Guzmán, et al., *La violencia en Colombia,* 2 vols., Bogotá, 1962.

Capron, E. S., *History of California,* Boston, 1854.

Carles, Rubén D., *A 150 años de la Independencia de Panama de España 1821-1971,* Panama, n.d.

Carles, Rubén D., *Crónicas de Castilla del Oro,* Panama, 1965.

Carles, Rubén D., *Crossing the Isthmus of Panama,* trans. Phyllis Spencer, Panama, 1946.

Carles, Rubén D., *Cuándo fueron fundados los pueblos y ciudades del Istmo de Panamá,* Colón, 1960.

Carles, Rubén D., *220 años del período colonial en Panamá,* Panama, 1959.

Carles, Rubén D., *La gente de "Allá Abajo,"* Panama, 1947.

Carles, Rubén D., *Homenaje a la ciudad centenaria de Colón 1853-1952,* Panama, 1952.

Carles, Rubén D., *Horror y paz en el Istmo, 1899-1902,* Panama, 1950.

Carles, Rubén D., *Old Panama (Panama la Vieja),* trans. Patrick J. Smyth, Panama, 1960.

Carles, Rubén D., *Reminscencias de los primeros años de la República de Panamá, 1903-1912,* Panama, 1968.

Carles, Rubén D., *Victoriano Lorenzo: el guerrillero de la tierra de los Cholos*, Panama, 1966.

Carrington, John W., *The Passage of the Isthmus: or, Practical Hints to Persons about to Cross the Isthmus of Panama*, New York, 1849.

Castillero Calvo, Alfredo, *La fundación de la Villa de Los Santos y los orígenes históricos de Azuero*, Panama, 1971.

Castillero Calvo, Alfredo, *1821—La independencia de Panama de España*, Panama, 1971.

Castillero Calvo, Alfredo, *Los negros y mulatos libres en la historia social panameña*, Panama, 1969.

Castillero Calvo, Alfredo, *Políticas de poblamiento en Castilla del Oro y Veraguas en los orígenes de la colonización*, Panama, 1972.

Castillero Pimentel, Ernesto, *Historia de Panamá*, Panama, 1962.

Castillero Pimentel, Ernesto, *Panamá y los Estados Unidos*, Panama, 1953.

Castillero Pimentel, Ernesto, *Política exterior de Panamá*, Panama, 1961.

Castillero Reyes, Ernesto J., *El Canal de Panamá*, Panama, n.d.

Castillero Reyes, Ernesto J., *La causa inmediata de la emancipación de Panama*, Panama, 1933.

Castillero Reyes, Ernesto J., *Chirquí. Ensayo de monografía de la Provincia de Chiriquı*, Panama, 1968.

Castillero Reyes, Ernesto J., *Episodios de la independencia de Panamá*, Panama, 1957.

Castillero Reyes, Ernesto J., *El Ferrocarril de Panamá y su historia*, Panama, 1932.

Castillero Reyes, Ernesto J., *Galería de presidentes de Panamá*, Panama, 1936.

Castillero Reyes, Ernesto J., *Historia de la comunicación interoceánica y de su influencia en la formación y en el desarrollo de la entidad nacional panameña*, Panama, 1941.

Castillero Reyes, Ernesto J., *Historia de los símbolos de la Patria Panameña*, Panama, 1964.

Castillero Reyes, Ernesto J., *Historia de Panamá*, Panama, 1962.

Castillero Reyes, Ernesto J., *"El Palacio de las Garzas," historia del Palacio Presidencial de Panamá*, Panama, 1961.

Castillero Reyes, Ernesto J., *El profeta de Panamá y su gran traición: el tratado del canal y la intervención de Bunau-Varilla en su confección*, Panama, 1936.

Castillero Reyes, Ernesto J., *El doctor Manuel Amador Guerrero, prócer de la independencia y primer presidente de la república*, Panama, 1933.

Castillero Reyes, Ernesto J., *Dr. Rafael Lasso de la Vega—prelado, legislador y prócer—(1764-1831)*, No. 5 of *Panameños Ilustres*, Panama, 1952.

Castillero Reyes, Ernesto J., and Juan Antonio Susto, *Rincón histórico*, Panama, 1947.

Caughey, John W., *Rushing for Gold*, Berkeley, 1949.

Chase, Lucien B., *History of the Polk Administration*, New York, 1850.

Chiché, *L'affaire de Panamá*, Bordeaux, 1896.

Chong M., Moisés, *Historia de Panama*, Panama, 1968.

Cochrane, Charles S., *Journal of a Residence and Travels in Colombia*, 2 vols., London, 1825.

Codman, John, *The Round: By Way of Panama, Through California, Oregon, Nevada, Utah, Idaho, and Colorado, with Notes on Railroads, Commerce, Agriculture, Mining, Scenery, and People*, New York, 1879.

Coffin, George, *A Pioneer Voyage to California*, Chicago, 1908.

El Congreso de Panama (1826), ed. Raul Porras Barrenechea, Lima, 1930.

Congreso Panamericano conmemorativo de Bolívar; 1826-1926, Panama, 1927.

Cook, Elliott Wilkinson, *Land Ho! The Original Diary of a Forty-Niner*, ed., Jane J. Cook, Baltimore, 1935.

Coope, Anna, *Anna Coope Sky Pilot of the San Blas Indians, An Autobiography*, New York, 1917.

Core, Sue, *Panama's Trails of Progress*, New York, 1931.

Cornish, Vaughan, *The Panama Canal and its Makers: A Historical Review*, London, 1909.

Correa D., Noris L., *Apuntes de Historia Patria*, Panama, n.d.

Cortázar, Roberto and Luis A. Cuervo, *Congreso de 1823 Actas*, Bogotá, 1926.

The Course of Empire: First Hand Accounts of California in the Days of the Gold Rush, ed., Valeska Bari, New York, 1931.

Crosby, Elisha Oscar, *Memoirs*, San Marino, California, 1945.

Cullen, Edward, et al., *Over Darien by a Ship Canal*, London, 1856.

Cullen, Edward, *The Isthmus of Darien Ship Canal*, London, 1852.

Davis, Charles H., *Report on Inter-Oceanic Canal and Railroads*, Washington, 1867.

Davis, Richard Harding, *Three Gringos in Venezuela and Central America*, New York, 1896.

de Andagoya, Pascual, *Narrative of the Proceedings of Pedrarias Davila in the Provinces of Tierra Firme or Castilla del Oro, and of the Discovery of the South Sea and the Coasts of Peru and Nicaragua*, trans., and ed. Clements R. Markhan, London, 1865.

DeGrummond, Jane Lucas, *Caracas Diary, 1835-1840*, Baton Rouge, 1954.

de la Guardia, Ernesto, *Teoría y práctica de la democracia, conversaciones con el Pueblo*, Panama, 1960.

de la Rosa, Diógenes, *Ensayos varios*, Panama, 1968.

de la Rosa, Domingo S., *Recuerdos de la Guerra de 1899 a 1902, Cauca y Panamá*, Barranquilla, 1940.

de Leon, César A., *Significado histórico de la actual crisis entre Panamá y los Estados Unidos*, Panama, 1964.

de Lesseps, Ferdinand, *Recollections of Forty Years*, New York, 1888.

de Mosquera, Tomás C., *Examen crítico: del libelo publicado en la imprenta del comercio en Lima, por el reo prófugo José María Obando*, Valparaíso, 1843.

de Mosquera, Tomás C., *Memoir on the Physical and Political Geography of New Granada*, New York, 1853.

Dénain, Adolphe, *Ensayo sobre los intereses políticos i comerciales del Istmo de Panamá*, Panama, 1844.

Dennis, A. L. P., *Adventures in American Diplomacy, 1896-1906*, New York, 1928.

Desarrollo económico y social de Panamá, Washington, 1962.

Destruge, Camilo, *Biografía del Gral. Don Juan Illingworth*, Guayaquil, 1914.

Diez Castillo, Luis A., *Los Cimarrones y la esclavitud en Panamá*, Panama, 1968.

Dimock, Marshall E., *Government Operated Enterprise in the Panama Canal Zone*, Chicago, 1948.

Duane, Colonel William, *A Visit to Colombia, in the Years 1822 and 1823*, Philadelphia, 1826.

Dubois, Jules, *Danger Over Panama*, Indianapolis, 1964.

Dunlop, Alexander, *Notes on the Isthmus*, London, 1852.

DuVal, Jr., Miles P., *And the Mountains Will Move: The Story of the Building of the Panama Canal*, Stanford, 1947.

DuVal, Jr., Miles P., *Cadiz to Cathay: The Story of the Long Diplomatic Struggle for the Panama Canal*, New York, 1968.

Ealy, Lawrence, *The Republic of Panama in World Affairs, 1903-1950*, Philadelphia, 1951.

Ealy, Lawrence, *Yanqui Politics and the Isthmian Canal*, University Park, Pennsylvania, 1971.

Edwards, Albert, *Panama: The Canal, the Country and the People*, New York, 1912.

Fabens, Joseph W., *A Story of Life on the Isthmus*, New York, 1853.

Fábrega, José Isaac, *Escritos Varios*, Panama, 1969.

Forbes-Lindsay, Charles H. A., *Panama, the Isthmus and Canal*, Philadelphia, 1906.

Franck, Harry A., *Zone Policeman 88, A Close Range Study of the Panama Canal and Its Workers*, New York, 1970.

Gandasegui, Marco A., *La concentración del poder económico en Panamá*, Panama, 1967.

García de Paredes, Guillermo, *Cortos cuentos de Coto*, Panama, 1970.

García Monge, Diego, *Manual del Registro Civil*, Panama, 1951.

Garella, Napoleon, *Projet d'un canal de jonction de l'ocean Pacifique et de l'ocean Atlantique à travers l'isthme de Panama*, Paris, 1845.

Gasteazoro, Carlos M., *Introducción al estudio de la historia de Panamá*, Mexico, 1956.

El General Volvió, David, Chiriquí, n.d.

Gibson, William Marion, *The Constitutions of Colombia*, Durham, 1948.

Gilbert, James S., *Panama Patchwork*, New York, 1911.

Gillis, William Robert, *Gold Rush Days with Mark Twain*, New York, 1930.

Gisborne, Lionel, *The Isthmus of Darien in 1852*, London, 1853.

Goldrich, Daniel, *Radical Nationalism*, East Lansing, 1962.

Goodwin, John Marston, *The Panama Ship Canal and Inter-Oceanic Ship Railway Projects*, Cleveland, 1880.

Gorgas, William C., *Sanitation in Panama*, New York, 1915.

Goytía, Victor F., *Bolívar el estadista*, Panama, 1968.

Graebner, Norman A., *Empire on the Pacific: A Study in American Continental Expansion*, New York, 1955.

Grant, U.S., *Personal Memoirs*, New York, 1885.

Gregory, Joseph W., *Gregory's Guide for California Travellers Via the Isthmus of Panama*, New York, 1850.

Griswold, Chauncey D., *The Isthmus of Panama, and What I Saw There*, New York, 1852.

Groh, George W., *Gold Fever, Being a True Account, Both Horrifying and Hilarious, of the Art of Healing (so-called) During the California Gold Rush*, New York, 1966.

Groot, José Manuel, *Historia eclesiástica y civil de Nueva Granada*, 5 vols., Bogotá, 1889-1893.

Grotius, Benjamin, *A Review of the Monroe Doctrine and the American Theory of the Panama Canal*, Washington, 1882.

Gunther, John, *Inside South America*, New York, 1967.

Gutiérrez, Samuel A., *El problema de las "Barriadas Brujas" en la ciudad de Panamá*, Panama, 1965.

Hale, Richard L., *The Log of a Forty-Niner*, Boston, 1923.

Hammond, R., and C. Lewis, *The Panama Canal*, London, 1966.

Harding, Earl, *The Untold Story of Panama*, New York, 1959.

Haskin, Frederic J., *The Panama Canal*, New York, 1913.

Haskins, C.W., *The Argonauts of California*, New York, 1890.

Hauberg, Clifford A., *Latin American Revolutions (Mexico, Central America, Panama, and the Islands of the Caribbean)*, Minneapolis, 1968.

Hauradou, Ricardo L. Martínez, *Sangre en Panamá, Enero 7 de 1964*, Panama, 1967.

Hedrick, Basil C., and Anne K., *Historical Dictionary of Panama*, Metuchen, 1970.

Helguera, J. León and Robert Davis, eds., *Archivo Epistolar del General Mosquera: Correspondencia con el General Ramón Espina 1835-1866*, Bogotá, 1966.

Henao, Jesús María and Gerardo Arrubla, *History of Colombia*, trans. and ed. James Fred Rippy, Chapel Hill, 1938.

Henao, Jesús María and Gerardo Arrubla, *Historia de Colombia*, Bogotá, 1916.

Hill, Howard Copeland, *Roosevelt and the Caribbean*, Chicago, 1927.

Horan, James D., and Paul Sann, *Pictorial History of the Wild West*, New York, 1954.

Howarth, David, *Panama: Four Hundred Years of Dreams and Cruelty*, New York, 1966.

Howe, Octavius Thorndike, *Argonauts of '49: History and Adventures of the Emigrant Companies from Massachusetts, 1849-1850*, Cambridge, 1923.

Hoyt, Edwin C., *National Policy and International Law: Case Studies from American Canal Policy*, Vol. 4, Denver, 1967.

Huberich, Charles Henry, *The Trans-Isthmian Canal: A Study in American Diplomatic History (1825-1904)*, Austin, 1904.

Huertas Ponce, Esteban, *Memorias y bosquejo biográfico del general Esteban Huertas; Prócer de la gesta del 3 de noviembre de 1903*, Panama, 1959.

Isaza Calderón, Baltasar, *Panamá La Vieja y Panamá La Nueva*, Panama, 1969.

Jackson, B. Franklin, ed., *A Brief Description of the Facilities and Advantages Which a Road Across Central America from Chiriquí Lagoon or Admiral's Bay, on the Atlantic to Chiriquí Bay, on the Pacific Would Afford to the Commerce of the World*, Philadelphia, 1852.

Jackson, Joseph Henry, *Gold Rush Album*, New York, 1949.

Jenks, Leland Hamilton, *The Migration of British Capital to 1825*, New York, 1927.

Johnson, Allen, ed., *Dictionary of American Biography*, Vol. II, New York, 1929.

Johnson, E. R., *History of Foreign and Domestic Commerce*, Washington, D.C., 1915.

Johnson, Theodore Taylor, *Sights in the Gold Region and Scenes by the Way*, New York, 1849.

Johnston, W. E., *The True History of the Panama Canal Scheme*, Paris, 1884.

Johnston, William G., *Experiences of a Forty-Niner*, Pittsburg, 1892.

Jones, Chester L., *The Caribbean Since 1900*, New York, 1936.

Jones, Tom B., *An Introduction to Hispanic American History*, New York, 1939.

Karlin, Alma M., *The Death Thorn: Magic, Superstitions, and Beliefs of Urban Indians and Negroes in Panama and Peru*, London, 1933.

Kemble, John H., ed., *Gold Rush Steamers*, San Francisco, 1958.

Kemble, John H., *The Panama Canal: The Evolution of the Isthmian Crossing*, San Francisco, 1965.

Kemble, John H., *The Panama Route, 1848-1869*, Berkeley and Los Angeles, 1943.

King, Thelma, *El problema de la soberanía en las relaciones entre Panamá y los Estados Unidos de América*, Panama, 1961.

Kirkpatrick, Frederick A., *Latin America A Brief History*, New York, 1939.

Korngold, Ralph, *Thaddeas Stevens*, New York, 1955.

Landínez, Jorge M., *Historia militar de Colombia: La Guerra Civil de los Mil Días*, Bogotá, 1956.

Larsen, Henry and May, *The Forests of Panama*, London, 1964.

Latané, John H., *Caribbean Interests of the United States*, New York, 1906.

Latorre, Benjamín, *Recuerdos de campaña, 1900-1902*, Usaquén, Colombia, 1938.

Lavine, Harold, *Central America*, New York, 1964.

Lee, William Storrs, *The Strength to Move a Mountain*, New York, 1958.

Legters, Lyman H., et al., *Area Handbook for Panama*, Washington, 1962.

Lemaitre, Eduardo, *Panamá y su separación de Colombia*, Bogotá, 1971.

León, José Nicolás, *Firme, irrevocable y perentorio concepto de los habitantes del Tocuyo sobre la forma de gobierno que debe adoptarse en Colombia*, Tocuyo, 1829.

Letts, J. M., *A Pictorial View of California*, New York, 1853.

Liot, W.B., *Panama, Nicaragua and Tehuantepec*, London, 1849.

Liss, Sheldon B., *The Canal: Aspects of United States-Panamanian Relations*, South Bend, 1967.

Lloyd, John A., *An Account of Levellings across the Isthmus of Panama*, London, 1830.

Luna, Carlos Cabezas, *El derecho de Panamá*, Sevilla, 1961.

McCain, William D., *The United States and the Republic of Panama*, Durham, 1937.

McCormac, Eugene I., *James K. Polk: A Political Biography*, Berkeley, 1922.

Mack, Gerstle, *The Land Divided: A History of the Panama Canal and Other Isthmian Canal Projects*, New York, 1944.

Manzano, Juan Manzano, *Manuel José de Ayala—compilador y consejero de Indias (1728-1805)*, No. 2 of *Panameños Ilustres*, Panama, 1951.

Marsh, Richard Oglesby, *White Indians of Darien*, New York, 1934.

Martínez Delgado, Luis, *Obras completas del Doctor Carlos Martínez Silva*, 2 vols., Bogotá, 1934.

Megquier, Mary Jane, *Apron Full of Gold; the Letters of Mary Jane Megquier*, ed., Robert Glass Cleland, San Marino, 1949.

Mellander, Gustavo A., *The United States in Panamanian Politics: The Intriguing Formative Years*, Danville, 1971.

Méndez Pereira, Octavio, *Justo Arosemena*, Panama, 1919.

Méndez, Pereira, Octavio, et al., *Panamá en la Gran Colombia*, Panama, 1939.

Meyers, William H., *Journal of a Cruise to California and the Sandwich Islands in the United States Sloop-of-War Cyane, 1841-1844*, ed., John Haskell Kemble, San Francisco, 1955.

Miner, Dwight Carroll, *The Fight for the Panama Route, The Story of the Spooner Act and the Hay-Herran Treaty*, New York, 1940.

Minter, John E., *The Chagres: River of Westward Passage*, New York, 1948.

Miró, Rodrigo, *El cuento en Panamá (estudio, selección, bibliografía)*, Panama, 1950.

Miró, Rodrigo, *La cultura colonial en Panamá*, Mexico, 1950.

Miró, Rodrigo, *La literatura panameña*, Panama, 1970.

Miró, Rodrigo, *El hermano Hernando de la Cruz y su significación dentro de la pintura quiteña*, Panama, 1960.

Miró, Rodrigo, *Mariano Arosemena, (el político, el periodista, el historiador)*, Panama, 1960.

Miró, Rodrigo, *Sentido y misión de la historia en Panamá*, Panama, 1969.

Morales, David Turner, *El crimen de los Yanquis en Panamá, respuesta a un genocida*, Panama, 1964.

Morales, David Turner, *Estructura económica de Panamá*, Mexico, 1958.

Morrel, Martha M., *"Young Hickory": The Life and Times of President James K. Polk*, New York, 1949.

Morrell, William Parker, *The Gold Rushes*, London, 1940.

Morrison, H. A., *List of Books and Articles in Periodicals Relating to Interoceanic Canal and Railway Routes* (Nicaragua; Panama, Darien and the Valley of the Atrato; Tehuantepec and Honduras; Suez Canal) Washington, 1900.

Moscote, José D., and Arce, Enrique J., *La vida ejemplar de Justo Arosemena*, Panama, 1956.

Munro, Dana G., *Intervention and Dollar Diplomacy in the Caribbean 1900-1921*, Princeton, 1964.

Narrative of the Expedition under General MacGregor against Porto Bello: Including an Account of the Voyage; and of the Causes which Led to Its Final Overthrow, London, 1820.

Nathaniel Niles' Plan for the Construction of a Ship Canal Between the Atlantic and Pacific Oceans, New York, 1868.

Nelson, Wolfred, *Cinco años en Panamá (1880-1885)*, estudio preliminar y notas por Armando Muñoz Pinzón, Panama, 1971.

Nelson Wolfred, *Five Years at Panama*, New York, 1889.

New Granada Canal and Steam Navigation Company, *Remarks on the Canal or "Dique" of Cartagena, New Granada, and Its Navigation by Steam*, New York, 1855.

Nicolau, Ernesto J., *El grito de la Villa*, Panama, 1961.

Niemeier, Jean Gilbreath, *The Panama Story*, Portland, 1968.

Noriega, Manuel A., *Recuerdos históricos de mis campañas en Colombia y en el Istmo 1876-77, 1885-86, 1900-02*, Panama, n.d.

Nourse, J. E., *The Maritime Canal of Suez; and Comparison of Its Probable Results with Those of a Ship Canal across Darien*, Washington, 1869.

Ortega B., Ismael, *La independencia de Panamá en 1903*, Panama, 1930.

Ortega C., Joaquín, *Gobernantes de la República de Panamá, 1903-1960*, Panama, 1965.

Orton, A. R., *"The Derienni," or Land Pirates of the Isthmus*, New Orleans, 1853.

Osbun, Albert G., *To California and the South Seas: The Diary of Albert G. Osbun, 1849-1851*, ed., John Haskell Kemble, San Marino, 1966.

Otis, Fessenden Nott, *Illustrated History of the Panama Railroad Together with a Traveler's Guide and Business Man's Hand-Book for the Panama Railroad and its Connections with Europe, the United States, the North and South Atlantic and Pacific Coasts, China, Australia, and Japan, by Sail and Steam*, New York, 1861.

Otis, Fessenden Nott, *Isthmus of Panama, History of the Panama Railroad; and of the Pacific Mail Steamship Company. Together with a Traveller's Guide and Business Man's Hand-Book for the Panama Railroad, and the Lines of Steamships Connecting it with Europe, the United States, the North and South Atlantic and Pacific Coasts, China, Australia, and Japan*, New York, 1867.

Pacific Mail Steamship Company, *A Sketch of the Route to California, China and Japan, via the Isthmus of Panama*, San Francisco, 1867.

Padelford, Norman J., *The Panama Canal in Peace and War*, New York, 1942.

Panama; Canal Issues and Treaty Talks, Washington, 1967.

The Panama Canal: Twenty-Fifth Anniversary, Balboa, 1939.

The Panama Canal: Fiftieth Anniversary, La Boca, C.Z., 1964.

Panama, 50 años de república, Panama, 1953.

Panama Election Factbook, Washington, 1968.

Panama—el país—el gobierno—la política internacional, Panama, 1960.

The Panama Massacre: A Collection of Principal Evidence and Other Documents Including the Report of Amos W. Corwine, Esq., Commissioner, the Official Statement of the Governor and Depositions Taken before the Authorities, Relative to the Massacre of American Citizens at the Panama Railroad Station on the 15th of April, 1856, Panama, 1857.

Parks, E. Taylor, *Colombia and the United States, 1765-1934*, Durham, 1935.

Payne, Jame L., *Patterns of Conflict in Colombia*, New Haven, 1968.

Peacock, George, *Notes on the Isthmus of Panama and Darien*, Exeter, 1878.

Peña, Concha, *Tomás Herrera*, Panama, 1954.

Pereira Jiménez, Bonifacio, *Biografía del Río Chagres*, Panama, 1964.

Pereira Jiménez, Bonifacio, *Historia de Panamá*, Panama, 1969.

Pérez, Modesto, *Los Precursores españoles del Canal Interoceánico*, Madrid, 1915.

Picón-Salas, Mariano, *Los días de Cipriano Castro*, Caracas, 1953.

Pim, Bedford, *The Gate of the Pacific*, London, 1863.

Pippin, Larry L., *The Remón Era: An Analysis of a Decade of Events in Panama 1947-1957*, Stanford, 1964.

Polk, James K., *The Diary of James K. Polk: During His Presidency, 1845-1849*, ed., Milo M. Quaife, 4 vols., Chicago, 1910.

Porras, Belisario, *La Venta del Istmo*, Panama, 1967.

Porras, Belisario, *Memorias de las campañas del Istmo, 1900*, Panama, 1922.

Prebble, John, *The Darien Disaster*, London, 1968.

Radcliff, William, *Considerations on the Subject of a Communication Between the Atlantic and Pacific Oceans, by Means of a Ship-Canal across the Isthmus, Which Connects North and South America; The Best Means of Effecting It, and Permanently Securing Its Benefits for the World at Large, by Means of a Cooperation Between Individuals and Companies of Different Nations under the Patronage of Their Respective Governments*, Washington, 1836.

Rafter, M., *Memoirs of Gregor McGregor*, London, 1820.

Rebolledo, Alvaro, *El Canal de Panamá*, Cali, Colombia, 1957.

Reclus, Armando, *Exploraciones a los Istmos de Panamá y Darién en 1876, 1877 y 1878*, Panama, 1958.

Restrepo, Ernesto, *Estudios sobre los aborígenes de Colombia*, Bogotá, 1892.

Restrepo, Vicente, *A Study of the Gold and Silver Mines of Colombia*, New York, 1886.

Reuter, Bertha A., *Anglo-American Relations During the Spanish American War*, New York, 1924.

Ringwalt, John L., *Anécdotes of General Ulysses S. Grant*, Philadelphia, 1886.

Rippy, James Fred, *Latin America in World Politics: An Outline Survey*, New York, 1928.

Rippy, James Fred, *The Capitalists and Colombia*, New York, 1931.

Robertson, William S., *Hispanic-American Relations with the United States*, New York, 1923.

Robinson, Tracy, *Fifty Years at Panama*, New York, 1920.

Robinson, Tracy, *Panama, A Personal Record of Forty-Six Years, 1861-1907*, Panama, 1907.

Rodman, Selden, *The Road to Panama*, New York, 1966.

Rodrigues, José Carlos, *The Panama Canal: Its History, Its Political Aspects, and Financial Difficulties*, London, 1885.

Roig de Leuchsenring, Emilio, *Bolívar, el Congreso Interamericano de Panamá, en 1826, y la independencia de Cuba y Puerto Rico*, Habana, 1956.

Rubio, Angel, *La Ciudad de Panamá, biografía urbana, funciones, diagnosis de la ciudad, paisaje callejero*, Panama, 1950.

Russel, Robert R., *Improvement of Communication with the Pacific Coast as an Issue in American Politics, 1783-1864*, Cedar Rapids, 1948.

Salazar, Fernando Galvis, *Uribe Uribe*, Medellín, 1962.

Salazar, José María, *Obserbaciones sobre las reformas políticas de Colombia*, Filadelfia, 1828.

Salazar, Victor M., *Memorias de la Guerra (1899-1902)*, Bogotá, 1943.

Salmoral, Manuel Lucena, *Historiografía de Panamá*, Panama, 1967.

Sánchez, Diodoro, *Pedro J. Sosa–ingeniero civil–1851-1898*, No. 4 of *Panameños Ilustres*, Panama, 1952.

Santovenia y Echaide, Emeterio S., *Eloy Alfaro*, n.p., 1937.

Schott, Joseph L., *Rails across Panama; the Story of the Building of the Panama Railroad 1849-1855*, New York, 1967.

Scott, William R., *The Americans in Panama*, New York, 1912.

Scott, Michael, *Tom Cringle's Panama Log*, n.p., n.d.

Seeman, Berthold, *Narrative of the Voyage of H.M.S. Herald*, 2 vols., London, 1853.

Seeman, Berthold, *Historia del Istmo de Panamá*, Panama, 1959.

Shelbourne, Sidney F., *A Comparative View of the Panama and San Blas Routes for an Interoceanic Canal*, New York, 1880.

Siegfried, Andrew, *Suez and Panama*, New York, 1940.

Simon, Maron J., *The Panama Affair*, New York, 1971.

Sisnett, Manuel Octavio, *Belisario Porras o la vocación de la nacionalidad*, Panama, 1959.

La sociedad de los amigos del país, ed., *Documentos importantes sobre la apertura de un canal fluvial entre océanos Atlántico y Pacífico por el istmo de Panamá*, Panama, 1835.

Soler, Ricaurte, *Estudio sobre historia de las ideas en América*, Panama, 1966.

Soler, Ricaurte, *Formas ideológicas de la nación panameña*, Costa Rica, 1971.

Soler, Ricaurte, *Materialismo e idealismo: una alternativa*, Panama, 1971.

Soler, Ricaurte, *Panamá en el mundo Americano, Programa analítico-alegato*, Panama, 1971.

Soler, Ricaurte, *Pensamiento panameño y concepción de la nacionalidad durante el siglo XIX*, Panama, 1971.

Soler, Ricaurte and Rodrigo Miró, *Significación histórica y filosófica de Justo Arosemena.* Panama, 1958.

Sosa, Juan B. and Enrique J. Arce, *Compendio de historia de Panamá*, 2nd ed., Panama, 1971.

Steele, Pablo, *¿Quiénes son los dueños de América Latina?* Panama, 1972.

Stephens, John L., *Incidents of Travel in Central America, Chiapas, and Yucatán*, 2 vols., New York, 1841.

Stephen, Sir Leslie and Lee, Sidney, eds., *The Dictionary of National Biography*, Vol. XII, London, 1949.

Stewart, J., *Bogotá in 1836-7, Being a Narrative of an Expedition to the Capital of New Granada and a Residence There of Eleven Months*, New York, 1838.

Strain, I. C., *A Paper on the History and Prospects of Inter-oceanic Communication by the American Isthmus*, New York, 1856.

Susto, Juan Antonio, ed., *2 relaciones de viajes al Istmo de Panama en 1835*, Panama, 1961.

Susto, Juan Antonio, *A Dos Siglos del extrañamiento de los Jesuitas y clausura de la Real y Pontífica Universidad de Panamá*, Panama, 1968.

Susto, Juan Antonio, *Homenaje al doctor Manuel Amador Guerrero en el centenario de su nacimiento*, Panama, 1933.

Susto, Juan Antonio, *Sebastián José López Ruiz médico y naturalista (1741-1832)*, No. 1 of *Panameños Ilustres*, Panama, 1950.

Taylor, Bayard, *Eldorado or Adventures in the Path of Empire Comprising a Voyage to California, via Panama; Life in San Francisco and Monterey; Picture of the Gold Region, and Experiences of Mexican Travel*, New York, 1856.

Tamayo, Joaquín, *La Revolución de 1899*, Bogotá, 1940.

Tejeira, Gil Blas, *Pueblos perdidos*, Panama, 1962.

Thompson, R. W., *The Interoceanic Canal at Panama; Its Political Aspects: The Monroe Doctrine*, Washington, 1881.

Tomes, Robert, *Panama in 1855: An Account of the Panama Railroad, of the Cities of Panama and Aspinwall with Sketches of Life and Character on the Isthmus*, New York, 1855.

Trautwine, John C., *Rough Notes, on an Exploration for an Inter-Oceanic Canal Route by Way of the Rivers Atrato and San Juan, in New Granada, South America*, Philadelphia, 1854.

Troncoso, Julio C., *Vida anecdótica del General Eloy Alfaro: nacimiento, juventud, campañas y cronología de los combates, administración, obras realizadas y muerte sacrificada del notable estadista*, Quito, 1966.

Tuñón, Federico, *El Canal barato*, Panama, 1964.

Turner Morales, David, *Estructura económica de Panamá; el problema del Canal*, Mexico, 1958.

Urdaneta, Amenodoro and Nephtalí, eds., *Memorias del General Rafael Urdaneta adicionadas con notas ilustrativas y algunos otros apuntamientos relativos a su vida pública*, Caracas, 1888.

Urreta, Gregorio María, *Memoria que consigna el que la suscribe al Señor Manuel Antonio Jaramillo, nombrado para desempeñar el Gobierno de esta provincia*, Medellín, 1829.

Valdés, Ramón M., *La independencia del istmo de Panamá: sus antecedentes, sus causas y su justificación*, Panama, 1903.

Vásquez, V., Claudio, *La insurrección de Las Tablas, 8 de noviembre de 1821*, Panama, 1962.

Vásquez, Juan Materno, *Sobre el hombre cultural panameño*, Panama, 1971.

Velarde, Fabián and Felipe J. Escobar, *El Congreso de Panamá en 1826*, Panama, 1922.

Velasco, Donaldo, *La Guerra en el Istmo*, Panama, 1902.

Vidal, Mercedes Luisa, *La Catedral de Panamá*, Buenos Aires, 1956.

Von Hagen, Victor W., *The Four Seasons of Manuela: A Biography, the Love Story of Manuela Saenz and Simón Bolívar*, New York, 1952.

Warren, Thomas R., *Dust and Foam*, New York, 1859.

Warden, William W., and Charles A. Eldridge, *The Chiriquí and Golfito Naval Stations Matter*, Washington, 1882.

Weatherford, W.D., *An Account of the Late Expedition Against the Isthmus of Darien under the Command of Sir Gregor McGregor*, London, 1821.

West, Robert C., *Colonial Placer Mining in Colombia*, Baton Rouge, 1952.

Westerman, George W., *Sore Spots in United States-Panama Relations*, Canal Zone, 1952.

Wheelright, William, *Observations on the Isthmus of Panama*, London, 1844.

White, Stewart Edward, *The Forty-Niners: A Chronicle of the California Trail and El Dorado*, vol. 25 of *The Chronicles of America* Series, New Haven, 1918.

Wyse, Lucien N.B., *Le Canal de Panama: L'Isthme Américain, explorations; comparison des tracés etudiés; état des travaux*, Paris, 1886.

Wyse, Lucien N.B., *El Canal de Panamá, el Istmo Americano, exploraciones; comparaciones de los trazados estudiados; negociaciones; estado de los trabajos*, trans. Roque Javier Laurenza, Panama, 1959.

Yacup, Sofonias, *Litoral recóndito*, Bogotá, 1934.

Yau, Julio, *El Canal de Panamá, calvario de un pueblo*, Madrid, 1972.

Ycaza, Nes de, *Victoriano Lorenzo, el Cholo Guerrillero*, Panama, 1970. [published for educational purposes by the Ministry of Education; it is for popular consumption and is based on the works of Rubén D. Carles.]

Yepes, Jesús María, *Del Congreso de Panamá a la conferencia de Caracas 1826-1954*, 2 vols., Caracas, 1955.

ARTICLES

Abbot, Henry Larcom, "The Best Isthmian Canal," *Atlantic Monthly*, LXXXVI (December, 1900), 844-848.

Abrahams, Mercy Morgan de, "Reminiscencias de la Guerra de Coto: La Cruz Roja Chiricana," *Lotería*, XIII, No. 149 (April, 1968), 10-37.

"Across the Isthmus in 1850: The Journey of Daniel A. Horn," ed. James P. Jones and William Warren Rogers, *The Hispanic American Historical Review*, XLI (November, 1961), 533-554.

"Admiral Casey and the Colombian Situation," *The Outlook*, LXXII (October 18, 1902), 384-385.

Aizpurua, Armando, "Doctor Juan Nepomuceno Venero López," *Lotería*, No. 112 (March, 1965), 24-30.

Aizpurua, Armando, "Don Juan Manuel Lambert Gallegos," *Lotería* (March, 1962), 50-59.

Alexander, Thomas S., "The Truth about Colombia," *The Outlook*, LXX (December 26, 1903), 993-996.

Alfaro, Ricardo J., "La independencia de Panamá y su fecha," *Lotería* (February, 1962), 30-32.

Alvarado, Pablo J., "Recuerdo de la Guerra de los Mil Días," *Lotería*, XII (March, 1967), 64-96.

"American Steam Marine: The Great Lines of Sea Steamers Connecting American Ports, and the Old and New World," *Debow's Review*, XIV (June, 1853), 583-587.

Ameringer, Charles D., "The Panama Canal Lobby of Philippe Bunau-Varilla and Nelson Cromwell," *Hispanic American Historical Review*, LXVIII (January, 1963), 346-363.

Ameringer, Charles D., "Philippe Bunau-Varilla: New Light on the Panama Canal Treaty," *Hispanic American Historical Review*, XLVI (February, 1966), 28-52.

Ammen, Daniel, "American Isthmian Canal Routes," *Franklin Institute Journal*, CXXVIII (December, 1889), 409-439.

Ammen, Daniel, "Inter-Oceanic Ship-Canal across the American Isthmus," *American Geographical Society Journal*, X (November, 1878), 142-162.

Andrist, Ralph K., "The California Gold Rush," *American Heritage*, XIV (December, 1962), 6-27, 90-91.

Anguizola, Gustave, "Negroes in the Building of the Panama Canal," *Phylon*, XXIX, No. 4 (Winter, 1968), 351-359.

Aragon, Leopoldo, "Has the Panama Canal a Future?" *The New Republic*, CXLVII, No. 4-5 (July 30, 1962), 16-17.

Arosemena, Mariano, "Independencia del Istmo," *Lotería* XIII, No. 150 (Mayo, 1968), 27-66.

Baker, George, "The Wilson Administration and Panama, 1913-1921," *Journal of Inter-American Studies*, VIII (April, 1966), 279-293.

Bates, L., "History of the Panama Railroad," *The World Today*, (July, 1906), 714-724.

Beebe, Lucius, "Panamint: Suburb of Hell," *American Heritage*, VI (December, 1954), 64-69.

Bieber, Ralph P., ed., "Diary of a Journey from Missouri to California in 1849," *Missouri Historical Review,* XXII (October, 1928), 3-43.

Biesanz, John, "The Economy of Panama," *Inter-American Economic Affairs,* XI (Summer, 1952), 3-29.

Biesanz, John and Mavis, "Uncle Sam in the Isthmus of Panama: A Diplomatic Case History," *The Caribbean: Contemporary Trends,* ed. A. C. Wilges, Gainesville, 1953.

Congress of Panama (1826), "The Bolivarian Congress of Panama [an intterview with Dr. Eduardo Posada]," *Hispanic American Historical Review,* VI (November, 1926), 260-263.

Buell, Raymond Leslie, "Panama and the United States," *Foreign Policy Reports,* VII (January 20, 1932), 409-427.

Bunau-Varilla, Philippe, "Nicaragua or Panama," *Scientific American,* LII (December 21, 1901), 21713-21714.

Burlingame, Roger, "The 'great' Frenchman. A New Interpretation of Ferdinand de Lesseps and the Panama Scandal," *Scribner's Magazine,* XCIV (October, 1933), 208-213, 249-256.

Burns, E. Bradford, "The Recognition of Panama by the Major Latin American States," *The Americas* XXVI (July 1969), 3-14.

Burr, William H., "The Panama Route for a Ship Canal," *Popular Science Monthly,* LXI (July, 1902), 252-268.

Burt, George A., "A Comparison of the Isthmian Canal Projects," *Engineering Magazine,* XIX (April, 1900), 19-27.

Anonymous, "California by Panama in '49," *The Century Magazine,* LXI (November 1900-April 1901), 901-904, 1917.

"The Capture of Colon," *The Outlook,* LXIX (November 30, 1901), 800.

Carles, Rubén Darío, "Oro en Panamá," *Lotería* (April, 1962), 37-42.

Carter, John Denton, "George Kenyon Fitch, Pioneer California Journalist," *California Historical Society Quarterly,* XX, No. 4 (December, 1941), 329-340.

Caruso, John Anthony, "The Pan American Railway," *Hispanic American Historical Review,* XXXI (November, 1951), 608-639.

Castillero, C., Alfredo, "La independencia de Panama de España—factores coyunturales y estructurales en la capital y el Interior," *Lotería,* No. 192 (November, 1971), 4-18.

Castillero Calvo, Alfredo, "Política de poblamiento en Castilla del Oro y Veraguas durante los orígenes de la colonización 1502-1522," *Lotería,* XIV, No. 160 (March, 1969), 67-89.

Castillero Reyes, Ernesto, "Don Melchor Lasso de la Vega," *Lotería,* No. 112 (March, 1965), 5-10.

Castillero Reyes, Ernesto, "El General O'Connor y la historia de Panamá," *Lotería,* XIII (October, 1968), 21-24.

Castillero Reyes, Ernesto, "El sesquicentenario de la emancipación de España," *Lotería,* No. 192 (November, 1971), 76-83.

Castillero Reyes, Ernesto, "La causa inmediata de la emancipación de Panamá," *Academia Panameña de la Historia*, Boletín No. 3 (July, 1933), 250-433.

Chamberlain, Leander T., "A Chapter of National Dishonor," *North American Review*, DCLXXV (February, 1912), 145-174.

Chrystie, G. Kennedy, "Personal Experiences of a Colombian Revolution," *The Living Age*, CCXXXI (November 16, 1901), 418-424.

Clare, Horacio, "Detención provisional de Victoriano Lorenzo," *Lotería*, XI, No. 130 (September 1966), 69-79.

Clemens, Samuel L., "Open Letter to Commodore Vanderbilt," *Richards Monthly* (March, 1869).

Cochrane, James D., "Costa Rica, Panama and Central American Economic Integration," *Journal of Inter-American Studies*, VII (July, 1965), 331-344.

Coker, William S., "The Panama Canal Tolls Controversy: A Different Perspective," *The Journal of American History*, LV (December 1968), 555-564.

Colby, E., "Panama-American Relations in Chiriquí," *Current History Magazine*, (July, 1920), 682-685.

Collings, Harry T., "The Congress of Bolívar (Panama, June 18-25, 1926)," *Hispanic American Historical Review*, VI (November, 1926), 194-198.

Colne, Charles, "The Panama Inter-oceanic Canal," *Franklin Institute Journal*, CXVIII (November, 1884), 353-376.

"Colombia," *The Outlook*, LXIII (November 4, 1899), 520.

"Colombia and Venezuela in Convulsion," *The World Work*, V (December, 1902), 2826-2829.

"The Colombia Insurgents Defeated," *The Outlook*, LXX (April 22, 1902), 898.

"The Colombian Revolution near Panama," *Harper's Weekly* XLVI (August 23, 1903), 1156-1157.

Colquhoun, Archibald R.. "The Panama and Nicaragua Canals," *Graphic*, LXI (February 3, 1900), 162.

Crodes, Frederick, trans., ed., "Letters of A. Rotchev, Last Commandant at Fort Ross and the Resumé of the Report of the Russian-American Company for the Year 1850-51," *California Historical Society Quarterly*, XXXIX, No. 2 (June, 1960), 97-115.

"The Crisis at Colón," *The Outlook*, LXXII (September 20, 1902), 148.

Cushing, John M., "From New York to San Francisco Via the Isthmus of Panama," *Quarterly of the Society of California Pioneers*, VI, No. 3 (1929).

DeGrummond, Jane Lucas, "The Jacob Idler Claim against Venezuela 1817-1890," *Hispanic American Historical Review*, XXXIV (May, 1954), 131-157.

Dilke, Charles W., "U.K., U.S., and the Ship Canal," *Forum,* XXIX (June, 1900), 449-454.

"The Disturbances in South America," *The Outlook,* LXIX (September 14, 1901), 101-102.

Domínguez, Rafael Rivera, "Estructura social de una comunidad negro-colonial panameña," *Hombre y cultura* (Revista del Centro de Investigaciones Antropológicas de la Universidad Nacional de Panamá), I, No. 4, (December, 1965), 47-64.

"A Double Revolution," *The Outlook,* LXVI (November 10, 1900), 627-628.

Drury, Clifford M., "John White Geary and His Brother Edward," *California Historical Society Quarterly,* XX, No. 1 (March, 1941), 12-25.

Dunlap, H., "Racial Pot-pourri on the Isthmus," *Lippincott,* (October, 1908), 489-495.

Ellison, William Henry, ed., "Memoirs of Hon. William M. Gwin," *California Historical Society Quarterly,* XIX, No. 1 (March, 1940), 1-26.

Fairchild, Mahlon D., "Reminiscences of a 'Forty-niner," *California Historical Society Quarterly,* XIII, No. 1 (March, 1934), 3-33.

Faye, Stanley, "Commodore Aury," *The Lousiana Historical Quarterly,* XXIV (July, 1941), 49-55.

Friedlander, R. A., "Reassessment of Roosevelt's Role in the Panamanian Revolution of 1903," *Western Political Quarterly,* XIV (July, 1961), 535-543.

Fuson, Robert H., "Communal Labor in Central Panama," *Rural Sociology,* XXIV (March, 1959), 57-59.

Gardner, Walter, "A Yankee Trader in the Gold Rush; Letters of Walter Gardner, 1851-1857," John W. Caughey, ed., *Pacific Historical Review,* XVII (November, 1948), 411-428.

Gatell, Frank Otto, "The Canal in Retrospect—Some Panamanian and Colombian Views," *The Americas* XV (July, 1958), 23-36.

Gies, Joseph, "Mr. Eads Spans the Mississippi," *American Heritage,* XX (August, 1969), 16-21, 89-93.

Goldrich, Daniel, "Requisites for Political Legitimacy in Panama," *Public Opinion Quarterly,* XXVI (Winter, 1962), 664-668.

Goldrich, Daniel, "Towards an Estimate of the Probability of Social Revolutions in Latin America: Some Orienting Concepts and a Case Study," *Centennial Review,* VI (Summer, 1962), 394-408.

Graham, Leopold, "Canal Diplomacy: A British View," *North American Review,* CXCVII (January, 1913), 30-39.

Graham, R. B. Cunningham, to *The Saturday Review,* XCII (October 5, 1901), 430-431.

Hackett, Charles Wilson, "The Development of John Quincy Adams' Policy with Respect to an American Confederation and the Panama Congress,

1822-1825," *Hispanic American Historical Review*, VII (November, 1928), 496-526.

Hackett, E. A., "A Central American Revolution," *Harper's Weekly*, XLIV (December 1, 1900), 1134-1135.

Hafen, L. R., "Butterfield's Overland Mail," *California Historical Society Quarterly*, II (October, 1923) 211-222.

Harrison, John P., "The Archives of United States Diplomatic and Consular Posts in Latin America," *Hispanic American Historical Review*, XXXIII (February, 1953), 168-183.

Hasbrouck, Alfred, "Gregor McGregor and the Colonization of Poyais, Between 1820 and 1824," *Hispanic American Historical Review*, VII (November, 1927), 438-459.

Hauberg, C. A., "Panama: Pro Mundi Beneficio," *Current History*, XXXII (April, 1957), 228-236.

Hayne, F. Bourn, ed., "A Boy's Voyage to San Francisco, 1865-66. Selections from the Diary of William Bowers Bourn Ingalls," *California Historical Society Quarterly*, XXXVI, No. 3 and No. 4 (September and December, 1957), 205-211; 293-306.

Headley, Joel Tyler, "Darien Exploring Expedition, under Command of Lieut. Isaac C. Strain," *Harper's New Monthly Magazine*, X (March, 1855), 433-458.

Herrera, Francisco, "Bibliografía de Panamá de 1960-1963," *Lotería*, X, No. 118 (September, 1965), 67-97.

Hildebrando A., Luna R., "Natá de los Caballeros," *Lotería*, X, No. 116 (July, 1965), 52-76.

Hill, Robert T., "The Panama Canal Route," *National Geographic Magazine*, VII (February, 1896), 59-64.

Holden, Erastus D., "Condemned Bar in 1849. An Excerpt from the Journal of Erastus Saurin Holden," *California Historical Society Quarterly*, XII, No. 4 (December, 1933), 312-317.

Hoskins, Halford L., "The Hispanic American Policy of Henry Clay, 1816-1828," *Hispanic American Historical Review*, VII (November, 1927), 460-478.

Huck, Eugene R. and Edward H. Mosely, "The Forty-Niners in Panama: The Canal Prelude," *Militarists, Merchants and Missionaries*, University, Alabama, 1970.

Hurtado, Alberto M., "Don Pedro Prestán y su destino trágico," *Lotería*, XIII, No. 149 (April, 1968), 44-49.

Hyde, Charles C., "The Isthmian Canal Treaty," *Harvard Law Review*, XV (May, 1902), 725-732.

Jones, Chester, Lloyd, "Loan Controls in the Caribbean," *Hispanic American Historical Review*, XIV (May, 1934), 141-162.

Jones, John, "A Case of Gold Fever," *Graham's Magazine* XXXV (December, 1849), 356-359.

Kahn, Edgar Myron, "Andrew Smith Hallide," *California Historical Society Quarterly*, XIX, No. 2 (June, 1940), 144-156.

Keasbey, Lindley M., "The Terms and Tenor of the Clayton-Bulwer Treaty," *American Academy of Political and Social Science Annals*, XIV (November, 1899), 285-309.

Kemble, John H., ed., "Andrew Wilson's 'Jottings' on Civil War California," *California Historical Society Quarterly*, XXXII, No. 3, 4 (September and December, 1953), 209-224; 303-312.

Kemble, John H., "The Genesis of the Pacific Mail Steamship Company," *California Historical Society Quarterly*, XIII (September, 1934), 240-254; XIII (December, 1934), 386-406.

Kemble, John H., "The Gold Rush by Panama, 1848-1851," *The Pacific Historical Review*, XVIII (February, 1949), 45-56.

Kemble, John H., "Naval Conquest in the Pacific. The Journal of Lieutenant Tunis Augustus Macdonough Craven, U.S.N., During a Cruise to the Pacific in the Sloop of War *Dale*, 1846-49," *California Historical Society Quarterly*, XX, No. 3 (September, 1941), 193-234.

Kemble, John H., "Pacific Mail Service Between Panama and San Francisco, 1849-1851, *The Pacific Historical Review*, II (December, 1933), 405-417.

Kemble, John H., "The Panama Route to the Pacific Coast, 1848-1869," *The Pacific Historical Review*, VII (March, 1938), 1-13.

Kennedy, John C., "Incident on the Isthmus," *American Heritage*, XIX (June, 1968), 65-72.

King, Charles A., "Apuntes para una bibliografía de la literatura de Panamá," *Revista Interamericana de Bibliografía*, XIV, No. 3, (July-August, 1964), 262-302.

Kinnaird, Lucia B., "Creassy's Plan for Seizing Panama, with an Introductory Account of British Designs on Panama," *Hispanic American Historical Review*, XIII (February, 1933), 46-78.

Langley, Lester D., "The U.S. and Panama: The Burden of Power," *Current History*, LVI, No. 329 (January, 1969).

Langley, Lester D., "Negotiating New Treaties with Panama: 1936," *Hispanic American Historical Review*, XLVIII, No. 2, (May, 1968), 220-233.

Lesley, Lewis B., "The International Boundary Survey from San Diego to the Gila River, 1849-50," *California Historical Society Quarterly*, IX, No. 1 (March, 1930), 3-15.

Lewis, Samuel, "The Cathedral of Old Panama," *Hispanic American Historical Review*, I (November, 1918), 447-453.

Lewis, William S., "Reminiscences of Delia B. Sheffield," *Washington Historical Quarterly*, XV, No. 15 (1924), 49-62.

Lloyd, John A., "Notes Respecting the Isthmus of Panama," *The Journal of the Royal Geographical Society of London*, I (1831), 69-101.

Loosley, Allyn C., "The Puerto Bello Fairs," *Hispanic American Historical Review*, XIII (August, 1933), 314-335.

McCullough, David G., "A Man, A Plan, A Canal, Panama!" *American Heritage*, XXII (June, 1971), 64-71, 100-103, 111.

Maack, G. A., "The Secret of the Strait," *Harpers Magazine*, XLVII (November 1873), 801-820.

Marden, Luis, "Panama, Bridge of the World," *National Geographic* LXXX, No. 5 (November, 1941), 591-630.

Martin, Harold, "Venezuela and Colombia," *The Independent*, LII (October 26, 1901), 2527-2532.

Massey, S.F., "The Late Revolution in Colombia," *Journal of the Military Service Institution*, XXII (July-December, 1897), 288-311.

Meagher, Thomas Francis, "The New Route Through Chiriquí," *Harper's New Monthly Magazine*, XXII (January, 1861), 198-209.

Metford, J. C., "Background to Panama," *International Affairs*, XL (April, 1964), 277-286.

Minger, Ralph E., "Panama, the Canal Zone and Titular Sovereignty," *Western Political Quarterly*, XIV (June, 1961), 544-554.

Miró, Rodrigo, "Mariano Arosemena, Maestro de Periodistas," *Lotería*, XIII (Mayo, 1968), 14-18.

Mitchell, C. Bradford, "Pride of the Seas," *American Heritage*, XXI (December, 1967), 64-88.

Molina, Edwin R., "La invasión del Dr. Porras al Istmo," *Lotería* (March, 1962), 42-45.

Morse, Edwin Franklin, "The Story of a Gold Miner: Reminiscences of Edwin Franklin Morse," *California Historical Society Quarterly*, VI. No 3. (September, 1927), 205-237 and No. 4 (December, 1927), 332-359.

Murgas, Rafael, "Los Recuerdos de Don Pablo (Prólogo a 'Recuerdos de la Guerra de los Mil Días')," *Lotería*, XII (March, 1967), 59-63.

Murphy, Robert Cushman, "The Earliest Spanish Advances Southward from Panama along the West Coast of South America," *Hispanic American Historical Review*, XXI (February, 1941), 2-28.

Navarro, José Oller, "El municipio de Taboga," *Lotería* (April, 1962), 43-52.

Navarro, José Oller, "Tomás Arias," *Lotería*, XIV (April, 1969), 29-31.

Naylor, Robert A., "The British Role in Central America Prior to the Clayton-Bulwer Treaty of 1850," *Hispanic American Historical Review*, XL (August, 1960), 361-382.

Nelson, Henry Loomis, "The Revolution and War in South America," *Harper's Weekly* XLV (October 12, 1901), 1040-1041.

Nettles, H. Edward, "The Drago Doctrine in International Law and Politics," *Hispanic American Historical Review*, VIII (May, 1928), 204-223.

Noli, Luis C., "Buscando la libertad declaran los Istmeños su independencia," *Review*, (November, 1969), 5-8.

184   BEFORE THE FIVE FRONTIERS

Oehler, Helen I., ed., "Nantucket to the Golden Gate in 1849. From Letters in the Winslow Collection," *California Historical Society Quarterly*, XXIX, No. 1 (March, 1950), 1-18.

"On the Isthmus," *The Outlook*, LXIX (December 7, 1901), 861.

Oran, "Tropical Journeyings in Route for California," *Harper's New Monthly Magazine*, XVI, No. 94 (December to May, 1857-1858), 457-471; No. 95 (December to May, 1857-1858), 572-593; XVII, No. 97 (June to November, 1858), 19-30; XVIII, No. 104 (January, 1859), 145-169; XIX, No. 112 (September, 1859), 433-454.

Otero D'Costa, Enrique, "Communication (discussing the name Portobelo)," *Hispanic American Historical Review*, XIV (November, 1934), 554-558.

Otis, Fessenden Nott, "A History of the Panama Railroad," *Harper's Magazine*, XXXV (June to November, 1867).

"Panama and Colombia," *Outlook*, LXXV (December 19, 1903), 966-967.

"Panama Railroad in Second Century of Service," *Illinois Central Magazine*, XXXXV (November, 1956) 10-12.

"The Panama Revolution," *Outlook*, LXXV (November 21, 1903), 624-625.

"Panama to Chagres," *Chamber's Journal*, XV (1851), 248-251.

Pattee, Richard, "Historical Activities in Panama," *Hispanic American Historical Review*, XVII (February, 1937), 106-109.

Patterson, John, "Latin-American Reactions to the Panama Revolution of 1903," *Hispanic American Historical Review*, XXIV (May, 1944), 342-351.

Patterson, Richard S., "The New Granadian Draft of a Convention for the Settlement of the Panama Riot Claim," *Hispanic American Historical Review*, XXVII (February, 1947), 87-91.

Penfield, Frederic Courtland, "Why Not Own the Panama Isthmus?" *North American Review*, CLXXIV (February, 1902), 269-274.

Pérez-Venero, Alejandro, "Reseñas históricas sobre varios proyectos para la construcción de una vía transístmica," *Lotería*, No. 192 (November, 1971), 60-75.

Pérez-Venero, Alejandro, "The 'Forty'Niners Through Panama," *Journal of the West*, XI (July, 1972), 460-469.

Pierre, C. Grand, "Panama's Demand for Independence," *Current History*, XIX (October, 1923), 128-130.

Pierson, William Whatley, Jr., "The Political Influences of an Inter-Oceanic Canal, 1826-1926," *Hispanic American Historical Review*, VI (November, 1926), 205-231.

Poindexter, Miles, "Our Rights in Panama," *Forum*, LXV (February, 1921), 129-144.

Porras, J. Conte, "Reflexiones en torno a la Guerra de Coto y de las primeras demandas Panameñas para reformar el Tratado del Canal," *Lotería*, No. 192 (November, 1971), 19-34.

Porras, Herán, "Papel histórico de los grupos humanos en Panamá," *Lotería*, XIV, No. 161 (April, 1969), 40-73.

Posada, José Restrepo, "A Santa María la Antigua del Darién," *Boletín Cultural y Bibliográfico*, Bogotá.

Powell, Anna I., "Relations Between the United States and Nicaragua, 1898-1916," *Hispanic American Historical Review*, VIII (February, 1928), 43-64.

Pratt, Julius H., "To California by Panama in '49," *The Century Illustrated Monthly Magazine*, XLI (April, 1891), 901-917.

Raymores, Franklin, "Quién fue Victoriano Lorenzo?" *Lotería*, XIII (Mayo, 1968), 82-96.

Read, Georgia W., "The Chagres River Route to California in 1851," *California Historical Society Quarterly*, VIII (March, 1929), 3-16.

"The Rebellion in Colombia," *The Outlook*, LXV (August 4, 1900), 760.

Reinhold, Frances L., "New Research on the First Pan-American Congress Held at Panama in 1826," *Hispanic American Historical Review*, XVIII (August 1938), 342-363.

"Revolutionary Disturbances in Venezuela, Colombia and Hayti," *The Outlook*, LXXI (August 9, 1902), 901.

"The Revolution in Colombia," *The Outlook*, LXV (May 5, 1900), 8.

Rippy, J. Fred, "Dawn of the Railway Era in Colombia," *Hispanic American Historical Review*, XXIII (November, 1943), 650-663.

Rippy, J. Fred, "The Development of Public Utilities in Colombia," *Hispanic American Historical Review*, XXV (February, 1945), 132-137.

Rippy, J. Fred, "Notes on the Early Telephone Companies of Latin America," *Hispanic American Historical Review*, XXIV (February, 1946), 116-118.

Rippy, J. Fred, "Political Issues in Panama Today," *Current History*, XXVIII (May, 1928), 226-227.

Robinson, Edgar Eugene, ed., "The Day Journal of Milton S. Latham, January 1 to May 6, 1860," *California Historical Society Quarterly*, XI, No. 1 (March, 1932), 3-28.

Robinson, Edwin V. D., "The West Indian and Pacific Islands in Relation to the Isthmian Canal," *Independent*, LII (March, 1900), 523-526.

Robledo, Alfonso, "Elogio a Henry Clay," *Hispanic American Historical Review*, VI (November, 1926), 199-204.

Rodríguez, Angel D., "American Powers in Panama," *Current History* XIV (May, 1921), 300-302.

Rodríguez, Mario, "The Prometheus and the Clayton-Bulwer Treaty," *Journal of Modern History*, XXXVI (September, 1964), 260-278.

Ronan, Elena Vinade, "All Aboard," *Américas*, III (January, 1951), 24-27, 46-47.

Roosevelt, Theodore, "How the United States Acquired the Right to Dig the Panama Canal," *Outlook*, XCIX (October 7, 1911), 314-318.

Rothlisberguer, Ernst, "Como vio un suizo a Colón y Panamá en 1886," ed., Juan Antonio Susto, *Lotería*, X (March, 1965), 82-89.

Rubio, Angel, "Bibliografía básica de la geografía de Panamá," *Revista Geográfica del Instituto Pan-Americano de Geografía e Historia*, Río de Janeiro, (1951-1952), 11-12, 31-36; (1953), 100-110.

Rydell, Raymond A., "The Cape Horn Route to California, 1849," *Pacific Historical Review*, XVII (May, 1948), 149-163.

"Sad Condition of the Panama Canal," *Scientific American*, LXIV, No. 3 (January 7, 1891), 38.

Salandra, Dominic, "Porto Bello, Puerto Bello, or Portobelo?" *Hispanic American Historical Review*, XIV (February, 1934), 93-95.

Salmoral, Manuel Lucena, "Historiografía de Panamá—fichero bibliográfico, letras *s, t, u, v, w,* y *z*," *Lotería*, No. 145 (December, 1967), 56-75.

Sander, Ralph, "Congressional Reactions in the United States to the Panama Congress of 1826," *The Americas*, XI (October, 1954), 141-154.

Scott, George W., "Was the Recognition of Panama a Breach of International Morality?" *Outlook*, LXXV (December 19, 1903), 947-950.

Sensabaugh, Leon F., "The Attitude of the United States toward the Colombia-Costa Rica Arbitral Proceedings," *Hispanic American Historical Review*, XIX (February, 1939), 16-30.

Seeman, Berthold, "The Aborigines of the Isthmus of Panama," *Transactions of the American Ethnological Society*, III (1853), 175-182.

Sevareid, Eric, "The Man Who Invented Panama," *American Heritage*, XIV (August, 1963), 106-110.

Sharpe's London Journal, XIV (1851), 121-125.

Shaw, Carey, Jr., "Church and State in Colombia as Observed by American Diplomats, 1834-1906," *Hispanic American Historical Review*, XXI (November, 1941), 577-613.

Sherman, Edwin A., "Sherman Was There: The Recollections of Major Edwin A. Sherman," *California Historical Society Quarterly*, XXIV, No. 1 (March, 1945), 47-72.

Shutes, Milton H., "Colonel E. D. Baker," *California Historical Society Quarterly*, XVII, No. 4 (December, 1938), 303-324.

Sinán, Rogelio, "Rutas de la novela panameña," *Letras de Panamá*, (December 1, 1947), 7.

"Sketches Along the Route of the Panama Railroad," *Harper's Weekly*, XXI, No. 1058 (1877), 268-269, 270.

Smalley, E. V., "The Panama Canal Scheme," *Outlook*, LX (December, 1898), 911-913.

Smeeton, Beryle, "Forsaken Port of the Spanish Main," *The Geographical Magazine*, London, XL (June, 1968), 1210-1213.

"Some Inside Panama History," *The Outlook*, LXXV (December 12, 1903), 890-893.

Spinney, Frank Oakman, "A New Hampshire Minstrel Tours the Coast, Rhodolphus Hall and His Letters," *California Historical Society Quarterly*, XX, No. 3 (September, 1941), 243-258.

Steele, Catherine Baumgarten, "The Steel Brothers, Pioneers in California's Great Dairy Industry," *California Historical Society Quarterly*, XX, No. 3 (September, 1941), 259-273.

Stowell, Levi, "Bound for the Land of Canaan, Ho! The Diary of Levi Stowell," *California Historical Society Quarterly*, XXVII, No. 1 (March, 1948), 33-50.

"The Struggle in Colombia," *The Saturday Review*, XCII (September 14, 1901), 326-327.

"Summary of the Survey of the Isthmus of Darien," *Royal Geographical Society Journal*, XXVII (1857), 203.

Susto, Juan Antonio, "Evolución histórica de las loterías panameñas," *Lotería*, XIV, No. 160 (March, 1969), 7-34.

Susto, Juan Antonio, "Historia de las historias de Panamá escritas por panameños," *Revista de Historia de América*, Nos. 35-36 (January-December, 1953), 97-103.

Susto, Juan Antonio, "Maceo en Panama," *Lotería*, (April, 1962), 53-58.

Susto, Juan Antonio, "National Bibliography of Panama, 1938," *The Pan-American Bookshelf*, II, No. 9 (September, 1939), 61-70.

Susto, Juan Antonio, "Panorama de la bibliografía en Panama," *Inter-American Review of Bibliography*, XVIII (January-March, 1968), 3-27.

Susto, Juan Antonio, "Panorama de la Bibliografía en Panama," *Lotería*, XII (March, 1967), 17-43.

Susto, Juan Antonio, "El Puente de Calidonia," *Lotería* (July, 1959), 34-50.

Susto, Juan Antonio, "La Villa de Los Santos: foco de la independencia de 1821, ante la historia," *Lotería* (November, 1964), 6-13.

"Textos de M. Arosemena," *Lotería*, XIII, No. 150 (May, 1968), 19-27.

Thayer, William Roscoe, "John Hay and the Panama Republic from the Unpublished Letters of John Hay," *Harper's Magazine*, CXXXI (June to November, 1915), 165-175.

Trény, "California Unveiled, or Irrefutable Truths Based upon Numerous Testimonies about that Part of the World," translated Desiré Fricot, *California Historical Society Quarterly*, XXIII, No. 1 (March, 1944), 41-68.

Triplen, Charles S., "Crossing the Isthmus in 1852: Report of the Regimental Surgeon, 4th Infantry, USA," *Panama Canal Record*, Vol. I (July 1, 1908), 347-348.

"The Trouble in South America," *The Outlook*, LXVIII (August 24, 1901), 941-942.

"The United States, Venezuela, and Colombia," *The Outlook*, LXXII (October 4, 1902), 239-240.

Valentine, Alan, "Vigilante Justice," *American Heritage,* VII (February, 1956), 72-95.

Van Alstyne, R.W., "British Diplomacy and the Clayton-Bulwer Treaty, 1850-60," *Journal of Modern History* XI (1939), 149-183.

Van Alstyne, R.W., "The Central American Policy of Lord Palmerston, 1846-48," *Hispanic American Historical Review,* XVI (1936), 339-59.

Vaughan, Edgar, "La colonia escocesa en el Darién (1698-1700) y su importancia en los anales británicos," *Boletín cultural y bibliográfico,* Bogotá, IX, No. 2 (1966), 189-218.

Von Hagen, Victor W., "Artist of a Buried World," *American Heritage,* XII (June, 1961), 8-19, 100-103.

Warren, Viola Lockhard, ed., "Dr. John S. Griffin's Mail, 1846-53," part III (*California Historical Society Quarterly,* XXXIV, No. 1 (March, 1955) 21-39.

Wheat, Carl I., ed., " 'California's Bantam Cock': the Journals of Charles E. De Long, 1854-1863. The Journal for the Year 1859," *California Historical Society Quarterly,* X (March, 1931), 165-201.

Wheat, Carl I., ed., "The Old Ames Press—A Venerable Pioneer," *California Historical Society Quarterly,* IX No. 3 (September, 1930), 193-195, 200.

Westerman, G.W., "Historical Notes on West Indians on the Isthmus of Panama," *Phylon,* XXI (Winter, 1961), 340-350.

White, Chester Lee, "Surmounting the Sierras," *California Historical Society Quarterly,* VII, No. 1 (March, 1928), 3-19.

Wiltsee, Ernest A., "Hawes and Co.'s San Francisco and New York Express," *California Historical Society Quarterly,* XI, No. 1 (March, 1932), 30-32.

Wong, Zósimo, "Posibilidad de un Canal Panameño," *Tareas* (July-March, 1972), 5-56.

Wright, Doris Marion, "The Making of Cosmopolitan California. An Analysis of Immigration, 1848-1870," *California Historical Society Quarterly,* XIX, No. 4 (December, 1940), 323-344.

"A Yankee Trader in the Gold Rush: Letter of Caughey," *The Pacific Historical Review,* XVII (February, 1948), 411-428.

NEWSPAPERS

Bogotá, *El correo nacional,* September 1890-June 1891.

Bogotá, *El heraldo,* July 4, 1889-Jauary 28, 1898.

Bogotá, *El taller,* April 28, 1888-October 2, 1890.

Bogotá, *El tiempo,* November 23, 1952.

Colón *Starlet,* 1899-1902.

London *Times*, 1897-1902.
New York *Herald*, December 8, 1860.
The New York Times, 1851-1858; 1894-1902.
Panama Herald, April 14, 1851-April 27, 1854.
Panama Mercantile Chronicle, January 2, 1865-October 16, 1868.
Panama Star, February 1849-1854.
Panama *Star and Herald*, 1854-1870; 1899-1902.
Panama *Star and Herald Steamer Edition*, January 3, 1856-December 25, 1870.

PERIODICALS

American Heritage, 1954-1972.
California Historical Society Quarterly, 1922-1961.
Loteria, 1950-1972.
The Nation, LVI, March 30, 1893
Niles Weekly Register, 1819-1825.
Overland Monthly, LXIV, XLVII.
Panama Canal Review, 1960-1972.
Scientific American, XIV, Supplement 346; LXIV, Supplement.

Ph.D. DISSERTATIONS

Allen, Cyril, "The Career of Felix Belly in Connection with the Canal Projects in Central America," Ph.D. dissertation, University of Minnesota, 1949.
Ameringer, Charles D., "Never Abandon Panama: The Story of Philippe Bunau-Varilla and the Panama Canal," Ph.D. dissertation, Tufts University, 1958.
Anguizola, Gustave A., "Fifty Years of Isthmian-American Relations: An Analysis of the Causes Jeopardizing Isthmian-American Friendship," Ph.D. dissertation, Indiana University, 1954.
Arbena, Joseph Luther, "The Panama Problem in Colombian History," Ph.D. dissertation, University of Viriginia, 1970.
Arragon, Reginald F., "The Panama Congress of 1826," Ph.D. dissertation, Harvard University, 1923.
Broggi, Arnold R., "La societé de Panama," Ph.D. dissertation, Fordham University, 1942.
Cameron, Duncan H., "Panama's Unusual Guest: The Canal Zone in United States–Panamanian Relations," Ph.D. dissertation, Columbia University, 1965.

Carter, Victor Patterson, "The Postwar Growth in the Flow of Funds from the Canal Zone to the Republic of Panama," Ph.D. dissertation Western Reserve University, 1970.

DeWitt, Donald L., "Social and Educational Thought in the Development of the Republic of Panama, 1903-1946: An Intellectual History," Ph.D. dissertation, University of Arizona, 1972.

Favell, Thomas Royden, "The Antecedents of Panama's Separation from Colombia: A Study in Colombian Politics," Ph.D. dissertation, Tufts University, 1950.

Findling, John E., "The United States and Zelaya: A Study in the Diplomacy of Expediency," Ph.D. dissertation, University of Texas, 1971.

Fletcher, William Glover, "Canal Site Diplomacy: A Study in American Political Geography," Ph.D. dissertation, Yale University, 1940.

Folkman Jr., Davis Izatt, "Westward via Nicaragua—The United States and the Nicaragua Route, 1826-1869," Ph.D. dissertation, University of Utah, 1966.

Gossett, Thomas Frank, "The Idea of Anglo-Saxon Superiority in American Thought, 1865-1915," Ph.D. dissertation, University of Minnesota, 1953.

Hauberg, Clifford Alvin, "Economic and Social Developments in Panama, 1849-1880," Ph.D. dissertation, University of Minnesota, 1950.

Hoffman, Theodore, "A History of Railway Concessions and Railway Development Policy in Colombia to 1943," Ph.D. dissertation, American University, 1947.

Jiménez, Georgia Isabel, "Panama in Transition Period of 1849-1940," Ph.D. dissertation, Columbia University, 1953.

Kemble, John H., "The Panama Route to California, 1848-1869," Ph.D. dissertation, University of California, 1937.

Langley, Lester D., "The United States and Panama, 1933-1941: A Study in Strategy and Diplomacy," Ph.D. dissertation, University of Kansas, 1965.

Lear, Julia Graham, "Allies and Adversaries: United States Relations with Panama, 1939-1947," Ph.D. dissertation, Tufts University, 1971.

Leonard, Thomas Michael, "The Commissary Issue in United States-Panamanian Relations," Ph.D. dissertation, American University, 1969.

Levett, Ella P., "Negotiations for Release from the Inter-Oceanic Obligations of the Clayton-Bulwer Treaty," Ph.D. dissertation, University of Chicago, 1941.

McCain, William D., "The United States and the Republic of Panama," Ph.D. dissertation, Duke University, 1935.

MacGregor Rob Roy, "The Treaty of 1846 (Seventeen Years of American-Colombian Relations) 1830-1846," Ph.D. dissertation, Clark University, 1929.

Mellander, Gustavo Adolfo, "The United States in Panamanian Politics, 1903-1908," Ph.D. dissertation, The George Washington University, 1966.

Miner, Dwight C., "The Fight for the Panama Route: The Story of the Spooner Act and the Hay-Herran Treaty," Ph.D. dissertation, Columbia University, 1940.

Mock, James R., "Panama and Nicaragua Canal Rivalry, 1870-1903," Ph.D. dissertation, University of Wisconsin, 1930.

Moral Pérez, Carlos R., "The Sovereignty and Jurisdiction of the Republic of Panama over the Panama Canal Zone," Ph.D. dissertation, New York University, 1948.

Mount, Graeme Stewart, "American Imperialism in Panama," Ph.D. dissertation, University of Toronto, 1969.

Mullen, Sister Mary Christine, "Diplomatic Relations Between the United States and Colombia about the Panama Canal," Ph.D. dissertation, Fordham University, 1935.

Nichols, Theodore E., "The Caribbean Gateway to Colombia: Cartagena, Santa Marta, and Barranquilla and their Connections with the Interior, 1820-1940," Ph.D. dissertation, University of California, 1951.

Ohl, Arden William, "A Study of the Trans-Isthmian Canal Problems with Emphasis on the Nicaragua Route," Ph.D. dissertation, University of Michigan, 1965.

Parks, E. Taylor, "Colombia and Its Relations with the United States, 1765-1848," Ph.D. dissertation, Duke University, 1931.

Pérez-Venero, Mirna M. Pierce, "Raza, color y prejuicios en la novelística panameña contemporánea de tema canalero," Ph.D. dissertation, Louisiana State University, 1973.

Richard Jr., Alfred Charles, "The Panama Canal in American National Consciousness, 1870-1922," Ph.D. dissertation, Boston University, 1969.

Rollins, Audrey, "The Emergence of Modern Panama," Ph.D. dissertation, Texas Technological University, 1967.

Ropp, Stephen Chapmen, "In Search of the New Soldier Junior Officers and the Prospect of Social Reform in Panama, Honduras and Nicaragua," Ph.D. dissertation, University of California, 1971.

Rorer, William D., "Spanish Isthmian Projects and the American Canal," Ph.D. dissertation, Yale University, 1907.

Sullivan, Ward W., "A Study in Relations Between Colombia and the United States, 1900-1924," Ph.D. dissertation, University of Illinois, 1925.

Tascher, Harold, "American Foreign Policy Relative to the Selection of the Trans-Isthmian Canal Route," Ph.D. dissertation, University of Illinois, 1933.

Turk, Richard W., "United States Naval Policy in the Caribbean, 1865-1915," Ph.D. dissertation, Tufts University, 1968.

Williams, Mary W., "Anglo-American Isthmian Diplomacy, 1815-1915," Ph.D. dissertation, Stanford University, 1914.

Zukowski, Walter Henry, "The Panama Canal: A Public Venture," Ph.D. dissertation, Clark University, 1957.

M. A. THESES

Alzamora, Alicia, "La participación de los franceses en la construcción del Canal Interoceánico," B.A. graduation thesis, University of Panama, 1952.

Bartlett, Esther, "The Secession of Panama," M.A. thesis, University of Wisconsin, 1933.

Benítez, Enrique Ney, "The Remon-Eisenhower Treaty of 1955 Between the United States of America and the Republic of Panama," Master's thesis, George Washington University, 1959.

Boelens, Ann Gordon, "The Panama Canal Problem 1944-58: Sea Level Canal Versus Terminal Lake Third Locks Canal," M.A. Thesis, Lousiana State University, 1972.

Bois, Florence P., "American Interest in a Central American Canal, 1825-1885," Master's thesis, Columbia University, 1931.

Brigham, Lawrence Whitney, "The History and Diplomacy of the Panama Canal," Master's thesis, Clark University, 1913.

Brooks, Earl Clayton, "The Controversy with Colombia over the Panama Canal, 1900-1914," Master's thesis, University of Southern California, 1932.

Butler, Howard R., "Public Opinion Concerning the Canal Policy of Theodore Roosevelt as Reflected in the Newspapers of Louisiana," Master's thesis, Louisiana State University, 1965.

Carey, Tom F., "The Diplomatic History of the Panama Canal and the Acquisition of the Canal Zone," Master's thesis, University of Oklahoma, 1908.

Carr, Isaac Newton, "The Relations of the United States with Panama since 1903," Master's thesis, University of North Carolina, 1925.

Cathey, Franklyn Warren, "The United States Policy in Regard to the Panama Canal," Master's thesis University of Washington, 1930.

Christie, Mabel H., "Diplomacy Leading up to Cession of the Panama Canal Zone to the United States," Master's thesis, Northwestern University, 1914.

Cochran, Mary Elizabeth, "Panama, Colombia and the United States," Master's thesis, University of Chicago, 1921.

Derbyshire, Ruth A., "A Diplomatic History of the Panama Canal," Master's thesis, University of Vermont, 1937.

Faley, Geneva Fern, "Diplomatic Relations Between the United States and Panama, 1903-1928," Master's thesis, Kansas State Agricultural College, 1928.

Ford, George Kenneth, "The Suez and Panama Canal Crisis: A Comparative Study of United States Foreign Policy and Interests," Master's thesis, Louisiana State University, 1965.

Frierson, Mary Elizabeth, "Colombian-American Isthmian Diplomacy," Master's thesis, Columbia University, 1922.

Galt, Sara Elizabeth, "The Acquisition of the Panama Canal Strip," Master's thesis, Columbia University, 1915.

Handley, Frank McDonald, "A Diplomatic History of the Acquisition of the Panama Canal Zone," Master's thesis, Vanderbilt University, 1925.

Hedrick, Edith Vail, "The Dispute Between the United States and Colombia over Panama," Master's thesis, University of Missouri, 1923.

Heiz, W. A., "United States Private Direct Investment in Central America," Master's thesis, Louisiana State University, 1956.

Hill, Kenneth Miller, "American Intervention in Panama," Master's thesis, American University, 1927.

Hodges, Claudius Brashier, "Diplomatic Relations Between the United States and the Republic of Panama, 1903-1918," Master's thesis, University of Texas, 1935.

Hownshell, A. C., "The Political and Diplomatic History of the Panama Canal," Master's Thesis, University of Kentucky, 1933.

Kaufman, Daniel Webster, "Diplomatic Relations Between the United States and the Republic of Panama," Master's thesis, University of California, 1942.

Lane, Alice Sarah, "Panama and the United States since 1903," Master's thesis, University of Oregon, 1933.

Lower, Iva Evaline, "The Acquisition of the Panama Canal Zone by the United States and the Subsequent Demands of Colombia for Reparation," Master's thesis, University of California, 1923.

Ludewig, Charles, Keech, "Relations Between United States and Panama," Master's thesis, Georgetown University, 1930.

McCall, Margery (Stewart), "The Life and Works of Stewart Edward White," M.A. Thesis, Louisiana State University, 1939.

McCollom, Ina Mae, "United States Mediation Between Colombia and Panama, 1903-1924," Master's thesis, University of Texas, 1933.

McCormich, W. B., "The United States, the Republic of Panama and the 1936 Isthmian Treaty," M.A. thesis, Louisiana State University, 1960.

McIntosh, Russell Hugh, "Isthmian Diplomacy: A Study of American Politics and Negotiations for an Interoceanic Canal," Master's thesis, University of Florida, 1941.

Mellander, Gustavo Adolfo, "Magoon in Panama," Master's thesis, George Washington University, 1960.

Metcalf, Clyde Hill, "American Naval Intervention on the Isthmus of Panama, 1848-1914," Master's thesis, George Washington University, 1936.

Pérez-Venero, Alex, "The Thousand Days' War: A Prelude to Panamanian Independence," Master's thesis, Mississippi State University, 1967.

Richards, Arthur Lee, "A Brief History of the Panama Canal," Master's thesis, University of Oklahoma, 1933.

Riehl, Joseph A., "The Monroe Doctrine and the Panama Canal," Master's thesis, Georgetown University, 1933.

Schumacher, Max George, "President Hayes and the Isthmian Canal," Master's thesis, University of California, 1933.

Simon, Henry, "The Acquisition of Panama," Master's thesis, Columbia University, 1915.

Stonier, Harold J., " A History of the Diplomacy concerned with the Acquisition and Operation by the United States of an Interoceanic Canal in Central America," Master's thesis, University of Southern California, 1915.

Strauss, Emma Marion, "Diplomatic Relations Between the United States and Republic of Colombia Regarding the Panama Canal Zone," Master's thesis, Columbia University, 1920.

Thrash, E. E., "The Competing Position of Air Cargo Between the Gulf States of the United States and Central America, Master's thesis, Louisiana State University, 1951.

Triolo, James S., Jr., "Diplomatic Relations Between the Republic of Panama and the United States, 1903-1936," Master's thesis, Stanford University, n.d.

Turner, Phyllis M., "Diplomatic History of Panama and the United States, 1903-1928," Master's Thesis, East Texas State Teachers College, 1940.

Wallin, Ruth E., "Diplomatic Relations Between the United States and the Republic of Panama, 1903-1935," Master's thesis, New York Teachers College in Albany, 1938.

Wallis, Charles Braithwaite, "The Word and Policy of the United States in Panama, " Master's thesis, Cambridge University, 1939.

Willoughby, George Wilson, "International Servitudes Relative to the Panama Canal," Master's thesis, University of Iowa, 1939.

White, Laura Cornelia, "The Universal Interoceanic Panama Canal Company, 1871-1889," Master's thesis, George Washington University, 1935.

Index